the
highly
sensitive
child

the highly sensitive child

Helping Our Children Thrive
When the World
Overwhelms Them

ELAINE N. ARON, PH.D.

Thorsons
An Imprint of HarperCollins*Publishers*
77–85 Fulham Palace Road,
Hammersmith, London W6 8JB

The website address is: www.thorsonselement.com

and *Thorsons* are trademarks of
HarperCollins*Publishers* Ltd

First published in the USA in 2002 by Broadway Books,
a division of Random House, Inc.

This edition published in 2003 by Thorsons

8

Designed by Chris Welch

Elaine N. Aron asserts the moral right to be
identified as the author of this work

A catalogue record of this book is
available from the British Library

ISBN-13   978-0-00-716393-9
ISBN-10   0-00-716393-2

Printed and bound in Great Britain by
Clays Ltd, St Ives plc

To sensitive children everywhere,
and to those who gently raise them so that they grow up
to be secure in a difficult world

Acknowledgments

This book exists thanks to—

The generous parents, teachers, and children who let me interview them or answered my questionnaires, and who offered so many insights I would never have thought of.

My energetic editor, Ann Campbell, and my dear agent, Betsy Amster.

Temperament counselor Jan Kristal, friend and consultant.

And always, my husband, Art, so lighthearted, protective, and patient with his sensitive family, and my son, who taught me firsthand much of what I have passed on in this book.

Contents

Introduction xi

Is Your Child Highly Sensitive: A Parent's Questionnaire xvii

PART I: AN OVERVIEW OF THE SENSITIVE CHILD 1

CHAPTER 1. Sensitivity: A Better Light on "Shy" and "Fussy" Children 3

CHAPTER 2. Fasten Your Seat Belts: The Challenges of Raising an Exceptional Child 39

CHAPTER 3. When You the Parent Are Not Highly Sensitive: Blessings in Disguise 68

CHAPTER 4. When You and Your Child Are Both Highly Sensitive: And What About the Rest of Your Family's Temperament? 90

CHAPTER 5. Four Keys to Raising a Joyous HSC: Self-esteem, Shame Reduction, Wise Discipline, and Knowing How to Discuss Sensitivity 113

PART II: FROM INFANCY TO YOUNG ADULTHOOD 151

CHAPTER 6. Off to the Right Start: Soothing and Attuning to Highly Sensitive Infants 153

CHAPTER 7. **Toddlers and Preschoolers at Home: Adapting to Change and Dealing with Overstimulation** *178*

CHAPTER 8. **Toddlers and Preschoolers Out in the World: Helping Them Feel Successful in New Situations** *206*

CHAPTER 9. **School-Age HSCs at Home: Resolving Problems** *228*

CHAPTER 10. **School-Age HSCs Out in the World: Helping Your Child Enjoy the Classroom and Social Life** *250*

CHAPTER 11. **Sensitive Adolescents and Young Adults: The Delicate Task of Launching a Spirited, Seaworthy Vessel** *279*

Twenty Tips for Teachers *311*

Resources *318*

Notes *323*

Introduction

If you are reading these words, there is something about your child that makes you think he or she is highly sensitive. To best understand what that means, read over the checklist on pages xvii–xviii. If many of these statements apply to your child, read on . . . and welcome.

Almost everyone knows that even at birth children have their own personalities. "She always knew what she wanted, even as a baby, and she was going to have it or else." "He was always good-natured. Feed him or not, change him or not—it hardly mattered." Like every other child, yours has inherited her own unique combination of innate temperament traits. Yet each trait taken by itself is probably not unique, but is typical of a group of children, and so it can be easily described. "Strong-willed." "Good-natured." And so forth.

One such common inherited trait is high sensitivity, found in about 15 to 20 percent of children (the percentage is the same in boys and girls). Some infants seem fairly oblivious to whatever you feed them and whatever the temperature of the room may be; it does not matter to them if the stereo is on loud or the lights are bright. But highly sensitive infants seem to notice every slightly new taste, every change in temperature; they startle at loud noises and cry when a bright light is in their eyes. When they are older, they are often emotionally sensitive, too. They cry easily when their feelings are hurt, they worry more, and they can be so happy they "can't bear it." They also reflect before they act, so that they often come across as shy or afraid when they are merely observing. When they grow older still, they are often remarkable for their kindness and conscientiousness; they are upset by injustice, cruelty, or irresponsibility.

Even though it is possible to say a great deal about highly sensitive children (HSCs), no description will fit every child perfectly because, again, each HSC is unique, thanks to a unique combination of inherited traits plus different upbringings and school experiences. Your HSC may be outgoing or prefer to play alone, persistent or easily distracted, bossy and demanding or so adaptable he's "almost too good." But there is still a common thread of sensitivity you can recognize.

THE REASON FOR THIS BOOK

Now might be the time to tell you a little more about my study of high sensitivity in adults and how I came to extend my work to children and child-rearing. I am a research psychologist as well as a licensed clinical psychologist; I am also a highly sensitive person and the parent of one. As I describe in Chapter 1, I began researching high sensitivity as a trait about twelve years ago, and so far I have interviewed or consulted with hundreds, maybe thousands, of sensitive adults, parents, and children. I have gathered questionnaire data from thousands of others. This research has also been published in the leading journals in my field. The information you will find in this book is based on solid evidence. In fact, it has been studied for fifty years in infants and children but described in other terms, such as low sensory threshold, innate shyness, introversion, fearfulness, inhibitedness, negativity, or timidity. So one could say that the basic reason for this book is that the trait needed renaming, especially when the old terms are applied to children. And in renaming it, we gain not only a more accurate description but new ways to think about our sensitive children.

For example, when a child is just watching, we tend to say she is shy or fearful without considering the possibility that this may be the expression of a sensitive individual's innate preference to pause and observe before proceeding. Or we may hear that a child is "over-reacting" or "cannot screen out irrelevant information" when he notices every mood and detail. But what is wrong with having a nervous system that is extremely good at registering the subtle nuances in a given situation? (Besides, who can say what is irrelevant? Noticing where the exit is might seem to most people like seeing "too many details"—until there's a fire.)

Probably one reason I had this insight about renaming the trait was that, being highly sensitive myself, I knew a little better what was going on inside a sensitive person. True, we are a bit more likely to become shy or anxious after being exposed to certain adverse circumstances. But I am now convinced that it is sensitivity, not shyness or anxiety, that is the fundamental trait. Furthermore, both my research and the research of others indicate that it is primarily parenting that decides whether the expression of sensitivity will be an advantage or a source of anxiety. There are simply too many highly sensitive individuals—again, about 20 percent of the population—for this trait to be a consistent disadvantage. Evolution would not have permitted it. When we understand this trait as sensitivity, we can see its many assets, notice the many sensitive individuals who are thriving, speak of the trait accurately, and above all, parent sensitive children better.

Describing this trait as high sensitivity has been justified best, however, by the response to the concept from the hundreds of thousands who read *The Highly Sensitive Person* or *The Highly Sensitive Person in Love,* many of whom have told me, "That's me—it fits me perfectly, and I never knew anyone else had these feelings . . . this hunger for enough down time and quiet, the almost constant awareness of others and concern for doing things right." (This response has not been trivial. My first book, *The Highly Sensitive Person,* became a best-seller and has been translated into Dutch, Japanese, Chinese, Greek, and Polish so far.) Many who contacted me also went on to say that they wished their parents had known about this trait when raising them, or they wanted advice on how to raise their own sensitive child.

Thus it seemed important to write *The Highly Sensitive Child*, particularly because the advice in the many generally good, one-size-fits-all parenting books leaves out issues that are important for HSCs, such as the need to maintain an optimal level of stimulation and how to do that. Missing just this point about arousal can lead to real problems, such as when a book suggests discipline methods that would so overarouse HSCs that they would be too upset to take in the moral lesson behind the correction. There is simply no other parenting book written with HSCs in mind.

Above all, this book was written because I know some of you are having considerable trouble raising an HSC. This should not be happening. Some of you may have even concluded that there is something wrong with your child or with you as a parent. This book will help alleviate that feeling. It really will. You will relax about your child and your child will be able to relax as well.

HOW TO USE THIS BOOK

I strongly urge you to read the whole book. The first half is about sensitivity, how your parenting is affected by your own temperament, and the biggest issues to be faced with HSCs, regardless of the age of your child. The second half focuses on specific age groups, all the way from infancy to the young adult who has left home. You should read about all ages of HSCs because (1) there are fresh ideas in each chapter that also apply to children of other ages; (2) under stress, HSCs can return to the behaviors and problems of a younger age, and when feeling good HSCs can act older than their age, so the advice for an age that your child is not may still apply right now; and (3) understanding what was happening during the years before you read this book and what will happen in the years ahead can help you a great deal with your child today.

The "Applying What You Have Learned" sections at the end of some chapters are, of course, optional, but should be helpful and enjoyable. And the case studies provided are all of real parents and children, with the names and identifying details changed, of course.

Above all, I hope that you use this book with pleasure. Having an HSC is a great blessing. Yes, there are some complications because your child is "different," but here is this book's motto (it was mine even before I understood that my son was an HSC): *To have an exceptional child you must be willing to have an exceptional child.* You have one. And this book will teach you how to raise him to be not only exceptional, but healthy, loving, well-adjusted, and happy.

Is Your Child Highly Sensitive?
A Parent's Questionnaire

Please answer each question as best you can. Answer TRUE if it is true or at least moderately true of your child, or was for a substantial time in the past. Answer FALSE if it has not been very true of your child, or was never true.

My child . . .

1. T F startles easily.
2. T F complains about scratchy clothing, seams in socks, or labels against his/her skin.
3. T F doesn't usually enjoy big surprises.
4. T F learns better from a gentle correction than strong punishment.
5. T F seems to read my mind.
6. T F uses big words for his/her age.
7. T F notices the slightest unusual odor.
8. T F has a clever sense of humor.
9. T F seems very intuitive.
10. T F is hard to get to sleep after an exciting day.
11. T F doesn't do well with big changes.
12. T F wants to change clothes if wet or sandy.
13. T F asks lots of questions.
14. T F is a perfectionist.
15. T F notices the distress of others.
16. T F prefers quiet play.
17. T F asks deep, thought-provoking questions.
18. T F is very sensitive to pain.
19. T F is bothered by noisy places.

20. T F notices subtleties (something that's been moved, a change in a person's appearance, etc.).
21. T F considers if it is safe before climbing high.
22. T F performs best when strangers aren't present.
23. T F feels things deeply.

Scoring

If you answered TRUE to thirteen or more of the questions, your child is probably highly sensitive. But no psychological test is so accurate that you should base how you treat your child on it. If only one or two questions are true of your child, but they are extremely true, you might also be justified in calling your child highly sensitive.

PART I

AN OVERVIEW OF THE SENSITIVE CHILD

Chapter One

Sensitivity

A Better Light on "Shy" and "Fussy" Children

This chapter helps you decide if you have a highly sensitive child and explores the trait thoroughly. It also provides more knowledge about all of your child's inherited temperament traits. Our goal will be to free you of any misconceptions you may have heard about sensitive children. Finally, we will distinguish high sensitivity from actual disorders (which it is not).

Well, if he were my child, he'd eat what was set before him."

"Your daughter is so quiet—have you considered seeing a doctor about that?"

"He is so mature, so wise for his age. But he seems to *think* too much. Don't you worry that he isn't more happy and carefree?"

"Jodie's feelings are so easily hurt. And she cries for other kids, too, when they are teased or hurt. And during the sad parts of stories. We don't know what to do for her."

"In my kindergarten class, everyone participates in group time, but your son refuses. Is he this stubborn at home?"

Are these sorts of comments familiar to you? They are to the parents I interviewed for this book. They had heard all sorts of well-intentioned comments like these from in-laws, teachers, other parents, and even mental health professionals. If you've received such comments, it is almost surely a sign that you are the parent of a highly sensitive child (HSC). And, of course, they are troubling, because you're hearing that something is odd or wrong with your child, yet you find your child marvelously aware, caring, and *sensitive*. Furthermore, you *know* that if you followed the well-intentioned advice, like forcing your child to eat foods he dislikes, socialize when he does not feel like it, or taking him to a psychiatrist, your child would suffer. On the other hand, if you follow the lead of your child, he thrives. Yet the comments keep coming, so you wonder if you're a bad parent and if your child's behavior is your fault. I have heard this same story over and over.

THE OPERATING MANUAL FOR *YOUR* CHILD

No wonder you worry that you may be doing something wrong. You have no one to help you. You have probably noticed that most parenting books focus on "problem behaviors"—restlessness, distractibility, "wildness," and aggression. Your child is probably anything but a problem in these senses. You're struggling with issues that the books don't talk about so much—eating problems, shyness, nightmares, worrying, and intense emotions that are not directed so much at others as they are simply outbursts. The usual advice that you eliminate unwanted behaviors through "consequences" (punishment) often does not work—your child seems crushed by punishment or even criticism.

In this book you will receive advice, but only for sensitive children and from parents of sensitive children, myself included, plus specialists in this trait. And our first advice is not to believe people when they imply there is something wrong with your child, and do not let your child believe it either. Nor are your child's differences your fault. Of course parenting can always be improved, and this book will "improve" you more than others, because, again, it is written entirely with your "different" child in mind. But forget the idea that the problem is some basic flaw in parent or child.

"DISCOVERING" HIGH SENSITIVITY

According to my own scientific research and professional experience as well as that of many others who have studied this trait under different, less accurate labels, your child has a normal variation in innate human temperament. She is one of the 15 to 20 percent born highly sensitive—far too many for them all to be "abnormal." Furthermore, the same percentage of sensitive individuals is found in every species that has been studied, as far as I know. With evolution behind it, there must be a good reason for the trait's presence. We will get to that in a moment, but first, a little bit about this "discovery."

I began studying high sensitivity in 1991, after another psychologist commented to me that *I* was highly sensitive. I was curious personally, not planning to write a book or even to try to tell anyone about my findings. In my community and the university where I was teaching, I merely asked to interview people who were "highly sensitive to physical or emotionally evocative stimuli" or "highly introverted." At first I thought sensitivity might really be the same as introversion, which is the tendency to prefer to have one or two close friends with whom one can talk deeply, and not to be in large groups or meet strangers. Extroverts, on the other hand, like large gatherings, have many friends but usually talk less intimately with them, and enjoy meeting new people. It turned out that introversion was not the same as high sensitivity: Although 70 percent of highly sensitive people (HSP) are introverts, a tendency that is probably part of their strategy to reduce stimulation, 30 percent are extroverts. So I knew I had uncovered something new.

Why would a highly sensitive person be extroverted? According to my interviews, they were often raised in close, loving communities—in one case even a commune. For them, groups of people were familiar and meant safety. Others seemed to have been trained to be outgoing by their families—it was imperative, and as good HSPs they tried to do what was expected of them. One woman recalled the day and hour she decided to become an extrovert. She had lost her best and only friend and decided then and there not to depend anymore on having just one friend.

Since discovering that the trait of sensitivity is not the same as introversion, I have found other evidence that sensitive people are also not inherently shy or "neurotic"—that is, anxious and depressed. All of these descriptors are secondary, noninnate traits found in some sensitive people as well as in many who are not sensitive.

When I made my request to interview sensitive people, I was swamped with volunteers, and finally spoke individually with forty men and women of all ages and walks of life, for three hours each. They really wanted to talk about this—the term and why it meant so much to them the moment they heard it. (Many adults purchase *The Highly Sensitive Person* simply because they recognized themselves in the title, and likewise you may have bought this book because you recognized your child in its title.)

After discerning the many details of sensitivity from these interviews, I was able to create a long questionnaire about it, and later a shorter one (see pages 88–89), and have since given these to thousands of individuals. The 20 percent or so who are highly sensitive usually immediately grasp the concept as describing them. The nonsensitive 80 percent or so truly do not "get it" and some answer "no" to every item. I found the same results through a random phone survey. Sensitive people really are different.

Since then I have written and taught on the subject extensively, and soon saw the need for a book on raising highly sensitive children. There were too many sad stories from adults about their difficult childhoods, in which well-meaning parents caused tremendous pain because they did not know how to raise a sensitive child. So I interviewed parents and children, and from those talks developed a questionnaire that was given to over a hundred parents of all types of children. That survey, when honed down to the questions that best distinguish HSCs from non-HSCs, became the parent's questionnaire at the end of the Introduction.

WHAT *IS* HIGH SENSITIVITY?

Highly sensitive individuals are those born with a tendency to notice more in their environment and deeply reflect on everything before acting, as compared to those who notice less and act quickly and impulsively. As a result, sensitive people, both children and adults, tend to be empathic, smart, intuitive, creative, careful, and conscientious (they are aware of the effects of a misdeed, and so are less likely to commit one). They are also more easily overwhelmed by "high volume" or large quantities of input arriving at once. They try to avoid this, and thus seem to be shy or timid or "party poopers." When they cannot avoid overstimulation, they seem "easily upset" and "too sensitive."

Although HSCs notice more, they do not necessarily have better eyes, ears, sense of smell, or taste buds—although some do report having at least one sense that is very keen. Mainly, their brains process information more thoroughly. This processing is not just in the brain, however, since highly sensitive people, children or adults, have faster reflexes (a reaction usually from the spinal cord); are more affected by pain, medications, and stimulants; and have more reactive immune systems and more allergies. In a sense, their entire body is designed to detect and understand more precisely whatever comes in.

How HSCs Sort Oranges

When I was little my father liked to take our family to visit factories, where he would talk the managers into taking us on a tour. The steel mills and glass manufacturers overwhelmed me, of course, because I was highly sensitive. They were too loud, hot, and fiery, and I would cry, so that I dreaded these trips. My nonsensitive family members, on the other hand, were annoyed by my tour-stopping behaviors. But I liked one tour—the orange-packing plant. I liked the ingenious invention that moved the oranges down a shaking conveyer belt until they fell into one of three sized slots—small, medium, or large.

I now use that experience as a way to describe the brains of HSCs. Instead of having three slots for processing what comes down the conveyer belt to them, they have fifteen slots, for making very fine distinctions. And all goes well until too many oranges come down the belt at once. Then you have a huge jam up.

So of course HSCs probably will not like the loud mariachi band in the Mexican restaurant, noisy birthday parties, playing fast-paced team sports, or everyone watching while they give an answer in class. But if you need a guitar tuned, a clever idea for party favors, a witty play on words, or to win a game like chess that requires anticipating consequences or noticing subtle differences, your HSC is the one to have around.

Is It All or None?

Can your child be just a little sensitive? Some researchers say you either have the trait or you do not; others say it is a continuum. My own research says both—that is, some HSCs seem more sensitive than others, probably because there are so many ways that a child's environment can increase or decrease how much sensitivity is expressed. But if it were a true continuum, like height or weight, most people would be in the middle. In fact, the distribution of highly sensitive people is more like a flat line, perhaps even with a few more people at either end.

Inside the Highly Sensitive Child

Let's go farther inside the mind of your HSC. Yes, he notices more, but he may have a "specialty." Some tune in to social cues, mainly noticing moods, expressions, or relationships. Some HSCs mainly notice the natural world, such as changes in the weather or the qualities of plants, or they seem to have an uncanny ability to communicate with animals. Some express subtle concepts, or the humorous and ironic. And some are mainly vigilant in new surroundings while others are mainly bothered by a change in the familiar. Still, in all cases, they are noticing more.

Your HSC is also thinking more than other kids about what she has noticed. Again, there is always variation. She may be pondering and asking you questions about social dilemmas—why you did what you did, why one kid teased another—or larger social issues. Another HSC might be trying to solve difficult math or logic puzzles, or worrying about "what would happen if," or making up stories or imagining their cat's thoughts. All kids do these things, but HSCs do them more.

The HSCs' reflecting on "what's come in," particularly whatever they have seen or heard, may be quite conscious and obvious, as when they ask for more time to decide something. (You have probably noticed that trying to get an HSC to decide quickly is like trying to walk a male dog quickly past fire hydrants.) But often HSCs' processing is entirely unconscious, as when they just intuitively sense what is going on with you. Indeed, intuition might be defined as knowing something without knowing how you know it, and sensitive people are generally highly intuitive.

The processing may be rapid, as when a child instantly knows "something's up" or "you changed my sheets" when other children would not notice. Or it may be slow, as when HSCs think about something for hours, then announce some startling insight.

Finally, as a result of taking in more and processing it more completely, if the situation is creating an emotional response (and all situations do to some extent), your HSC is going to feel stronger emotions. Sometimes it's intense love, awe, or joy. But because all children are dealing with new, stressful situations every day, HSCs will also have to feel fear, anger, and sadness, and feel these more intensely than other children.

Because of these strong feelings and deep thoughts, most HSCs are unusually empathic. So they suffer more when others suffer and become interested early in social justice. They are also brilliant interpreters of what is happening in anything or anyone that cannot speak—plants, animals, organs in bodies, babies, those not speaking the sensitive person's language, and the very elderly when they suffer from dementia. They tend to have rich inner lives. And again, HSCs are conscientious for their age—they can imagine for themselves or understand when you say "what if everybody did that." They also tend to seek the meaning of their lives very early.

Mind you, HSCs are not saints. In particular, with a few bad experiences, they are more likely than others to become shy, fearful, or depressed. But with a little gentle guidance, they are exceptionally creative, cooperative, and kind—except when overwhelmed. And whatever they are doing—or not doing—HSCs do stand out, even though they are not "problems" in the usual sense.

Long before I knew I was raising a highly sensitive child, I just knew my son was "different." He was aware, incredibly creative, conscientious, cautious in new situations, easily hurt by his peers, not fond of "rough and tumble" play or sports, and emotionally intense. He was hard to raise in some ways, easy in others, and always stood out, even if only as the kid who was not joining in. So I developed the motto that I shared with you in the Introduction: *If you want to have an exceptional child, you must be willing to have an exceptional child.*

The Problem of Becoming Easily Overstimulated

Although I could sing the praises of HSCs for many pages, you are reading this book because you need help. Unfortunately, most people—and that includes parents—tend to notice mostly the down side of sensitivity. This is, again, because HSCs are easily bothered by things other children do not notice, and can become totally overwhelmed by a noisy, complex, constantly changing situation, like a classroom or a family reunion, especially if they are in that environment for too long. How could they not be bothered, when they sense so much in every situation? But given the fact that HSCs are in the minority, their reactions and solutions often seem odd to others. Hence all those hints from others, or perhaps suspicions in your own mind, that your child is abnormal.

What are some of the ways in which HSCs try to deal with overstimulation? No child will do all of these, but some will likely be familiar to you. Often HSCs complain a great deal—it's too hot, too cold, the fabric is too itchy, the food is too spicy, the room smells too weird—things other children would not even notice. And they may choose to play alone, watch quietly from the sidelines, eat only familiar foods, or stay in one room or indoors or in a certain spot outside. They may refuse for a few minutes, hours, days, or even months to speak to adults, strangers, or in class. Or they may avoid "typical, fun kid activities" like summer camp, soccer, parties, or dating.

Some HSCs throw tantrums and have rages to avoid what irritates or overwhelms them or as a reaction to it. Others try to cause no trouble, to be perfectly obedient, hoping no one will notice them or expect more of them. Some stay glued to the computer or read all day, mastering a smaller world. Others will begin to overcompensate for what seems to them to be a flaw, by striving to be stars or perfect.

Some overstimulated HSCs bounce off the walls and seem to have attention deficit disorder, ADD (but their attention is fine when they are not overstimulated and have their priorities straight—more about that later). Or they have "meltdowns," lying on the floor and screaming. Others become very still and quiet when overstimulated. Some develop stomachaches or headaches—their body's reaction and also its solution if that means they can go and rest.

Finally, as we will see, some HSCs feel they have tried everything and finally give up. They become afraid and withdrawn and lose hope.

Children can exhibit any of these behaviors for other reasons, and all children can become overstimulated without being HSCs. But too often sensitivity is the last explanation adults think of when children rage, are depressed, bounce off the walls, have stomachaches, or become stressed-out overachievers. It is my hope that, with the publication of this book, people will no longer overlook that possibility. At the end of the chapter I will discuss how to distinguish an over-aroused HSC from children who are not sensitive and children with more serious problems.

If There Are So Many HSCs, Why Haven't I Heard of This Before?

Today, we know that about 50 percent of personality is caused by innate temperament differences such as high sensitivity. The other 50 percent is caused by experiences or the "environment." But not so long ago psychologists believed that a person's personality was completely determined by experiences, especially experiences within the family.

When psychologists did begin to study temperament, it was easy to describe the actions and feelings of active children as they were observed in the laboratory or at school, but harder to describe those who stood in the back of the room or were quiet. You might say that this difference of doing less was the easiest to observe—all cultures observe this difference in people—but the hardest to describe. So observers tended to assume that the quiet ones were shy, afraid, unsocial, or inhibited. In identifying the trait of high sensitivity, we have simply gained a more accurate label.

I see no evidence that children are *born* afraid, timid, shy (afraid of social judgments), negative, or preferring to avoid human contact. Such innate fear would be a terrible flaw in a social species such as ours. It would not have withstood the tests of evolution and been passed on over generations, as this trait clearly has been. All of these reactions or characteristics, if they arise, can be better understood as a vulnerability due to something more basic, sensitivity. (Or in some shy, fearful, inhibited nonsensitive people, these reactions are purely due to bad experiences, but not genetics.)

What we call this trait *does* matter. Labels tell us what we are dealing with as well as affect how children are viewed and view themselves. Naturally, those in the majority, the nonsensitive, have developed assumptions about what is going on inside sensitive children. Sometimes they may be projecting a bit—seeing in the "other" what they do not like and want to be rid of in themselves (perhaps fear or what they see as "softness" or "weakness"). But from the inside, sensitive children and their parents know the rest of the story—these children are *sensitive*.

IS YOUR CHILD HIGHLY SENSITIVE?

If you have not already done so, fill out the questionnaire at the end of the Introduction. Every "true" is a statement about an HSC. These questions are the result of research involving thousands of children. However, not all the statements will be true of every HSC. Children, like adults, vary enormously, in both their other inherited traits and the environment in which they grow up. So another way to decide is to do what you are doing—reading this chapter—and then seeing if it seems to fit your child.

Parents often know right away that they have an unusually sensitive child. Any newborn can be fussy or colicky, but sensitive infants cry mainly when there's too much (for them) happening around them for too long. And for a sensitive infant, it takes much less to be "too much." Sensitive children are also more affected by the moods of their parents—for example, anxiety. You can imagine the vicious circle that can create—you will find more on this topic in Chapter 6.

On the other hand, some sensitive babies don't cry very much at all. Their parents have caught on to their infant's sensitivity, perhaps because they are sensitive themselves, and have kept their child's world calm and not too stimulating. Yet sensitive infants are still noticeable—they seem to follow everything with their eyes, respond to every sound or change in tone, and react to the fabrics against their skin or the temperature of their bathwater. As they grow, HSCs notice even more—that you are wearing a new shirt, that the broccoli has some spaghetti sauce on it, that there aren't any trees growing here, that Grandma moved the sofa. And again, they are even more easily overwhelmed as they grow because they are experiencing so much more and have not yet become familiar with what they see, or learned how to reduce what their senses are absorbing.

So Why Is My Child Sensitive but Others Aren't?

Any temperament trait is an innate, and thus very basic, aspect of a person's behavior. It is genetically determined and usually present from birth. The basic temperament traits are found not only in humans but in all higher animals. Think of the temperaments typical in different breeds of dogs—the friendly Lab, the aggressive pit bull, the protective sheep dog, the proud prancing poodle. How they are raised matters, too, of course, but you cannot make a bulldog act like a Chihuahua. These *personalities* evolved, or were developed by breeders, because they are highly adaptive in certain situations. Therefore they are *not* disorders or impairments. All of them are normal dogs.

Biologists used to think that evolution guided every species toward a perfectly adapted prototype for living in a particular ecological niche. There is a design for an elephant that will work perfectly—a perfect length of trunk, height, thickness of skin. Elephants born with these features will survive while those that do not will die out.

Yet it turns out that in most or perhaps all animal species we find two "personalities." A sizable minority are like your child—more sensitive, aware of subtleties, checking everything before proceeding—while the majority go boldly ahead without paying close attention to the situation or their surroundings.

Why would this difference exist? Imagine two deer at the edge of a meadow with grass that looks especially nutritious. One deer will pause a long time to be certain no predators are lurking. The other will pause briefly, then rush out and eat the grass. If the first deer was right, the second deer is dead. If the second deer is right, the first deer misses out on the best grass and, if this happens often, may suffer from malnutrition, become diseased, and die. So having two strategies, two "breeds" of deer in a herd, increases the odds of that group of deer surviving no matter what happens in the meadow that day.

Interestingly, even a study of fruit flies found this difference—and the gene that causes it. Some fruit flies have a place on their "forage" gene that makes them "sitters"—they do not forage far when food is present. Others are called "rovers" and do forage afar. Even more interesting, the gene causes the sitters to have the more sensitive, highly developed nervous systems!

In another animal experiment, looking at the "personality types" of pumpkinseed sunfish, a pond was filled with traps. According to the researchers, the majority of fish were "bold" and behaved "normally" by going into the traps, while the minority, the "shy" fish, escaped the traps. (What I want to know is why the two types weren't called the stupid and the smart sunfish? Or at least the nonsensitive and sensitive!)

HOW THE HUMAN SPECIES WILL BENEFIT FROM YOUR HSC

In human groups there are enormous advantages to having a large minority who reflect before acting. They notice potential danger sooner; the others can then rush out to take care of it (and even enjoy the excitement of it all). The sensitive ones think carefully about consequences, too, and often insist that the others pause, see what may happen, and develop the best strategy. Clearly the two work best in combination.

Traditionally, sensitive people have been the scientists, counselors, theologians, historians, lawyers, doctors, nurses, teachers, and artists (for example, at one time sensitive people naturally became their town's schoolmaster or -mistress, preacher, or family doctor). But, increasingly, sensitive persons are being nudged out of all these fields due to what seems to be a cycle that starts with the nonsensitive moving aggressively into decision-making roles, where they, quite naturally due to their temperaments, devalue cautious decision making, emphasize short-term profits or flashy results assertively presented over a quieter concern for consistent quality and long-term consequences, and do not need and so eliminate calm work environments and reasonable work schedules. Sensitive people are discounted, have less influence, suffer, or quit. Then the nonsensitive control the profession even more.

My description of this cycle is not meant as a complaint—merely an observation about a probable reason for these professions becoming more profit-oriented and less satisfactory in their results. In today's world, too, if decision makers are not thinking enough about complexities and consequences, there is also danger as well as discomfort when there is an imbalance between the influence of the sensitive and nonsensitive. So it is critical for all of us that your HSC emerge from your home feeling confident and important, so he can share his gifts and have a solid influence on others.

Your Child Is Still Utterly Unique—Like Rhoda's Three

Now that I have made a case for "sensitive" as the best label for this trait, let's admit one problem with labels (there are others of course). It seems as though as soon as we give something a label, we think we know quite a bit about it, whether it is a camellia, a German shepherd, or an HSC. In fact, we still know very little about each individual camellia, German shepherd, or HSC.

As I interviewed parents and children specifically for this book, I was stunned by the uniqueness of each HSC, even more than in adults. It made me agree yet again with Margaret Mead, who said that children are born with a great variety of traits, like the many hues of a palette, but the culture encourages only certain ones. The others are ignored or flatly discouraged, so that by adulthood there is less variety.

In childhood, however, there is a vast palette, even among HSCs. Consider Rhoda, a highly sensitive person with three older HSCs— ages twenty-two, twenty, and sixteen. As children, they were all more aware of stimuli than other kids. They all needed more rest and "down time" than their peers. People told all three of them at various times that they were "overreacting" and "too sensitive." Each found some form of artistic endeavor to express their intense awareness.

But such different children! Ann, the oldest, is a photographer. She likes fresh experiences—she rides motorcycles, jumps out of airplanes. Andrew, the middle child, is conservative, particular, and "fussy." He is a visual artist. His work is very detailed and careful. From birth he was always the most sensitive to sound and to scents.

All three are intensely emotional, but Ann and Andrew do not let it show. Tina, the youngest, has always been more dramatic and expressive. As a child she threw tantrums. As a teenager she has dark depressions. Her art form is poetry—something she can read out loud. Her colds are more likely to become bronchitis or even pneumonia, something that takes her to the doctor's office.

WHY DO EVEN HSCS VARY SO MUCH?

One reason for the variation among HSCs is that temperament traits seem to be caused by several genes, each having small, cumulative effects. Thus each different flavor of sensitivity—sensitivity to the subtle, the overwhelming, the new, the emotional, the social, or the physical and nonsocial—may be caused by a different gene. Yet there is still something common to these different sensitivities and they may tend to be inherited together. (If the underlying trait was not *one* trait, my questionnaire would have uncovered several different "factors," but there was only one.)

Here are more examples of the range of HSCs. Yes, Rhoda's youngest, Tina, had tantrums, as do many HSCs when young and overstimulated. But in this book you will also meet Alice, who is three and has never had a tantrum. She is strong-willed and opinionated, but when she wants something, she says it in a way that is almost uncanny in its maturity.

You will meet Walt, seven, who hates sports (but loves chess); Randall, nine, who will only play baseball, and only if his mother coaches the team; and Chuck, also nine, who will play any sport and be good at it. He climbs high and loves to ski, but he knows his terrain and his limits. (On a recent skiing trip, Chuck was caught at the top in a blizzard. He cried from the stress of it, but insisted on going down anyway.)

Chuck is an indifferent student; Walt and Randall are doing great academically. Catherine has been advanced almost every grade, starting with a move from preschool to kindergarten. And Maria was her high school's valedictorian and graduated summa cum laude in chemistry from Harvard.

You already read about Tina being an extrovert. Chuck is also extroverted, popular, already discovered by the girls. In contrast, Randall has limited friendships, mainly because he does not like to go to other homes—he dislikes the unfamiliar family members, food, and routines.

Sometimes the quality that parents notice most is their child's emotional sensitivity. You'll meet River, a teenager so aware of others' emotions that he begged his mother to take in a homeless person he found in the park. (His mother decided to let the man stay until her son realized the problems with the situation and found another solution, which he did after three months.)

Melanie, eight, is another HSC with emotional sensitivity. She cries if she feels embarrassed or if someone else is teased. Her sensitivity also extends to physical pain. Afraid of falling, she did not learn to ride a bike without training wheels until her sister, three years younger, learned. Her pride finally forced her to take the risk.

Walt is mostly sensitive to new situations and people. Consider Walt's first experience with grass: He crawled to the edge of a blanket, continued onto the grass, and cried from the shock of it. His mother remembers that two years later his sister crawled to the edge of the blanket, felt the grass, and just kept going.

Larry, thirteen now, is mostly sensitive to sound, clothing, and foods. Until kindergarten he only wore sweatshirts and sweatpants. He could not bear the roughness of jeans. Like Walt, he also doesn't like new situations—he refuses to go to camp or take long vacations.

Mitchell, five, seems to have all the characteristics of an HSC. He is sensitive to social novelty, so he's really struggling with starting school. He does not like birthday parties and will not wear a costume at Halloween, not wanting everyone looking at him. He is slow verbally because he's thinking so much before he speaks—he developed some stuttering after his older cousins came to visit because he had trouble speaking as quickly as they did. He has the physical sensitivity, too, so that he does not like foods that have been mixed or socks that rub. His mother cuts the tags from his clothing because they bother his neck and waist.

THEN THERE IS EMILIO

Emilio, seven, is not quite like any of the others, yet he has the same underlying "feel." He is very sociable and has no trouble meeting new people. He eats everything, eagerly, and is not fussy about what he wears. Yet despite his extroversion, he dislikes noise and parties and needs plenty of down time and a schedule. His sensitivity was clearly manifested in his self-imposed solution to overstimulation in infancy—in fact, it showed signs of true genius.

For the first two months of life Emilio had been crying every night at the same time, right on schedule, and was obviously miserable. Then his parents bought a playpen. From then on he was happy in it and nowhere else. He ate there, slept there, played there. If his mother took him out, he howled, and as soon as he was old enough, he crawled right back to it. He had no interest in exploring the cupboards or closets. He wanted his playpen!

Neighbors and relatives felt sorry for him, and told Emilio's mother she had to get rid of that baby prison and stunter of exploration—a perfect example of that familiar, well-meaning advice that implies something is wrong with either the child or the parents.

But Emilio's mother could not bear to separate her infant from his playpen. It made him too happy. The playpen was in the living room, so he was included in most family life, and to Prince Emilio it seemed to be more like a castle than a dungeon. So his mother decided to stop making an issue of it—as long as the floor of it did not break under her chubby son's bouncing! She knew he would not be there when he was twenty. And in fact, at two and a half, when his younger brother needed it, he gave it up, not wanting to seem like a baby.

Another Source of Variation—Two Competing Systems

Another reason for the variations in the behavior of HSCs is suggested by one of the scientific models for the cause of sensitivity, which is that sensitive persons have a very active "behavioral inhibition system." All brains have this system, but in the highly sensitive it is thought to be especially strong or active. For example, this system is associated with an active right hemisphere of the thinking part of the brain (the frontal cortex), and babies with more electrical activity and blood flow on the right side of the brain are more likely to be HSCs.

I prefer to call this system in the brain the "pause-to-check system" because that is what it really does. It is designed to look at the situation you are in and see if it is similar to any past situations stored in your memory. So it only causes "inhibition" for a moment—unless, of course, the prior similar situation was threatening. Otherwise, after a brief pause to check, one could just as easily decide to rush ahead.

For the highly sensitive, the pause-to-check urge is probably strong because they have so much input to process from every situation. Consider the two deer pausing at the edge of the meadow. The highly sensitive deer is noticing subtle scents, shadows, shades of color, tiny movements caused by the wind—or perhaps not caused by wind but by a predator. The less sensitive deer is not noticing all of this so has less to process, less reason to pause.

What the less sensitive deer has is a stronger "behavioral activation system"—it sees some good grass in the meadow and after a very brief check, it heads for it. This system, which I will call the "go-for-it system," causes us to be eager to explore, succeed, and pursue the good things in life. It makes us want new experiences, try new things, all in the interest of knowing, acquiring, thriving.

Again, everyone has both systems, and these two systems are controlled by separate genes. Thus one can have a very strong inhibition system or a strong activation system, or both, or neither. HSCs who are high on both are like Ann or Chuck—always exploring, trying new things, climbing higher. But being HSCs, too, they do it carefully, usually without taking big risks. They know their limits.

So, another major source of variation among HSCs is the relative strength of these two systems. I will discuss this more in Chapter 3.

Now It Really Gets Complicated—So Many Other Traits

Yet another source of variation besides different genes for different kinds of sensitivity and the relative balance of the aforementioned two systems are your child's other inherited traits. Those who study temperament have come up with several different lists. (I think of them as different ways to slice the same pie.) The best-known list is of nine traits, arising from the work of Alexander Thomas and Stella Chess. As you seek to better understand your HSC, it is important to know something about these other temperament traits. So let's consider each, in the light of high sensitivity (the definitions are from Jan Kristal's *The Temperament Perspective*).

1. *Low sensory threshold.* On this list from Thomas and Chess, low sensory threshold is the equivalent of high sensitivity, although their term seems to imply that the five senses are the main source of the trait and does not emphasize the deeper processing of experiences, including imagined or remembered experiences, with all their emotional implications.

2. *Activity or energy level.* Active children have a great zest for life. They are independent and approach everything with their entire mind and body *on*. They are usually well coordinated, quick to walk and talk, eager to learn, but exhausting to parent. Less active children are calm, seldom fidgety or restless, better at fine motor skills than gross ones, and in no hurry. HSCs can vary on this as much as other children (it is probably affected more by the go-for-it system). Being high in activity can help an HSC move out into the world. But when considering activity level, I like to think about both inner and outer activity. Some children, HSCs in particular, may be outwardly quiet but their minds are buzzing.

3. *Intensity of emotional response.* Intense children put considerable energy into their emotional expression. They seem dramatic and loud; you do not have to guess what they are feeling. Low-intensity children are subdued, showing their displeasure with little fuss, never a tantrum. Most HSCs have intense responses, but many would be considered low on this trait because they do not express their reactions outwardly, in dramatics, so much as inwardly, with stomachaches or anxiousness. It is usually not hard to see their intense response if you are paying attention. And HSCs who are outwardly intense—there are some—at least grow up with the advantage that they let the world know when they are overwhelmed.

3. *Rhythmicity.* Children with this trait are very predictable. You know what time they will be hungry, sleepy, or have bowel movements. When older, they are creatures of habit, keep their rooms orderly, eat regular meals and snacks, and get their work done on time. Most HSCs are fairly predictable, probably because they

thrive on order, and this can be a great advantage to you and your child. But your HSC may also be quite unpredictable.

5. *Adaptability.* Children who are very adaptable go with the flow; they can handle changes, transitions, and interruptions; they make good travelers. Slow-adapting children need to know what to expect and when to expect it, and don't like change that happens suddenly. They want to control situations when they don't know what to expect. A simple statement like "Time to eat" may be met with stalling or a complete tantrum. Most HSCs *seem* to be poor adapters, but in reality they are being asked to adapt to too much. They are overwhelmed, or afraid of being overwhelmed, by all the new stimulation that must be processed before they can relax. On the other hand, HSCs can see the consequences if they do not adapt, both for themselves and those around them, and will try their best to be flexible. What is frustrating for parents is that these children often keep it together when away from the family, then when they come home, they "lose it" when asked to make a small transition. For the sake of being socially appropriate, they have overtaxed their ability to handle change. At home they feel free to let go.

6. *Initial Reaction* or approach/withdrawal. One child rushes into things, another is slow to warm up. Most HSCs pause to check, but if the HSC also has a strong go-for-it system, she might be fairly quick to engage with new people and things if it feels safe.

7. *Persistence.* Some children stick to a task no matter what. They like to finish what they start; they will practice something until they master it. We say they have a long attention span, until it becomes a problem, then we call it stubbornness. Other children stay with an activity briefly, then move on. It may be that they are easily frustrated and give up more easily. This is a separate trait from sensitivity, but sensitivity affects it. For example, since HSCs process things so deeply, they tend to be persistent. But their vision of how to do something perfectly can make them frustrated when they cannot achieve it, which leads to overarousal

and a sense of failure, and then they want to quit and are not persistent. Or some will drop everything—not persist—if they see that someone needs or desires them to do something different.

8. *Distractibility.* This refers to how easily a child can be taken "off task" or shifts on his own from one activity to another. How does this differ from low persistence? A distractible child will look up from reading if someone walks by; if he is also persistent, the child will return to reading. A less persistent child keeps watching. A less distractible child would not even notice the person walking by. If he's also not persistent, he will not read for long either, but not necessarily because of any distraction. HSCs are fairly distractible, since they notice so much, but their deep processing usually overrides their distractibility—that is, in a quiet place with no inner worries they have deep concentration.

9. *Predominate Mood.* Some children are said to be naturally cheerful, some irritable, some pessimistic. Many temperament counselors no longer use these labels, because they recognize that a child's mood is deeply affected by her environment and experiences. I do not see any one mood predominating in HSCs, although I do see their moods affected more by life experiences than non-HSCs.

CLEARING UP AGAIN THOSE OLD MISCONCEPTIONS

As we come to the end of our introduction to highly sensitive children, it is equally helpful to pinpoint what your child is not. People have probably labeled your HSC in various ways that sound so true you may find it difficult to ignore those labels. So let's consider some of these and whether they have any real merit.

First, is your child "fussy"? Yes, HSCs are definitely bothered more by "little" discomforts, changes, or oddities. But "little" is in the eyes of the beholder. What seems neat, clean, comfortable, or scent-free to one person is dirty, miserable, and reeking to another. If it is the same macaroni to you whether it's shell-shaped or elbow-shaped, it is not to your tearful child. Respecting the reality of your HSC's experience is basic to getting along with her. It's okay if you do not like your child's reactions—you each have likes and dislikes—but you each have to be respectful. You can allow your child not to like the macaroni's shape, and she should be polite about it. Chapter 7 has advice on handling your child's discomforts. But we will not call this type of response "fussy."

Second, your child is not inherently timid or fearful. Again, I doubt any individual—animal or human—is born highly afraid of everything. Except for a few specific fears, such as the fear of falling, we learn what to fear from experience. It is actually rather easy to tell the difference between fear due to past bad experiences and sensitivity—people who like to pet dogs or cats know what I mean. Both the "shy" and the sensitive animals may hang back and watch you rather than rush forward. But the sensitive ones are alert, curious, and come forward eventually, deciding about you and then sticking to that decision the next time you meet. The frightened ones can barely look at you, are tense, distracted, and miserable, and may never come forward, or if they do, you have to go through it again the next time around.

It is also true that once HSCs have had bad experiences or feel unsupported, then when they do pause to check they cannot compare the new situation to old ones and assume all is well, so they truly are fearful. But to think of these children only as fearful is to miss their essence and especially their assets. When we see a lovely fair-skinned person with blond hair and blue eyes, we don't say, "Oh, look at that skin cancer–prone person." So why focus on the greater potential for fear in HSCs? It is important to regard every personality trait as having a purpose and to focus on the situations in which it is adaptive as well as the times when it is not.

In the same vein, HSCs are not born "shy." I doubt anyone is born shy in the sense of fearing the negative opinions of others and being seen as not good enough. Of course, the word *shy* is loosely tossed around, especially about those who hang back for any reason. "Shy" is even used with animals—people will say that one in every litter is born "shy." But when it is used in this loose way to describe any kind of hesitance, again, you are probably inaccurately labeling a child who is actually an HSC.

I was present on the first day of preschool for both my son and, fifteen years later, my nephew. Both boys, both HSCs, stood at the back of the room, just stunned by all the kids, toys, and activity. I could tell they were not afraid. They were just watching, fascinated. Both times a teacher came up and asked them if they were "shy" or "afraid." The labeling had already begun for them.

Third, introverted HSCs do not "dislike people." Introverts simply prefer being with one or two close friends rather than in large groups or meeting strangers. Another way to think of introverts is that they prefer to step back and reflect on what they encounter; extroverts prefer to rush forward. Introverts value the inner, subjective experience of what they encounter; extroverts value the outer, "actual" objective experience.

As I said earlier, when I began my research, I thought sensitivity might be the same as introversion, and by the last definition, it is. But most people think of introversion and extroversion as a description of how sociable one is. And by that definition, as I've said, about 70 percent of HSCs are introverts, but not all; some are extroverts. And not all social introverts are highly sensitive. Are introversion and extroversion inherited differences? We do not know for sure. What matters is that you know your child's preferred, most comfortable style.

Fourth, your child is not even "overly sensitive." Professionals with a medical background tend to think of sensitivity as a disorder, a problem of being "too sensitive" and unable to filter or coordinate the information they take in. For example, occupational therapists who use Sensory Integration Therapy to treat real problems include "oversensitivity" as a problem, as if it can be cured.

I do not wish to be critical of Sensory Integration, however. Certainly, sensitive children, like all children, may have a sensory integration problem. These show up as difficulty with balance, awkwardness or stiffness of motion, lack of coordination, and so forth. Many parents have told me that they found Sensory Integration very helpful for their HSCs, although it takes time. But I do not think being sensitive as I have defined it is a problem to be treated, much less cured. (Whenever anyone says an HSC is "overly" sensitive or taking in "irrelevant" information, I think of Sherlock Holmes, who found everything relevant.)

Finally, HSCs are not mentally ill and will not become mentally ill unless put under unusual stress. As Jerome Kagan of Harvard said about "highly reactive infants," 90 percent do not become consistently inhibited or anxious as adults. Studies of adolescent anxiety finds it unrelated to shyness in early childhood, except in rare cases in which the families already had members with anxiety disorders. Finally, there is my own research, which indicates that those HSCs with reasonably normal childhoods were no more prone to anxiety, depression, or shyness than non-HSCs.

Furthermore, two studies have found that "reactive" children (HSCs) with good childhoods are actually *less* likely to have physical illnesses or injuries than non-HSCs (suggesting they are emotionally healthier as well).

STILL UNSURE IF YOUR CHILD IS AN HSC?

At the start of the chapter I said that a good way to know if your child is an HSC is simply to read this chapter and see if it fits. To help you draw your conclusion I need to make a few more comments.

First, your child is probably not an HSC if he is sensitive about only one thing, or only about something that would be expected for his age. For example, most children develop a fear of strangers in the second half of the first year, and become fussy about how things are done when they are two. Most young children are bothered by very loud noises and separations from their parents. They almost all have some nightmares.

Your child is also probably not an HSC if there was no sensitivity or fearful reactions until a big stress or change in the child's life—a new sibling, move, divorce, or change of caregivers, for example. If your child's personality has undergone a sudden, persistent, disturbing change—such as becoming withdrawn, refusing to eat, developing obsessive fears, picking fights constantly, or developing a sudden, very negative self-image or sense of hopelessness—that needs to be checked by a professional team, which usually includes at least a child psychologist, child psychiatrist, and pediatrician. An HSC's reactions are fairly consistent from birth, not a sudden change, and not purely negative.

HSCs have responses that are more pronounced than those of a non-HSC, but they are within the normal range for HSCs, and the normal range on most other behaviors. They start to talk and walk at about normal times, although slight delays are common in toilet training or giving up a pacifier. They are responsive to people as well as to their environment, and eager to communicate with those they know well. And while young HSCs may refuse to talk at school at first, they should be talking at home and with close friends—that is, they should be relaxed in familiar surroundings.

HSCs and ADD

I am always asked about the relationship between the trait of sensitivity and attention deficit disorder (ADD). On the surface, there are similarities, and some professionals think many HSCs are misdiagnosed as having ADD. And, I suppose, it is possible for HSCs to have ADD. But the two are not the same at all, and in some ways are, in fact, opposites. For example, there is more blood flow to the right side of the brain in most HSCs, more to the left in those with ADD.

Children with ADD probably have *very* active go-for-it systems and *relatively* inactive pause-to-check systems.

Why are the two confused? Like children with ADD, HSCs can be easily distracted because they notice so much (although at times they are so deep in thought they notice very little). But ADD is a disorder because it indicates a general lack of adequate "executive functions," such as decision making, focusing, and reflecting on outcomes. HSCs are usually good at all of this, at least when they are in a calm, familiar environment. For whatever reason (the cause is not known), children with ADD find it very difficult to learn to prioritize, to return their attention to what they are doing once they have glanced outside or know the teacher is not talking to them personally.

Again, HSCs can generally tune out distractions when they want to or must, at least for a while. But it requires mental energy. Thus another reason HSCs can be misdiagnosed as having ADD is because, if the distractions are numerous or prolonged, or they are emotionally upset and thus overstimulated already from within, they may very well become overwhelmed by outer distractions and behave as if agitated or "spacey." They may tire midway through a long, noisy school day because they have to make a greater effort than others to screen out distractions. Also, if they fear they will perform worse in a given situation because of overarousal and distractions—for example, during an important exam—they very often do become overaroused and therefore notice some distraction they could ordinarily tune out.

Teachers may suggest that an HSC has ADD because there is usually money for treating ADD, so the student who is thus diagnosed will receive special help—as discussed, high sensitivity is a less familiar explanation for unusual behavior. (There is also considerable controversy among those who study temperament about whether much of ADD is simply normal temperament variation that is, like sensitivity, misunderstood. For an interesting cultural discussion of ADD, with much to say to highly sensitive people as well, take a look at *Ritalin Nation* by Richard DeGrandpre.)

Autism and Asperger's Syndrome

Usually, when a child has a serious problem, such as autism or Asperger's disorder, the parents or pediatrician have spotted it early on. Autistic infants do not smile, imitate facial expressions, follow a pointing finger with their eyes, or mouth the syllables of language. At two or three they have little interest in others or responses to others' needs and feelings. They apparently do not wish to communicate and do not engage in imaginary play, as far as we know. This is all very different from the behavior of an HSC, who is eager to communicate except when very overstimulated. High sensitivity is found in about 20 percent of the population; autism affects two to four children in ten thousand, and three quarters of them are boys. One is a normal variation, the other is a true disorder.

Asperger's syndrome affects about one in five hundred children and is five times more common in boys. Such children often exhibit motor problems, such as strange postures, gestures not matching their speed, awkwardness, poor rhythm, and unreadable handwriting. An HSC during the stress of an examination might show poor coordination but not the other symptoms. Children with Asperger's do seem to wish to communicate, but do so very poorly because they apparently lack an intuitive understanding of how to listen and when to talk. They cannot take hints, understand irony, keep secrets, or decipher facial expressions. They often talk monotonously on a subject no one else is interested in. None of this is true of a normal HSC.

The reason there is sometimes confusion here is that children with autism or Asperger's are usually very highly sensitive to sensory input. But again, they are not sensitive to social input, or at least not in an adaptive way, which makes them very, very different from HSCs. I do not believe that HSCs are on some normal end of an "autistic spectrum," although that argument has been made. A better description of children on the more normal end of the autistic spectrum would be those who are socially "odd"—eccentric, pedantic, or emotionally remote.

Again, normal children, HSCs included, are born ready and eager to relate; they are programmed for it. As we will see in Chapter 6, they are probably already emotionally responsive to their mother even in the womb; children with these other disorders are not.

What to Do If You Are Not Sure

If in doubt, have a team of professionals evaluate your child. Start by getting the name of a highly respected professional who takes a team approach, then get the names of the other professionals with whom he or she works. This may be costly, but problems caught early can usually be changed and with far less expense. You need a team because a pediatrician alone may emphasize physical symptoms or solutions. A psychiatrist will be looking for mental disorders that might be helped with medication. A psychologist will want to teach new behaviors but may miss a physical problem. Occupational therapists will emphasize sensorimotor problems and solutions; speech therapists will attend to verbal skills; a social worker will examine the family, school, and community environment. Together, they are great. Indeed, there may be some problem in each area that needs attention. (In my opinion, medication alone is never a sufficient treatment for a behavioral problem in a child, who should be learning how to cope with whatever problem she has.)

A thorough evaluation will take weeks, not hours. Those involved should want reports from you, your child's teachers or child-care providers, and any professionals who have already seen your child. They should ask for your family's medical records and history, and someone should observe your child and possibly you and your child together. Above all, they should talk about temperament as part of the total picture and sound knowledgeable on the subject. Unfortunately, many professionals are not, and they can make serious mistakes with an HSC. (See Resources at the end of the book for names of temperament counselors.)

Finally, during and after this evaluation, these professionals should be giving you support and encouragement. You need to be able to trust and respect these people; they are going to have a tremendous effect on your child's life. If you have doubts about an opinion, get a second one. Those who provide the first opinion should encourage that. Do not be rushed into any treatment unless there is a good reason for speed.

Remember, HSCs are normal kids who most of the time are relaxed and outgoing with those they know well. They listen and express themselves easily. When under stress, they are temporarily out of commission, perhaps very upset. But you will also have seen them feeling good, friendly, curious, and proud of themselves.

Should you look for a "cure" for your child's sensitivity? No. Temperament traits can be worked with so that the child learns how to cope and fit into a given culture, and parents can learn how to help with that. Trying to cure, remove, or hide a trait, however, is likely to lead to more trouble. Sensitive older boys and men in our society often feel they have to hide their sensitivity, and they do so usually at great personal cost. Variety in temperament is the "spice of life"— and perhaps the best hope of a species' survival.

A FINAL WORD: HSCS *ARE* ON THE WAY TO SUCCESS AND HAPPINESS

Do you have any lingering concern that your child may find it difficult to be truly happy or successful? If so, stop worrying. Many highly sensitive people have told me that they believe they feel far *more* joy and contentment far *more* deeply than others. And a host of them are prominent professors, judges, doctors, research scientists, widely published authors, famous artists, and renowned musicians.

Yes, your child will be more aware of the problems and the pain in the world. But perhaps the best definition of happiness came from Aristotle: We are happiest when doing what, by nature, we were born to do best. The born dancer is happiest dancing, not quite as happy when baking pies. The born gardener is happiest gardening, not quite so happy trying to write poetry. But one thing all humans were born to do, by nature, is simply to be aware, fully aware. In that sense HSCs are superb humans. Being superb at what they do best by nature provides them with this highest form of happiness, even when, in their case, it may also bring a greater awareness of suffering and loss, even death. You will be part of their working through the consequences of this awareness, which means your life, too, will be deepened.

As we will discuss in the next chapter, parenting an HSC is one of life's greatest and happiest challenges. You make more of a difference with such a child, and so the rewards are greater, as are the issues to be addressed. If being a parent makes you happy, then using Aristotle's argument, a child who asks more of you as a parent should be a source of greater joy.

APPLYING WHAT YOU HAVE LEARNED

Appreciating Your Own Child

Now that you are familiar with the trait of sensitivity, its flavors, the other temperament traits, and are rid of some misunderstandings about HSCs, you are in a very good position to take a fresh look at your child. Fill out the following assessment. You might want to do it alone, with your child's other parent, or with your child's teacher or regular caregiver (or you can each do it and compare).

I. Types of sensitivity (check off each kind that applies):

__ Physical, low threshold—for example:

    Sensitive to fabrics, rough socks, tags in clothes.

    Notices low sounds, subtle scents.

__ Physical, intensity—for example:

    Reacts more to pain than other children.

    Bothered by loud noise.

__ Physical, complexity—for example:

    Does not like crowds or bustling places.

    Does not like foods mixed or complex seasonings.

__ Emotional, low threshold—for example:

    Picks up on the moods of others.

    Good with animals, babies, bodies, plants (beings that cannot talk).

__ Emotional complexity—for example:

    Has interesting insights about what is going on with people.

    Has complex, vivid dreams.

__ Emotional, intensity—for example:

    Cries easily.

    Deeply upset by another's suffering.

__ Novelty, low threshold—for example:

    Notices small changes in room or your clothing.

    Prefers little or only gradual changes.

__ Novelty, complexity—for example:

    Does not need or like many new things happening.

    Dreads a major change such as moving to a new town.

__ Novelty, intensity—for example:

    Does not like surprises, being startled, sudden changes.

    Hesitant in all new environments.

__ Social novelty, low threshold—for example:

    Slow to warm up again with someone she has not seen for a while.

    Notices small changes in people after not seeing them for a while.

__ Social novelty, complexity—for example:
   The more unusual or unknown the person, the more hesitant.
   Does not like to be in large groups when some are strangers.
__ Social novelty, intensity—for example:
   Does not like to be the center of attention among strangers.
   Does not like meeting a lot of new people at once.
   Does not like to be questioned by a stranger.

Next, rate your child on the seven traits from Thomas and Chess (leaving out "sensory threshold" because it is the same as sensitivity and you have already measured that in a better way, and leaving out "predominate mood" for the reasons given earlier in the chapter). You can look back at pages 22–24 if you have forgotten to what these traits refer.

1. *Activity or energy level:* Low Medium High
2. *Intensity of emotional response:* Low Medium High
3. *Rhythmicity:* Low Medium High
4. *Adaptability:* Low Medium High
5. *Initial reaction:* Approaches Variable Draws back
6. *Persistence* (attention span): Low Medium High
7. *Distractibility* (easily shifts attention to a new stimuli): Low Medium High

Now, check off what you regard as your child's other strengths:
   Artistic ability
   Scientific ability
   Skill at mental games
   Athletic ability
   Patience
   Empathy
   Conscientiousness
   Great sense of humor
   Spiritual interests

Intelligence
Kindness
Concern for social justice
Others _____

Your child's problem areas (in your opinion). Some examples might be:
Trouble with coordination or playing sports
Shyness, often afraid of being rejected
Negative mood or behavior
Stubbornness
Rudeness, selfishness, lack of consideration
"Too good"
Not able to make "small talk"
Spends too much time at computer or _____
Anger
Too noisy, boisterous
Rejected by others for being aggressive
Rejected by others for being too passive
Slow learner
Learning disability
Attention deficit disorder
Others _____

Would the above problem areas be a problem for any parent, or are they things that particularly bother you? (Could you imagine this problem being "no problem" in another family?)

Major events can shape your child's life; beside each that applies, write what you think has been the effect:
Move
Divorce
Illness
Death in family

Death of a close friend, including beloved pet
Illness in family, mental or physical
Past abuse, physical or sexual
Persistent poverty
Prejudice
Unusual successes, awards, accomplishments
Public notice
Acquiring a very close friend
A special mentor (including a close grandparent, teacher, etc.)
Trips or other experiences that made a lasting impression
Lessons (musical, athletics, etc.)
Consistent activities—soccer, Scouts, etc.
Unusual living environment (big city, inner city, country, a farm,
    etc.)
Religious training
Cultural resources (gets to see many plays, is taken to concerts,
    scientists or writers often visiting family)
Other _____

Now, write a page or two about your child, based on the above—a
kind of summary, as if you were explaining him to someone.

• Begin with his sensitivity, then the other temperament traits he has.
• List all of your child's strengths.
• Then mention the problems, in your opinion.
• How are these problems affected by your view of them (would
  someone else find them "no problem")?
• Write something about how these strengths and weaknesses have
  been increased or decreased by your child's history.
• Finally, looking back at your child's sensitivity, how has it con-
  tributed to your child's strengths?
• How has it contributed to the problems?
• How has it contributed to your child overcoming her problem
  areas?

- How has your child's sensitivity been interwoven with her major life experiences? Did it increase their impact in some cases? Decrease it in some cases?
- Go back and underline what you have learned that you did not know before. How do you think this will change how you treat your child?

Keep these pages—you may find a time when it would be useful to give them to a teacher, long-term caregiver, doctor, or interested family member.

Chapter Two
Fasten Your Seat Belts
The Challenges of Raising an Exceptional Child

> *In this chapter you learn why skilled parenting helps HSCs even more than other children, and why the skills are different with HSCs. We discuss the six qualities of HSCs that present the greatest challenges, and you will begin to learn how to respond effectively when they arise. We will also take note of all the joys that come with raising an HSC.*

In the last chapter I mentioned Maria, a "typical" HSC who graduated summa cum laude from Harvard. But it did not happen without skilled parenting.

Maria's parents did not have all the advantages that you might imagine come with the family of a Harvard graduate. Estelle, Maria's mother, has had a difficult life, starting with her own childhood. She was an HSC in a troubled family that made her the scapegoat because she was different from the rest of them. As she expressed it, "At least I knew what hurts a sensitive child."

When Maria was born, Estelle and her young husband were living below the poverty line and neither family was helpful. Indeed, Estelle felt she had to protect her new baby from the meddlers and disturbed people in *both* families. Her intuition was apparently right—one of Maria's grandfathers was later convicted of child molesting. These were not easy circumstances in which to raise a child, much less an HSC.

As soon as Estelle realized that Maria was as sensitive as she had been ("I knew it at two weeks—she could maintain solid eye contact as I walked around the room"), she decided to stay home and give full attention to her daughter during the formative years. She learned all that she could about parenting, but adapted it to fit the different kind of child she knew she had—one like herself. She automatically cut the labels out of clothing. She had always preferred simple foods, so food was never a problem between them. In raising Maria, Estelle applied the understanding of both parenting and sensitivity that she wished her parents had had.

For example, Estelle rarely pushed Maria into new experiences the way some parenting books urged. But there were important exceptions, when Estelle knew Maria would be all right and was too young to know for herself what she could reasonably do and enjoy. In one instance, as a teenager, Maria was invited by family friends to go to Sweden. Maria did not want to go. Her mother insisted. Ten days into the trip, Maria called from Stockholm to say how grateful she was to her mother for forcing her to go.

Mostly, however, Estelle defended her daughter's right to say no because of her sensitivity. In elementary school her class was obliged to watch a movie about animals being butchered. Deeply upset, Maria walked out—to her teacher's consternation. Estelle told her she was right—she did not have to watch anything that distressed her that much. The incident and others like it led Estelle eventually to place Maria in a private school. There she blossomed, became her school's valedictorian, and was encouraged to apply to Harvard.

Estelle always placed great emphasis on promoting Maria's self-esteem. In high school Maria grew and grew, to over six feet—yet another characteristic that made her feel different. But although Maria was "shy," the combination of self-esteem and sensitivity made her a natural leader. Starting even in kindergarten, kids listened to her, copied her ideas. She was cautious with new people but wanted to play with other children and did, with no obvious problems. According to her mother, she just played with fewer children than most kids did. It also seemed to Estelle that there was always a "sensitivity gap" between her daughter and other children. They were not as considerate or as aware as Maria.

Today, as a young adult, Maria's life is not completely easy. She still wishes she was not so sensitive or tall. She is twenty-seven and still not in a "permanent relationship." According to her mother, "she always finds something wrong with a man." That sounds like the "sensitivity gap" she felt in childhood, coupled with the ability of highly sensitive people to spot the flaws in a close other, especially one who is not as sensitive. Maria has changed residences several times since she left college, trying to find a quiet enough place to live. But she is successful in her profession and travels to foreign countries without hesitation—that trip to Sweden she resisted was only the first of many. She is healthy and confident about her future. She is an HSC who has grown up wonderfully, thanks to responsive, sensitive parenting.

WITH AN HSC, YOU MAKE A BIGGER DIFFERENCE

Every now and then someone is on the talk-show circuits arguing that genetics determine everything and parenting does not matter. Yes, at one time there was probably too much emphasis on the role of parenting, especially mothering, in shaping a child's personality. No one even considered the role of inherited temperament. So a balance was certainly needed.

Ironically enough, however, the research is now clear that parenting does matter, and much more, in raising children like HSCs, whose temperaments are at the extreme end of normal. And in studies done with monkeys, "reactive" (sensitive) monkeys randomly assigned at birth to be raised by especially calm mothers (studies we cannot do with humans) turned out to be far more resilient adults, even troop leaders, compared to those raised by nervous mothers.

Reactive monkeys who were randomly assigned to be subjected to separations from their mothers, on the other hand, were far more affected in adulthood by this trauma than less reactive monkeys.

Most HSCs do not have to deal with being totally separated from their caregiver, but research finds that they are more likely to be affected by caregivers who are mentally absent—due to stress or depression, perhaps—or who would just as soon not be there, or who may be overly afraid themselves about losing a close other. For example, Megan Gunnar and her colleagues at the University of Minnesota found that highly sensitive nine-month-olds left for a half hour with an attentive baby-sitter "playmate" were far less distressed physiologically during this separation from their mothers than they were when they were left with an inattentive caregiver. An attentive caregiver was almost as good as having mom present, but an inattentive one made the separation more stressful for HSCs than non-HSCs.

In another study, focusing on the general security or insecurity of the bond with the mother, these same researchers found that highly sensitive eighteen-month-olds who were generally insecure with their mothers (I will discuss this more in Chapter 6) had distressed bodily reactions in new situations, while secure HSCs were not affected. Non-HSCs were also not distressed by new situations, of course—whether their relationship with their mother was secure or not. That is, only the insecure HSCs' were deeply distressed in new situations. Several more studies have found the same general results.

The conclusion? "A history of responsive, sensitive caregiving . . . provided the securely attached infant with the resources to reduce activation of the [bodily distress] system, even though the child's temperament might bias him or her to experience novel events as 'potentially' threatening." In other words, when sensitive toddlers are in the stressful situation of being separated from their mothers, they are all right if left with a caring person and not all right if left with an inattentive person. If they are in an unfamiliar situation that is particularly stressful for them, they are more affected by an insecure attachment to their mothers. They are very affected by the sense they will receive help if they need it. Not only do HSCs need to perceive support in such situations because they are more aware of the dangers, but they are also probably more aware of the degree of support and caring of their mothers and other caregivers.

GOODNESS OF FIT—EACH CHILD EXPERIENCES A DIFFERENT FAMILY, A DIFFERENT FIT

Interestingly, researchers find that whatever a family does do to influence a child's personality, it affects each child differently, as if each is growing up in a completely different family. Some of this is due to the parents being in a different situation when each child is born, and some of it is that each child is different so parents respond differently, or conversely, the same parenting methods may affect two children quite differently, depending on their temperaments. Probably most parents are not "good" or "bad" so much as they are specialists, naturally working well with some temperaments more than others.

The implication is that if you have more than one child, one may thrive in your care, another may not do as well. But research also finds that a little understanding and training can affect that greatly— "goodness of fit" matters more than parent and child having the same temperament. A good fit is a family and school environment that supports and encourages a child's natural way of behaving. In one family, a quiet artist who does not like sports will be considered ideal. In another, this child will be a huge disappointment. *But there is always a good fit when parents accept their children for who they are,* then adapt their methods to suit the child. Studies in which parents are trained to understand their child's temperament consistently find that the children of these parents have far fewer problems.

One way to describe this book is to say it is essentially about what you can do to create a good fit between you and your child. Since each of you are individuals, this book will sometimes miss something important about one or both of you. That is why I am saying right here that it is smart to have a top-notch temperament counselor or therapist aware of temperament to whom you can turn while raising your HSC. That way you do not have to go looking for someone when you feel you're in a crisis. You have a professional to help you with your taxes or when buying a house. Why not with parenting?

This book can, however, take you a long way with your HSC, because there is so much that HSCs have in common that most "child experts" do not know. We will begin with one of the big ones: To create a "good fit" you must learn to appreciate your child's excruciating sensitivity to *you*, the One in Charge. Fortunately, although I did not know it, I had been forced to appreciate this reality even before I had my own HSC.

The Beagle and the Border Collie

As I said in Chapter 1, the fact that there are different breeds of dogs is a good way to understand that there can be different "breeds" of children, too. We know some dog breeds are well suited for some owners, but not for others—that's why there are so many. But the owners can also learn to adapt to the temperaments of their dog. If they learn in time.

When I was young, my parents bought me a beagle I promptly named Star. If you know beagles, they are generally tough little dogs with a nose that takes them exploring everywhere, at which times they could care less about you or anything else but The Scent. I suppose they are sensitive in their noses, but nowhere else. When Star was about a year old, my mother and I became involved in obedience training and eventually she, then I, tried to show Star in dog shows. In the show ring she was an angel while on a leash, but once off it, she was *out of there*, running sometimes for blocks, following the aroma of her Holy Grail. Later we bought poodles to train and show—they were perfect for obedience shows, but they were high-strung performers, terribly nervous and demanding of attention.

After I left home and married, I wanted another dog and another breed. I did not know why (not knowing yet that I was highly sensitive or that dogs could vary on this trait), but I had always admired border collies—those black-and-white dogs that herd sheep. I was sure they would be perfect for showing in obedience-training shows. So I bought one, and soon had a devoted, intelligent companion.

This dog, Sam, seemed able to read my mind. Housebreaking was easy—I just took her outside while she was "making her first mistake," and she never made another. She only tore up one object while teething—I was home later than usual one evening and I found bits of an old paperback for a psychophysiology course, appropriately titled *Animal Emotions,* all over the floor. Had she learned to read?

When Sam was nine months old I put on a choke collar and took her out for her first obedience lesson, learning to sit. I gave her backside a smart slap (I had been taught that a push would cause the dog to resist and push back), jerked the collar to bring her head up and get her attention, and said "sit." She collapsed on the ground, quivering. Since that was the wrong response, I got her to her feet and repeated the standard way to train a dog to sit—spank, jerk, order. She crouched lower to the ground, shook more, her eyes pleading with me, "Why? What have I *done?*"

I knew enough to stop and think it over. But the next day I tried the same method. I knew that once she did it right I could praise her and she would understand that better. But first she had to sit properly.

By the time I figured out that a gentle pressure and kind word would do it, I had almost ruined her. In fact, she never got over shaking and crouching when I brought out that collar. She learned to sit, stay, heel, and much more, once I got it that all she needed was to understand what I wanted: Wait here, go rest in the corner, meet me here later, fetch it, carry it, herd away the cows, gather up the puppies, keep the baby in the yard. Often she knew what was needed before I did—like bringing my husband and me together when we had lost each other in the woods at night, or driving off a burglar. (The joke in my family growing up was that Star the beagle would have gone off with any burglar with a hot dog in his pocket.)

It was natural for Sam to know what was needed and to care enough about us to do it because she was so *sensitive*. As for the dog shows, we never went to any—something about her made me not want to take advantage of her goodwill by making her a public spectacle.

I doubt that any method would have made Star the beagle consistently obedient when her leash was off, but the usual methods worked well enough to teach her what I wanted. Sam needed much more specialized skills and thoughtfulness on my part. That is how it is when an animal or child can almost read your mind and be quite overwhelmed by a harsh word from you, the beloved authority. I still did not "officially" know about this trait when my son was born. I did not know until he was grown and gone. But Sam had given me a good intuitive introduction.

Not Knowing How Makes Parenting Anything but Satisfying

I had thought of myself as a very good dog trainer when I started in with Sam, and there was a showcase full of trophies and ribbons to prove it. But Sam humbled me. She also made me feel guilty for causing her so much stress, bewildered as to why the usual methods did not work, depressed about myself for failing, angry with her for being such a wimpy dog, and isolated (if the standard methods did not work, who could I turn to for help?). I obsessed about why she was acting so strangely, and when I redoubled my efforts I only made her worse. At that point, training Sam was not satisfying.

Lack of skill in parenting an HSC can cause the same emotions. You think you are pretty good at parenting, especially if you have some experience with children. Then along comes this child who humbles you. I have heard parents talk about all of it: feeling guilty for their child's obvious suffering at their hands, public embarrassment about their child's shyness, fussiness, tears over "nothing," fears, and so forth. There is the bewilderment. And for some parents there is depression, especially as sleepless nights pile up. There is anger, a sense of inadequacy, isolation from other parents with "normal" children. Some parents feel victimized, trapped, overinvolved. It can affect a marriage, the other children, and a parent's health. And it is definitely not satisfying.

DIFFICULT VERSUS EASY HSCs

Parenting certain HSCs is also more difficult than parenting others. Some are real "drama queens" and demanding "little princes." This partly depends on other aspects of their temperament, such as their persistence, flexibility, and emotional intensity, plus the child's role models and general environment. (If your frustration, or anything else in your life, is making you upset, demanding, or out of control, you can hardly expect your child to be different.)

I also find that parents who are more accepting of the trait and generally available and responsive to their child are the ones, ironically, whose HSCs are more "trouble" when small. This is because their child feels free to express his feelings—to get angry, wildly excited, frustrated, hurt, frightened, and overwhelmed. Once the feelings are out, however, the skilled parent teaches the child how to cope with them.

Parents who are less available and responsive—perhaps they are overwhelmed themselves, or not comfortable with intense emotions—may cause an HSC to hide her feelings in order to be accepted and not cause any trouble. But the child never learns to cope with these bottled-up feelings, and they usually resurface in other ways in adulthood, when it is much harder to fix. So I always worry a bit when parents tell me that their HSC "never caused us any trouble at all."

The Vicious Cycle

With those of you who are trying so hard, only to find that your child is still not happy, outgoing, and "normal," I often see a vicious cycle: You worry, you try harder to shape your child to meet your expectations, your child does not behave the way you want (because he cannot), so you worry more, try harder, and so forth. Both you and he feel like failures. So we return to the first advice in this book: Realize that your child's unusual behaviors are not your fault and not your child's fault. HSCs are not being difficult on purpose!

This cycle is more common with nonsensitive parents of an HSC—a situation thoroughly discussed in the next chapter. But even highly sensitive parents can be unsure how to cope with an HSC and desperately wish their child was different.

Mitchell's Mother Finally "Gets Out of Her Own Way"

Mitchell's mother did not realize that she and her son were both highly sensitive. Sharon had been raised in a pretty tough, not very sensitive family. She did not remember consciously adapting to them. She just did.

But she was very sensitive to her new baby, Mitchell. She loved to sing, and she could not miss the signs that her baby did not like to be sung to. When he was older, he did not like to sing either—at least not in the children's choir in which she had planned to see him shine. Sharon was equally frustrated when he would not wear a costume at Halloween and still needed a pacifier at four. And she was sad that "he couldn't initiate—I saw him as always the follower, the imitator, never the leader."

Then a speaker came to Mitchell's preschool and talked about sensitive children. "Suddenly," Sharon said, "the light went on." She went on to tell me how much she wishes she had understood sooner and "gotten out of my own way and stopped judging my parenting. Deep down I had known what to do. But I was not doing it and was blaming myself for the results, especially when the rest of the family thought there was something wrong with what I was doing. Now all that is over. I mold myself to fit his behavior. I let him tell me what he needs.

"And he has so many wonderful qualities, too—his sweetness and gentleness. So if he doesn't want to run off and do a skit at our family reunion, now it's not a big deal to me. It's almost a pleasure to say, 'No, he doesn't want to do it.' It feels good to understand so well when others don't."

THE SIX MOST COMMON PROBLEMS

So let's get to work by discussing six facets of your child's high sensitivity and how each, although neutral in itself, can cause certain problems for you as a parent until you have the right skills. You will also begin to learn some of those skills in this chapter.

1. Awareness of Subtleties

What a wonderful quality in some situations: your daughter notices your every loving glance and returns it, can tell you when her little brother is hungry before you ever thought about a feeding, and functions like a living smoke alarm, letting everyone know if there is a bit of smoke anywhere, even from the next-door neighbor's chimney. In other situations, what a pain. In particular, HSCs notice when the smallest thing is not to their liking. "There's some skin left on this apple—you know I hate skin." "This room stinks" (you cannot smell a thing unusual). "You moved my computer, didn't you?" "Yes, that's the flavor I like, but the wrong brand—this kind tastes chalky."

Not all HSCs notice subtleties. There are a few who seem fairly oblivious, being more preoccupied with their inner world. Or they may be bothered more by intensity—loud noise, bright lights, or spicy foods—and less by subtle stuff. Or they may only notice subtleties in one area—just food or clothing or social nuances. But with an HSC, it's bound to come up somewhere.

Chapter 7 will focus on coping with the problems that arise with this quality of HSCs. In the meantime, here are some general pointers:

- *Believe your child.* When your child says it hurts, rubs, or stings, it does, even if the same thing doesn't bother you.
- *With little HSCs, keep them fed and rested*—they will be less irritable and better able to wait for you to relieve a discomfort.
- *When HSCs are old enough to understand you, first acknowledge your child's discomfort, then let him know when and how it will end* or that you simply cannot do anything about it if that is truly the case. If you have first conveyed sincere respect for your child's response and sympathy for his desperate need, and your own valid reason to delay or do nothing—you have to finish the shopping, get to the car where there are dry clothes, use up this brand because you cannot afford to waste it—he will grow in the ability to understand that and wait.
- *Put limits on what you can be expected to do.* Some children find their shoelaces uncomfortable, but even if you tie them fourteen times they will still feel all wrong, possibly because your child is so focused on this sensation and frustrated. Discuss it when you are not tying shoes—that you will try five times, trying to follow her instructions. The fifth time will have to suffice because you've become frustrated, too, or do not have the time to continue.
- *Stick to your standards* of politeness and good public behavior, but remember emotions are sometimes irrational and overwhelming, even for adults. If your child is losing all control over what seems like a "small matter," solve the situation for now as best you can, or if you cannot, let your HSC cry or scream while you simply hold her (if young) or stay with her and sympathize. When things are calm, perhaps the next day, the two of you can discuss what needs to be done so that she will behave better the next time.

• *When possible, put your child in charge of the solution.* A parent with a son who is fussy about socks has him choose the ones that will not bother him. If there are none, it is not mom or dad's fault.

2. Being Easily Overstimulated and Overaroused

As I said in Chapter 1, a child who notices subtleties will also become overwhelmed when too much is coming at once. (The "too much" can come from outside, but also from inside, as when a child imagines something very frightening or exciting.)

The more stimulation, the more the body becomes aroused to deal with it. Every animal and human seeks just the right level of arousal—it's as automatic as breathing. Too little and we are bored, restless. We put on the radio or call a friend. Too much and we are uncomfortable, rattled. We try to calm down, but if we can't, we perform poorly at whatever task we are doing—hitting a ball, solving a math problem, thinking of things to say in a conversation. HSCs become overaroused more easily. That means your daughter may be perfectly able to catch a softball when the two of you play catch at home, but in a game she drops the ball as often as she catches it. She starts to hate playing, she cries during games, yet she wants to play and you want her to. You think, why so much drama around a simple game of ball? Do you make her play or let her quit?

First, understand that HSCs will have areas in which overarousal causes great difficulty. These are usually activities in which, early on, they have had a failure or imagined they would have one. The next time they try they are more aroused and anxious rather than more relaxed, so they do even worse. But performance anxiety is not always the culprit—they can be eager to perform and confident and still be overaroused by the lights and the crowd.

Can we ever see this proneness to overarousal as a good thing? Overarousal itself is never helpful, but needing so little to reach a comfortable level has its uses. HSCs are usually less easily bored, for example. And they are more caring, involved performers in situations when others might not make an effort.

Are there HSCs who do not become easily overaroused? Most have some areas in which they are so at ease that they can function smoothly even under great pressure or conditions of high stimulation. But in other areas, the overarousal usually appears. Chapter 7 will help with dealing with overarousal in general, and Chapter 8 will help when it leads to shyness in social situations. In the meantime, here are some general pointers:

- *See that your child has an area of competence*—a sport, form of art or self-expression, academic subject, magic show, comedy routine, experiences of chatting with interested adults, or leading other kids in a fantasy game. Choose something he is interested in and start slowly, seeing that at first every attempt meets with success.

  With my son this worked with drama and writing. When I enrolled him in an acting class at age eight, I actually asked the teacher to praise him—he had had so many failures in sports. He came out of his first class beaming: "She says I'm a born actor!" He never missed a class after that.

  With writing, I made a point of seeing that he never handed in a paper that was not typed and well done. The good grades and praise made him love it.

- *See that your child is so overrehearsed and so skilled that nothing will faze her.* Practice in the same circumstances and setting as she will actually be performing the skill. Go to the baseball diamond to practice. And once your child is prepared for the arithmetic test, give him some problems to do with a time limit and that you will grade afterward. Never let an HSC go into a test or performance underprepared.

- *Talk about things that can go wrong and how to handle them.* Talk about mistakes and how to understand them. It is the bottom of the ninth, the score is tied, and your child strikes out. Discuss ahead of time that this is bound to happen at least once in every baseball career. What can your child say to herself and to others to make it bearable? (Does that seem like planting the expectation to fail? Usually, your child will have already imagined failure; you are planting the seed of coping.)

* *Explain the effect of overarousal on performance and comfort.* Explain that he has the skill, but nervousness (or noise, a new setting, an audience, or other overstimulation) can sometimes interfere. Tell your child this story: I knew a woman who could break world records in her sport at small contests, but could never do it at the Olympic trials. She and I had to conclude that the Olympics did not identify the best athletes, but the best athletes *under conditions of very high stimulation.*

* *See that some of your child's competencies are not ones that can be much affected by pressure*—for example, artwork, skilled care for a pet or plants, and physical activities like long-distance running or hiking in which one meets personal goals.

* *Help your child enjoy a variety of activities at a noncompetitive level*—singing with you in the car or doing a play for a supportive family audience. She does not have to try out for choir or join the drama club to enjoy these. If a talent does appear, you can always encourage it, but "being a pro" is less important than enjoying.

3. Deep Inner Reactions

Although reactions subside once an HSC is familiar with a situation, during the initial processing, reactions can spiral *higher.* As I said in Chapter 1, because HSCs process everything more fully, they also have stronger emotional reactions. The more that a new emotional situation is experienced and its full implications and consequences imagined, the more impact it will have. That means more happiness, joy, satisfaction, contentment, and ecstasy. And more miserable feelings, too.

These intense reactions do not require a fully developed, conscious mind. They start in infancy and are present in small children, even if they cannot talk about them. Older children, who can talk about feelings, still may not be conscious of them—we all repress feelings if they seem unacceptable. These repressed feelings show up as physical symptoms or inexplicable, displaced emotions. The classic example, seen frequently by child therapists, is a child who claims to be delighted with a new little brother or sister, a reaction that the parents of course brag about to everyone. But the child is now terrified, maybe, of being eaten by dogs or using the toilet or pictures of monkeys. These weird fears go away when a wise parent or therapist gets the child to play games like the big dog eating the baby dog, followed perhaps by an honest discussion of all the different, normal feelings people have, including anger, and some of the feelings a new brother or sister can create. Some feelings we only talk about—we do not do what they make us feel like doing—but they are still okay to have.

Even when the emotions are not worrisome, like hating one's baby sister, HSCs may not show their tumultuous inner life to the rest of the world. The introverts—70 percent of HSCs—will often keep it all inside. The intense and extroverted HSCs will express themselves more.

HSCs are often even more distressed than other children by unfairness, conflict, or suffering; for example, they may be deeply sad about the loss of the rain forests, racial injustice, or the mistreatment of animals. They tend to foresee dire consequences. They are usually quite disturbed at seeing other children teased. They lose their appetites if their parents have a fight. It is all typical stuff for children, except stronger.

Are there exceptions? Always. Some HSCs are able to develop strong self-regulation of their own emotions, perhaps even too strong. How much feeling to feel is a question all people face (although some have less choice), and the answer is often decided by culture and the family style, and particularly by what parents teach a child about emotional expression. Usually nothing needs to be said to teach an HSC to control her emotions. She senses what is wanted. For example, parents who are embarrassed or afraid of the strength of their own feelings or the feelings of their child will convey by their avoidance of emotions that feelings are best kept unexpressed. On the other hand, if an HSC lives with parents who often lose control emotionally and he has inherently strong emotional self-regulation abilities, he may decide total control is preferable to the chaos created by his parents.

We will talk more about handling strong emotions in Chapter 7, but here are some general suggestions:

- *Think about how you handle emotions and how you want your child to handle them.* Think about each emotion: sadness, fear, love, happiness, anger, and curious excitement. Which ones were not allowed when you were growing up? Are you teaching the same lessons to your child?

- *Read up on "emotional intelligence."* Mary Kurcinka's *Kids, Parents, and Power Struggles* is excellent for helping parents become sound emotional coaches for their children. Her book has whole lists of tips for the parents of any sort of child: For example, listen to the emotions first rather than lecture about the behaviors, teach your child what soothes and calms her, and get to know your child's emotional cues so you can help her recognize her feelings.

- *Talk to your HSC about emotions.* These children in particular need to be able to name what they are feeling and what might have caused it so that they can feel more in control over the inner tumult. Talk about how you have handled similar feelings.

- *Strive to "contain" your child's negative emotions* until your HSC can do it for herself. Ideally, you go off to a quiet place and let the child fully express the feelings while you remain calm and nondefensive. Your attitude should be "tell me more, tell me all about it, and what else, and what else. . . ." This full expression will allow both of you to later get at what was the real cause, and meanwhile your child can feel all that is happening inside without having to endure it alone. You will hold it with her until, with years and experience, she can hold it alone. We will consider this containing task more in Chapter 7.

- *Be attuned to positive emotions, too, matching their tone.* You want to respond to negative emotions with attention and respect, but do respond to positive feelings equally. Do not squash your HSC's enthusiasms and happy moods with comments like "If you're so happy, this is a great day to clean your room."
- *Be aware of how being overstimulated and overaroused can increase all emotional reactions,* especially the negative ones. A mood often passes with a good night's sleep, while staying up and trying to talk it away can only add to the overstimulation. Always try, "Shall we sleep on it?"
- *If any powerful emotion lasts for several days, you may want to seek some help.* This includes depression, anxiety, anger, and also happy but sleepless "hyper" states. You do not have to take your child to a psychologist—that may be quite distressing in itself. You might start with you and a professional trying to figure it out without your child around. And the goal should be understanding what caused these lasting feelings, not merely medicating them away. Medication should be a last (but invaluable) resort.

4. Awareness of Others' Feelings

Given that humans are social animals, if you combine an awareness of subtleties and an intense emotional life, you have a person who tends to be highly aware of others' feelings. What a wonderful attribute, making your HSC empathic, an intuitive leader (not to mention salesperson), skilled in knowing how to nurture just about anything, and having a good sense of when a close relationship needs attention.

Again, this awareness begins in infancy. All infants are highly aware of their caregiver's feelings—their survival depends on it. When psychologists emphasize the importance of early mothering and the security of the bond between mother and child, it is not to make mothers feel guilty. It is simply a reality due to our being primates. And for better or worse, HSCs are going to be exquisitely attuned to those who take care of them. And since 40 percent of par-

ents did not experience a secure attachment in childhood themselves, it is important for those of you with that sort of history to
learn to send secure messages to your own child. We will discuss
that more in Chapter 6.

For older HSCs, one of the biggest problems is that they can be
aware of another's feelings even when the other person is not. People often deny their fear or anger to be polite or avoid embarrassment, and may do so even to the point of being honestly unaware of
it. "Of course I'm not annoyed" or "I'm not even slightly afraid." But
the HSC may pick up on subtle signs, even the scent caused by the
emotion in the other's body. Then your child must deal with knowing about the other's feelings without seeming to know, while getting a different message in words. I know one sensitive woman who
in childhood confronted her best friend several times about how envious and competitive they were with each other. Her friend always
denied it—until adulthood. But all through childhood, the woman
had to wonder if she was crazy and making it all up.

It will help your child enormously if you can identify and be honest about your own feelings.

Similarly, people will say to a "shy" HSC, "Don't be so worried
about what other people think; they aren't even noticing you!" That
is hard for the HSC to believe when he is noticing everything about
everyone else, including how much others truly are subtly comparing themselves to each other. But, if you raise your HSC to feel confident—which you will learn to do in Chapter 5—he will notice
others watching but assume they are pleased or accept that it does
not matter.

As for empathy, when HSCs are overwhelmed, they can become
temporarily quite unaware of other's needs. But if your child is
chronically insensitive to others or remote, something is wrong that
is not simply overarousal.

As a result of all this awareness of others, an HSC may decide to
put the needs of others first to spare them (and the HSC) emotional
pain. This is usually not conscious, and the compliance may only
happen with some people. With others, yourself for example, your

HSC may be quite feisty, outspoken, and demanding. But when your child seems to be choosing to be a doormat, it is probably because she finds it easier than feeling the other's pain or burning need, or the threat of the other's anger or judgment. What can you do about making this awareness of others' feelings an asset for your child? We will discuss this more in later chapters, but here are some basic tips.

- *Be aware of how you handle your own awareness of others' feelings.* If you feel nothing or show no reaction to another's suffering, your child will be left alone with his reaction plus have less respect for you. If you deny the problem of worrying about what others think of you, your child will feel flawed for still having this concern. So think these issues through for yourself and discuss with your HSC how you resolve them. For example, if you and your child hear of some catastrophe in which many people have suffered, a child with religious instruction will want to know why God allowed all those people to suffer and what is a child's duty toward the victims? One of the joys (and trials) of having children, especially an HSC, is being forced to confront the big questions in life.
- *Teach your child what can be done,* like sitting down together at the "season of giving" at the end of the year and choosing which charities and causes your family will contribute to. And discuss what is not helpful, like feeling bad *all* the time about others' suffering. You do all you can, then move on. Regarding being aware of others' judgments, I like the "fifty-fifty rule"—you can always expect 50 percent of people will like what you do, 50 percent will not. So you may as well do what you think is best. You cannot please them all.
- *Look at how you balance the needs of others around you with your own needs.* Consider your own ability to say "no" to others or to disregard their opinion when it feels wrong. Your child will imitate you.
- *Teach your child that he has a right to say no or ignore another's opinion.* In particular, a person who is burned out from helping others or

trying to please them is no use to anyone. We each do our part, but we cannot do it all or lose sleep over it. As one Christian writer pointed out, Jesus knew he could heal every person in Judea, but as far as we know he slept okay at night without having done so.

- *Be careful about sharing too many of your own troubles or judgments of others with your child.* HSCs can become wonderful friends, confidants, and counselors, especially for parents without another close, understanding other. But this is too much for even the wisest child to handle. Your HSC is still learning to cope with an overwhelming world and needs to gain strength from you before she can handle the job of supporting a troubled adult. And when HSCs hear you judging others, they will be even more convinced that this is a common human behavior.

- *To promote your child's sense of his own needs and wishes, insist that he make choices whenever that is possible.* I will emphasize this often. Even if your child is slow at it or you think you know what he would choose, ask. "Do you want crackers or bread?" "Would you rather invite Jan here or see if you can go to Jan's house?" If his needs conflict with another's, displeases someone, or anyone says his choice is stupid or in poor taste, tell your child that it is correct to briefly and politely consider advice that sounds sensible and is said with good intentions, but that he has a right to his own needs and opinions and to learn from his own experience.

- *See that everyone's wishes in your family are heard and respected equally when that is possible*—that is, practice equal and reciprocal empathy, rather than the HSC being the one who complies more. One parent with two HSCs alternates "ruler for the day" rights. When Janie is ruler, she can ride in the front seat, answer the phone (or not), get the first serving of dessert, hold the dog's leash, or whatever the privilege is that one of the two children might enjoy. On the next day, Gareth gets to choose. On their day, they know and act on what they want, not having to think of the other. For an HSC, that can be a huge relief and important experience.

In our family, we can be considerate of each other to a fault. I used to say that I would love to have a day pass without hearing one of the three of us say "I'm so sorry." At times it seemed as though we were apologizing for breathing each other's air. Perhaps that is why we had a tradition that on a birthday we would all go to the grocery store and the one with the birthday could choose any special food he or she wanted for the family dinner. There was something about doing this with the others present that I think helped to override that sense of guilt about having one's own way.

5. Caution Before Proceeding in New, Possibly Dangerous Situations

Because sensitive children see so much in every situation, they will have some new aspects to notice even in a familiar one. Imagine two children coming into the kitchen in the morning. To the non-HSC, it's just like every other morning. The HSC, however, notices father's coat is gone so he has left early; mother is in a strange mood; there's a paper bag behind the door as if someone tried to hide it fast; a smell of burnt toast; a broken dish in the trash. Did they have another fight? Or maybe they're distracted, getting ready for my birthday tomorrow?

Given this sensitivity to even familiar situations, an entirely new situation has to be well processed before an HSC enters it. That is just how it is. This can be frustrating for nonsensitive parents especially, for whom a surprise party is just a party, or the ocean is just the ocean—something kids are supposed to love and dive right into. But their HSC wants to check it out, and if forced to proceed, may protest, not enjoy it, or refuse this "pleasure" altogether.

Yet this is a quality of HSCs that parents can easily appreciate, too. HSCs are not as likely to fall from trees, get lost, be hit by a car, try smoking, or be abducted or misused by a disturbed adult. You warned them of the dangers and they check every unfamiliar situation to see if those dangers are present. It is even better with teenagers. They are better drivers (or will not drive—my son did not wish to take on that huge responsibility until he was twenty-seven). They are cautious about drugs, sex, breaking the law, and who they hang around with.

But you also do not want your child to miss out on interesting new experiences, as when Maria, the HSC described at the beginning of this chapter, was invited as a teenager to travel to Sweden. She insisted that she would not go, but her mother insisted that she would; later, a happy call from Stockholm proved her mother correct.

There are times, of course, when HSCs are not so cautious in new situations. In Chapter 1 you learned about the pause-to-check and go-for-it systems in every brain. All HSCs are strong in the first, but the two systems are independent, so some HSCs are high on both. They are careful, but also adventuresome. In that chapter I described Ann, who rides motorcycles and jumps out of airplanes, but only her parents know how much she has studied the safety considerations and how much down time she needs to recover. You also met Chuck, who climbs trees like a monkey and loves to ski. But only his mother knows he has never broken a bone because he has checked out every unfamiliar branch and slope. Since the culture admires and encourages adventuresomeness, often only the parents know their child's secret, cautious side.

We will talk more about the problems associated with pausing before proceeding and how to deal with them in Chapters 8 and 9. But for now, here are some overall recommendations.

- *Remember the advantages of your child's caution—this will help you not be disappointed when it seems "uncool."*
- *See it from your child's viewpoint.* You have been in this situation many times, but he has not. You no longer notice the cliff beside the road or the shadows on the path. And there may be fewer risks for you. These are not your future playmates; you are bigger so dogs and waves and cars look smaller; you are used to heavy jet planes staying in the air.
- *Point out what is familiar or what resembles past situations that your*

child has mastered. "The family reunion will be a lot like Grandma Mae's birthday party." "The ocean is just a huge bathtub and the waves are like the kind you make when you move around in your bath." "There's Sue—you met her last week at Nancy's party."

- *Take it one step at a time.* See Chapter 7 for these steps. Keep each step small and easy so your child can hardly protest and will definitely succeed and look good. "You don't have to talk to anybody if you don't want to. Just come and watch. You can be busy with your Gameboy." After some watching, you can try saying, "I'll bet if you walk Tiger over to those swings, someone will ask you what kind of dog he is."
- *Provide a retreat* (if you can do so without drawing embarrassing attention to your child). "You can go to your room whenever you want to leave the party. Just slip out and I'll cover for you if anyone asks." "I've told the teacher you may want to go and rest—just tell her."
- *Success is the key to your child exploring new situations in the future.* Remember, all HSCs have a go-for-it system. They *want* to explore, as long as the risks do not seem too high. So point out all that they will gain from exploring (without going overboard) while minimizing the risks. "I was so impressed, seeing you out there in the deep end swimming like a fish. To think you couldn't swim at all last summer. Next week you'll be starting middle school and changing classes every period. Think of it—if one teacher's a drag or you don't like some kid in your class, you aren't stuck all day. And you get to take those two electives you signed up for. You already know enough about computers and Native Americans to practically teach those classes yourself. I'll bet it won't be long before you're 'in the swim' there, too."

6. Being Different—It Attracts Attention

The sixth challenge when raising an HSC is not due to the trait directly, but the way others view it. Unless your child becomes very good at hiding it, she will be known as someone who feels and notices more, someone who pauses before acting and thinks everything over afterward. And it seems to be a human fact that when we meet someone different, especially a member of a minority group (and sensitive people are in the minority), we immediately decide if they are superior or inferior, if they look up to us or if we should look up to them. This is what any child who seems "different" must face.

As with the other six, there are also advantages in having a child who is different. Remember our motto: To have an exceptional child you have to be willing to have an exceptional child. Some teachers, peers, and relatives will think your child's differences are marvelous. From these people your child will gain the self-esteem she will need when meeting up with some of the other people, the majority in our culture, who are less impressed with sensitivity.

Indeed, in some cultures it is a social advantage, an honor, to be sensitive. Peoples living close to the earth esteem their highly sensitive herbalists, trackers, and shamans. And a study comparing elementary school children in China and Canada found that being a "sensitive, quiet" child was associated with being popular in China, but with being unpopular in Canada. Perhaps "old" cultures with rich artistic, philosophical, and spiritual traditions such as China and Europe can afford to reward sensitivity more than "new" immigrant cultures such as the United States, Canada, Latin America, and Australia, which have rewarded pioneering "macho" men and "tough" women who gave little thought to the risks in a new land.

If you think about it, cultures that are tough, aggressive, impulsive, and quick to explore are the ones that expand and take over cultures with more peaceful, thoughtful, sensitive values—whether with an army, an aggressive economic style, or the dissemination of its culture. But this may be a story of the tortoise and the hare—the individuals and cultures that value sensitivity may yet be the survivors. Or, more likely, the cultures that succeed will be the ones combining both qualities, that balance impulsivity with a thorough awareness of the long-term consequences of despoiling natural resources; exploiting "inferior" groups until they become a burden or take their revenge; not bothering to educate the young; and so forth. A society in which sensitive people have equal respect and power will not make these mistakes. As I've said before, the world needs your HSC.

We will discuss in Chapter 5 what you can do to empower your HSC and protect her from prejudices about sensitivity, but here are some basic pointers:

- *Examine your own attitude toward this trait.* Research shows that almost everyone who grew up in North America has a subliminal, unconscious prejudice toward persons of color. Those who decide not to behave in a prejudiced way are those who actively override this built-in reaction. Likewise, since you grew up in a culture that thinks "sensitive, quiet" children are not as admirable, you must override this reaction for the sake of your child. And it can be quite real. Research indicates that "shy" sons, in particular, are often their mother's least favorite child (while "shy" daughters are often encouraged to stay home and be mother's special friend).

- *Talk about the trait with your child.* Acknowledge the problems it creates but also point out the assets. Some parents fear mentioning that their child is different. I had a European-American friend who adopted an African-American child, and when I sent the child a book about famous African-Americans, my friend returned it to me, telling me that they were not going to tell their child she was different! As if she hadn't noticed. Ignoring your child's difference will not work. Your silence will speak louder than words.

- *Think through how you want to respond to comments from others, especially when your child will overhear you.* Having developed some educated and clever responses, you can be almost invincible on this topic, since most people are ill-informed. You will learn how to do this in Chapter 5. Your child will use these same responses when alone with others, and also to counter self-criticisms internalized from others when you were not around.

• *When your child is old enough to understand a bit more about culture and human psychology, explain about the roots and history of people's reactions to sensitivity*—how it is admired in some cultures, and that when it is not, some people, especially men, are so afraid of revealing anything like that in themselves that they become quite peculiar about it. I have been on several talk shows with macho-type hosts who seemed on the verge of nervous breakdowns while discussing this subject with me. They had weird nervous laughter, inappropriate questions, and poor concentration. They were probably reliving the day they fell down and cried and somebody blasted them with "Stop crying and act like a man instead of a mama's boy!" Maybe you and your child can learn to enjoy these over-the-top reactions to bringing up the subject as much as I do.

• *Insulate your child from undo attention, praise, or pity.* On rare occasions certain people may find your child's sensitivity in and of itself to be extraordinary. But your child did nothing special to be born sensitive and should not be *overly* praised for that in itself or allowed to feel superior to others. Treat pity the same way, except that it is even more uncalled for. HSCs are not to be pitied. And even if they were, what counts is what we do with the cards we are dealt.

THE JOYS THAT ONLY PARENTS OF HSCS KNOW

Naturally, a book like this devotes the majority of its pages to identifying and solving problems. But that truly does the HSC an injustice and does not prepare you, the parent, to recognize and revel in all the joys involved. So let's take a moment to count your blessings.

• *Even the problems have a bright side.* By providing the understanding and help your child needs, you will be deeply appreciated by your HSC. Your child may even promote you to others as a saint among parents. And as you deal successfully with tough issues, in the family and from outside, you and your child can have moments of deep mutual appreciation. You will share electrifying success when you help your HSC master a fear, coming out of it even more confident than another child would. You will feel like comrades when you figure out together how to respond to teasing or prejudiced comments.

* *Your child will make you more aware of everything,* introducing you to beauty, nuances, social subtleties, and questions about life that you would not otherwise stop to consider. Even if you are highly sensitive, your HSC brings a child's fresh and highly receptive outlook on the world. You will be looking up the answers to all sorts of questions, or looking inside for those that are only answered there.

* *The two of you will connect in a deeper way.* Of course, a connection requires two people—you will have to learn to be receptive to those moments when your child wants to be especially close and also to those times when she needs her separateness.

* *You will have a child who is aware of you, both the conscious and unconscious parts, which will force you to be more aware of yourself.* "Mom, why did you tell that lady you like her when you told me you don't?" "Dad, you said you're so tired you could drop, but now you're sweeping the floor."

* *You will see your well-raised HSC grow up capable of amazing depths of feeling* and of pleasure from the full range of beauty to be known in the outer and inner worlds. He may even express it in ways that allow others to see the treasures he has brought up from these depths.

* *You will see your well-raised HSC make an exceptional contribution to the world,* whether backstage or front and center. Because sensitive people are such keen observers and thinkers, they are traditionally the inventors, lawmakers, healers, historians, scientists, artists, teachers, counselors, and spiritual leaders. They are the advisers to rulers and warriors, the visionaries and the prophets. In their communities, they are often the opinion leaders, the ones others seek out on how to vote or solve a family problem. They

make extraordinary parents and partners. They are compassionate and care deeply about social justice and the environment.

I am sure that you can add points that I have forgotten, that are the special joys *you* receive from raising your HSC. Quite a list, yes? So keep our motto in mind: To have an exceptional child you must be willing to have an exceptional child. And let's get to work.

Chapter Three

When You the Parent Are Not Highly Sensitive

Blessings in Disguise

This chapter should be read by sensitive as well as nonsensitive parents. You begin by taking a self-test, for high sensitivity in adults (and discuss another important temperament that you and your child may have—high novelty seeking). Then we concentrate on both the advantages and problems you may encounter raising an HSC if you (or your partner or the other adults helping to raise your HSC) are not as sensitive—with plenty of suggestions for handling the problems. (Chapter 4 looks at the advantages and problems to expect if you are highly sensitive.)

HIGH SENSITIVITY AND YOU, MOM AND DAD

Even though high sensitivity is an inherited trait, it is quite possible for one or both parents of an HSC to not be highly sensitive themselves. (Some close relative probably is, and that person and your child probably even have similar physical features.) To find out if you are, *take the self-test now at the end of the chapter.*

This chapter is important for all parents to read, since even highly sensitive parents will not always be sensitive in the same ways or to the same degree as their child. This chapter will also help you advise the nonsensitive people around your child. And you will definitely want to read it if you are just discovering that you are highly sensitive yourself, since up until now you may have had the perspective of a nonsensitive parent, as Sharon did in the previous chapter.

(Please note: For brevity's sake I will often say "nonsensitive" rather than "non-highly-sensitive," but I never mean it as "insensitive." Rather, I mean it very technically: not having this particular inherited trait.)

A SPECIAL NOTE TO FATHERS

Fathers especially need to read this chapter, whether they are highly sensitive or not, because men in this culture are more likely to have the perspective of a nonsensitive parent. That is because our culture tends to equate being a man with insensitivity—with not noticing subtleties and being able to "take it like a man," whatever the level of stimulation, stress, or pain, even though *just as many men as women are born with this trait.* (By the way, if you score only in the medium range on the self-test, you may still be highly sensitive.) In my research, fathers turned out to be unusually important in the adjustment of HSCs, since traditionally they teach children how to manage out in the world.

HIGH SENSITIVITY AND NOVELTY SEEKING

High novelty seeking is the term for the trait created by having a very strong go-for-it system (described in Chapter 1). High novelty seekers often like physical thrills, are bored easily with "the same old people," and love to explore. (In Thomas and Chess's terms, they are "highly approaching.") For example, they'd rather go to a new place than back to one they know they like, and if they're traveling, the more foreign the foreign country, the better. They often experiment with drugs at some point in their lives and they dislike routines.

As said before, it is possible to be highly sensitive and also high on this trait. But even if you are both, your trait of high novelty seeking will have some effects on you that will make you similar to a nonsensitive parent. The reason is that both high novelty seekers and nonsensitive people will enter into new situations more readily than their HSC, although for different reasons. Novelty seekers will do it because they want the fresh experience; nonsensitive types will simply not be so concerned about pausing to check.

In spite of the similarities, there is one situation where we need to discuss novelty seeking separately. That is when both you and your child are both highly sensitive and high novelty seekers. (I have not done enough research on novelty seeking to provide a child's test for it, but I think you can estimate your child's novelty seeking fairly well.)

The problem for types like you two is that you are easily bored, always craving fresh experiences, yet easily overwhelmed. Your optimal range of arousal is very narrow. You can seem almost self-destructive in that you will plan a day or an entire lifestyle that overwhelms you, then be exhausted, distressed, or even fall ill. When you consistently fail to contain your novelty seeking, you are inviting chronic illness because of your equally high sensitivity. And, of course, our culture supports the novelty-seeking side of you more. For example, corporate cultures often require or certainly encourage top managers to travel all over the world for their work. And high novelty seekers love all that travel and seeing new places. But if they are highly sensitive, they also burn out from it.

I say all of this because it will be your responsibility to figure out how to manage these two traits in yourself and then to teach your child how to do it. (Since this is not a book on that subject, I can only refer you elsewhere—to volume 4, issues 2 and 3 of *The Comfort Zone*, a newsletter for highly sensitive people—see Resources.)

WHEN YOU AND YOUR CHILD HAVE QUITE DIFFERENT TEMPERAMENTS

If you are all one way (a nonsensitive novelty seeker—and perhaps an extrovert, too) and your child is all the other way (an HSC, not a novelty seeker, and perhaps an introvert) then this is a very serious difference between you. Everything I am about to say is very, very important for you.

First, be assured that nonsensitive parents and HSCs can do extremely well together. In Chapter 2, I described "goodness of fit" and emphasized that it does not at all mean that a parent and child need to have the same temperament; indeed, we will see ways where differences in temperament are an advantage. A good fit refers to the fact that some environments—cultures, families, and parents—support a given temperament especially well. If parents realize that there has been a lack of fit up to this point, they can adapt.

But adapting means first realizing that you need to. As a nonsensitive person, you are used to kids like yourself and like the majority of kids—80 percent, in fact. So the first big step is accepting that the difference in your child is real, not a pretense or manipulation on his part, or a failure in parenting by you or your partner.

A key part of accepting your child is pinpointing all the things you like about a highly sensitive temperament. But perhaps more important is admitting all the things you find strange, frustrating, and disappointing; all the experiences that, because of it, you will not have as a parent or see your child have. All of this has to be grieved. You may never send this child to summer camp, or see her as a team captain, or have the phone ringing off the hook with party invitations, or see her being immediately happy and spontaneous in new settings. For some HSCs these will happen, but for some they will not. Ever. There will be other joys instead. It's a "package deal." But what is not in the package has to be accepted. No person or personality or life can be everything.

Only after you have accepted and grieved these limits can you fully engage in problem solving and start to come up with your own creative solutions. Before that, any suggestion will be met with "Yes, but"—"Yes, but he won't do that" or "Yes, but that's so difficult for me." Some part of you will still be resisting, not truly accepting your child's differences. (If all of this is difficult for you, I recommend you also read the chapter on relationships between highly sensitive people and nonsensitive people in my third book, *The Highly Sensitive Person in Love*—parenting is, after all, a love relationship.)

It always helps to know you are not alone, so let's return to Randall, the bright nine-year-old you met in Chapter 1 who has so few friends because he does not like to go to anyone else's house. I also mentioned that he liked baseball. But he could not bear to have an unfamiliar coach, so his mother became the coach. Quite a mother.

This mother, Marilyn, was a nonsensitive person who learned the hard way about goodness of fit, but learn she did.

"You Don't Coddle Boys"

Marilyn is a woman who "jumps right into things." Her husband is not. Her son, Randall, was clearly sensitive from birth, taking after his dad. As an infant he would only eat a few foods, as a toddler he wanted to stand back and look at things before approaching. But Marilyn had a demanding business and Randall had been in the care of a nanny whom he loved, so everything was pretty comfortable and orderly during his infancy. "He never cried as a baby," according to Marilyn.

Then Marilyn thought he was old enough to be in a play group. She would come home at two o'clock, and he was a happy child until they headed for the group. Then he would panic and scream, insisting that she stay with him. He also refused to go on playdates unless she went along. And he hated birthday parties unless he was the first to arrive. Even then Marilyn often had to take him home early.

Particularly difficult for Marilyn was that Randall never liked being kissed and hugged. He was a loving child, but he just could not tolerate that kind of proximity. Imagine how disappointing for Marilyn, and for the grandparents—Randall was their first grandchild. Was he "normal"? She was so worried about this that, looking back, she thinks she bent over backward to deny any noticeable personality differences between her son and herself.

It was Randall's starting kindergarten that broke through the denial and also gave her the answer. She had suspected that it would be difficult—she and Randall visited the class for a year before he was to start. Still, on the first day, he was terrified, and every day after that. At this point Marilyn decided to take a part-time job so she could take him to kindergarten herself, although relatives and family friends thought this was oddly "overinvolved." It was still six months before Randall said a word in class. *What* was going on?

Fortunately, Randall's teacher knew. Ms. Peterson happened to understand sensitive children, having been one herself and seen dozens in her classroom over the years. She let Randall take his time joining in, and she explained to Marilyn all about her son—that he was quite normal but needed extra time and could be easily overwhelmed by noise, strangers, and the unexpected. In particular, seeing Marilyn's style, she told Marilyn to pay attention to her son's anxiety, to believe it, and not to push so hard.

It was only at the end of the year that Randall relaxed in Ms. Peterson's class. And now that he is in fourth grade, he likes school (mainly thanks to Ms. Peterson). He knows what to expect, and by doing what is expected so well, teachers love him. (Teachers make such a difference for HSCs; you will learn more about finding the right ones in Chapter 8.)

How are Randall and Marilyn doing now? She calls him "a wonderful child." And according to her, he is very relieved to understand himself. He can tell her what he needs and she listens, supporting him. From her (and his year with Ms. Peterson) he learned that there is nothing wrong with his preferring to stay home and read books. He is friendly and social at school but does not want more activities after school.

Furthermore, Marilyn becomes quite eloquent when talking

about her own transformation as a parent. She realizes now that she had thought it was her job to push her son, to get him over his fears. Especially with a boy, she had thought if she "coddled" him that this would "enable" him and encourage his "dysfunction." Now she realizes she could not have been farther off. Her job is to understand, protect, and encourage him, while holding to her own standards of considerate behavior.

For example, she tells the relatives that Randall prefers to shake hands rather than kiss and hug, but she insists on the handshake and some polite words to reciprocate the expression of affection. But they arrived at this solution together.

Looking back, Marilyn still worries that her pushing him during those early years may have added to his panic when starting kindergarten. "Not being highly sensitive myself, we were often at odds, stressed," she recalls. But Marilyn and Randall are clearly on the right track now, and that is what counts. "I remind him that I still may put him into situations that are not good for him, but I try to make the best choice and I am willing to listen to his viewpoint. Frankly, I listen to him now more than ever before, and he's rarely wrong."

Another note to highly sensitive fathers: According to Marilyn, Randall's father shares his son's temperament. I did not interview him, but wonder where he was while his wife was insisting on raising a tough boy. But he seems involved now—for example, Randall is learning golf from his father. (Golf is a good game for an HSC— you weigh all the subtle factors, then take one shot to get it right.) Marilyn admits she always wanted Randall to excel at the big team sports, but this is one more area where she has learned to listen to Randall's preferences.

If You Are Not Highly Sensitive—The Many Benefits for Your HSC

Let's not overlook the advantages Randall has gained from Marilyn not being highly sensitive, and other benefits your HSC may enjoy because you are not as sensitive.

1. *You will give your child more adventures!* Marilyn involved Randall in activities he might not have tried otherwise. It turned out that he did like one team sport, baseball. (It is a good team sport for HSCs—slower than soccer or basketball, less rough-and-tumble, and involves more subtleties. In our culture, playing a team sport has become almost a necessity in order to be accepted, especially by other boys.)

   Whether it is sports or something else, the nonsensitive parent generally takes his or her HSC to new places and pushes the child to try new things, to have some adventures. If the child can tolerate it and then succeeds even a little, he will be more willing and even eager to try other new activities. All parents should gently, and at times strongly, encourage their HSCs to venture out into new territory. When a strong push is what is needed, nonsensitive parents probably more often dare to give it.

2. *You will, or can, provide grounding and balance.* When your child is "flipping out," overwhelmed by fear, anger, sadness, or any other emotion, or just overwhelmed—you will be feeling it less and be able to settle her down and "contain" her reaction (as described in Chapter 2)—provided you understand her sensitivity and are not infuriated by her *over*reaction. Your calm response will be catching; she will learn your emotional response to the same situation and adopt some or all of it as the appropriate response for that situation in the future.

3. *You will speak up and protect your child more readily than a more sensitive person might.* Marilyn defended Randall when the grandparents wanted to hug and kiss him. And in Chapter 8 we will tell you how she handled a bully (and not by stepping in and fighting it out for Randall—she was far more creative than that). A highly sensitive parent might have backed down, not wanting the high stimulation of a confrontation. Or if a sensitive parent has had an unsupported childhood and many similar experiences—grandmas insisting on a hug or bullies insisting on kicks—he or she might role model something like, "You'll have to take it, Randall."

4. *You are probably fairly communicative, saying what is on your*

mind without a lot of hesitation. This kind of "running commentary" gives an HSC a sense of how an adult thinks and copes. It also means your child does not have to worry about a silent parent who may be angry or upset and not saying so.

Where the Not–Highly Sensitive Parent Has to Be Very Careful

1. *You will have trouble believing that your child is having a different experience of the world.* It is always hard to believe that another's experience is valid when it is so different. Since you will think "no one could possibly feel that way," you may try to think of explanations that would fit if it were you—for example, when your HSC complains, thinking "he's faking it" or "she just wants attention."
2. *You will often feel impatient.* For you, someone who boldly speaks or acts without a lot of pausing beforehand, patience will be a real challenge—a good virtue to develop, however.
3. *Your volume will be too loud.* By that I do not mean just how loudly you speak, but the forcefulness of the words you choose. Everyone tends to put their thoughts into words with the same intensity as it takes for them to grasp another's thoughts. HSCs tend to communicate with hints, gestures, glances, nuances, and tones of voice. You will tend to communicate more bluntly, even harshly by your child's standards. If you speak like this with your child—and you will do it often, you can't help it—he or she will hear your thoughts expressed quite differently from how you mean them or from what she needs. Especially criticisms and your feelings of displeasure, but also suggestions—all will be taken too much to heart. Your child may be so overaroused by your style that she will not even hear the content. Or you will have *too much* influence, and your child will not be able to hear or speak her own thoughts.

Also, when HSCs are telling you about their deepest feelings, they especially need you to speak very gently, as if the two of you are handling sea creatures you brought up from the depths of the ocean that are not used to bright light.

4. *You may find your child boring at times.* Yes, HSCs have strange, deep, and often humorous insights. But they also like to be quiet. They can take forever to say what is on their mind. Taking a long trip? Do not count on nonstop conversation. He may stare out the window or want to read. Or your child may be entertaining you or trying new things, knowing you are easily bored, but he *needs* the down time. And it can be pretty boring waiting for an HSC to try something new.

5. *You may feel rejected by your child not wanting to be with you more or not wanting your physical touch.* It is easy to mistake these reactions as signs that your child does not like you. On top of that, as they get older especially, they may be much more friendly with others than with you. But it is usually the case that your child feels forced to do this with others, but likes and trusts you enough to be herself with you.

6. *You may find yourself unintentionally taking advantage of your child's sensitivity.* It is easy to ask a sensitive child to wait, to be good, to listen to your troubles, to do what you need. They usually try to comply. But it is unfair and damaging if others in the family are asked to do less or listen to fewer troubles because this is your "good, helpful, wise, mature child."

What You Can Do to Make a Better Fit

1. *When you have trouble believing that your child is having a different experience of the world:*
   - *Do all you can to understand your child's experience.* Ask your HSC how he perceives situations. Think of analogies that might help you—for example, a tag in a shirt that is bothering your child's neck is as unpleasant as having an allergic skin reaction. Get to know some highly sensitive adults and ask them about their experiences now and as children. Speak to other parents of HSCs, both those who are and are not sensitive themselves. Find out how they perceive and handle situations.

- *Consider temperament counseling* (see Resources), a huge source of help.
- *If your child has an experienced, understanding teacher, ask him or her about your child* relative to other children and how this teacher perceives and handles children like yours. Teachers get to know a great many children, and can often provide a wealth of information.
- *Do not attribute more familiar, mature, complicated, or Machiavellian motives* to explain a behavior just because it is something you yourself do not experience because you are not highly sensitive. It is always *possible* that your HSC is being cowardly, lazy, aloof, antisocial, overly sensitive, defiant, whiny, or just out to drive you crazy. But be certain before you act on one of those assumptions.
- *Do not expect your child to enjoy the same things you enjoyed as a child.* And do not feel too sorry for him for what you perceive as "missing out on things."
- *Do not push too hard.* This is a big one. You may have to push sometimes, but only if you truly think your child would be sorry if you didn't, as when Estelle (in Chapter 2) pushed Maria to go to Sweden. See Chapter 8 for how to gently encourage your child, step by step, out into the world.
- *Do not make your own childhood sound so wonderful that your HSC feels envious or inferior.* In the interest of tempting your HSC to go to summer camp or play football, you may try to paint such a wonderful picture of these that your HSC feels terrible. Yours was the wonderful, wild, daring, and *normal* childhood. The rest of the culture is going to give that impression to your child as it is, in every TV commercial, movie, and children's book. Keep in mind for both of you that your child is going to have other joys, perhaps greater ones, but of a very different nature.

2. *When you feel impatient:*
   - *Work on it!* Patience is a necessity for parenting an HSC. De-

velop strategies like counting to ten or taking a little time out yourself to express your frustration to an empty room.

- *If you ask a question, do not be impatient for the answer.* If you are not sure if your child is going to answer, ask if she is still thinking. Expressing impatience, natural as it may be to feel, will only lengthen the time it will take for your child to speak up.

- *If you ask your HSC to make a decision, give your child adequate time to make it.* If there isn't time for a slow decision or you can't be patient, don't ask.

- *If you want your child to try something new, be prepared to get her into it slowly,* step by step (again, see Chapter 8). If there isn't time to do this or you're not in the mood, don't suggest a new activity.

- *Watch your impatience about having to provide more physical security than you needed or other children need at the same age.* HSCs cannot help but hear about fires, break-ins, and murders. They have probably experienced the awful anxiety of almost missing something because of some unforeseen delay. They cannot help but imagine the consequences of such things. You may be annoyed about having to recheck that the doors are locked at night or leaving extra early to get to the movie, but both of your lives may be more relaxed as a result of attending to potential problems before they arise. (More about dealing with fears in Chapter 7.)

3. *Be aware of your louder "volume":*
   - *Always tone down expressions when speaking to your HSC.* Try to train other nonsensitive family members to do the same. Avoid harsh, sudden questions that might be mistaken as criticism, such as "Why did you do that?"

   - *Avoid teasing or jokes about them that can be misunderstood.* Teasing deeply upsets most HSCs, probably because they are hearing (or fearing) an undercurrent of hostility or superiority that the speaker may not even be aware of.

   - *If your child needs correction, start with a low volume—it is usually enough.* Do not use anger, withdrawal of love, or other threats (more on this in Chapter 5). Even "time outs" may be too much. A simple comment may be enough.

- *Do not make dire predictions about the consequences if your child does not obey.* Do not say, "Why did you pick those leaves? Haven't I told you not to? If you eat oleander leaves you will die." This will only create fear. With an HSC an instruction and a non-threatening explanation is usually enough. "See this plant? It's called an oleander. It has pretty flowers, but don't ever eat the leaves or the flowers—they are not good to eat. I have asked you not to pick any kind of leaves because I know you don't know yet one plant from another. We don't want the stuff in the leaves of plants like oleander to get onto your hands and then onto something you eat."

- *Be careful about which thoughts you speak out loud.* Speaking your thoughts out loud can be very helpful when they are reassuring thoughts or your child might otherwise fear you are angry or upset, but do not exclaim in frustration or worry out loud when it is not necessary—your sensitive child will take up your bad feeling with extra force.

- *Beware of talking so much that your child becomes quiet because he cannot think of things to say as fast as you can.* You tend to leap (or speak) first and look a little later. Your child is thinking over what you have said and what to say back, while you may have already changed the subject. Leave silences.

- *When discussing your HSC's deepest thoughts or emotions, do so with the most gentle, respectful, quiet tone.* If your child brings up something when you know you might be distracted, ask him to wait until you can be fully present. If you just speak off the top of your head or while distracted, your child may soon decide you're too casual and superficial to be an adequate confidante. (Many sensitive adults tell me no one understood them as children. I often wonder if others wanted to understand but were unable because of their ill-considered first responses.)

So if your child is telling you about having seen an angel, do not interrupt with a request that he take his feet off the coffee table. Parents have done it! It is a quick way to be rid of an angel conversation—and probably of angels, too.

4. *To avoid feeling bored:*
   - *Expect that you may be bored sooner by an activity than your child is.* Bring along something to do until your child is ready to stop. She may have spent a long time getting used to the water, for example, and is now delighted with it. As one parent put it, "He's just starting to enjoy Gymboree when it's over."
   - *Go back to practicing patience* while you are waiting for your HSC to act or respond. It's good for your blood pressure.
   - *Get a radio or CD player with earphones* for long car trips or other times you will be alone together in the same space. Encourage your child to interrupt you if she has something she wants to say, and be responsive if she does. Make a comment to her now and then—check in—to see if she is now ready to engage with you.
   - *Before giving up on contact, explicitly ask your child if he would like to talk or do something with you,* indicating that that would be your preference (if it is), but you will also be happy on your own. Your child may just need some encouragement or a topic, and certainly needs to know you enjoy his company.

5. *If you feel rejected when your child wants to be alone or not be touched:*
   - *Learn to believe that your child just really needs privacy, quiet, and down time.* Do not take it personally and do not try to talk your child out of these, even if you think he's missing out. These needs are greater than yours, so you must strive not to feel rejected, critical, or even surprised.
   - *Instead of feeling uncared for, think of yourself as your child's much appreciated protector,* and sometimes you must protect your HSC from your own need or tolerance for more stimulation—your ability to work, travel, and play hard. But paradoxically, this

can also bring you closer, because you understand each other better than others do. Others will also want your HSC's time, and you can help your child by explaining why she is not staying so long at the family reunion or not coming to the wedding. Remember how much pleasure Marilyn now gets from knowing she is the only one who really understands her son.

- *When doing things together, find some parental pleasure in providing what your child needs.* It feels good to nurture a sensitive child, providing the routines and rest that make him happier, even if you don't need them. Does it seem as though your child doesn't require this kind of care when with you? Look closely. Often, if a child senses a parent does not like making these adjustments, he attempts to forgo them, but there may be some seemingly unrelated problems, like your child getting sick on vacations or having nightmares or trouble sleeping. Your child will be happier, and happier with you, if you can be more attentive to his needs.

- *Learn to read the signs when your child is becoming fatigued and overstimulated, and stop*—stop *before* she reaches the breaking point and wants nothing more to do with you! (See the cues in Chapter 6.) This will be long before you might be tired, so you must be alert to this. But this way, rather than your child "rejecting" you, you will be the one stopping things.

- *Do not try to pry information out of your HSC*—even if you succeed, he will feel violated. Allow space for conversation, show interest, but do not insist on it. With my son, bedtime was when the floodgates opened. Being a night owl by nature, if it meant putting the lights out later, he would be willing to tell me long stories about what happened at school or discuss just about anything. It may not have been good "sleep hygiene" to let him get away with this, but I liked having my worries eased—that he could be hiding something that was troubling him—so I think we both slept better after these unburdenings.

- *If your child does not like physical affection, proximity, or conversation, keep reaching out in a gentle, nonjudging way.* Try alternative ways—a gentle pat on the shoulder may be appreciated more than hugs or kisses, and doing a special project together might be easier than a "talk." To want some closeness is a normal way to express love, and your child may appreciate the thought if not the action. And she will certainly need to learn to appreciate such reaching out when it comes from others.

- *Ask first: "Would you mind a hug?" "Would you like to hold hands while we walk?" "Shall we kiss good night?"* This way you do not surprise your child. Take a "no" matter-of-factly as his right, and a "yes" without a lot of gushing comment. Remembering this is especially hard for parents who have not seen their child all day. Many parents find that once they learn to ask first, their HSC is far more open to affection, then or soon after.

- *Try waiting until your child is more relaxed.* Overstimulation may be her problem, especially when you are reuniting at the end of her school day or your workday. Your child's rejection is a sign that she trusts you with her problem of overwhelming fatigue.

- *Encourage your child to express affection in other ways when he is in the mood*—perhaps through notes or gifts. Be very appreciative of these.

- *Do not give up on physical contact.* Just keep it light and brief. Maybe just holding hands. Try letting it happen casually during low-key games or make believe. Ask your child what he likes and does not like.

- *If you and your child are different in gender, consider whether your child may be at an age where he or she is struggling with some sexual information or misinformation, or simply frightening sexual feelings.* Children and sex is a difficult topic and beyond the range of this book, but HSCs cannot help but be strongly influenced by sexual messages between people and in the media. In the process, they will hear about inappropriate sexuality between adults and children. Now might be the time to let the parent of your child's gender (or a close relative) explore what's up for your child in this area. And be certain that all of your own nonverbal signals are clear: Nothing sexual is going to happen between the two of you. For example, a parent's nudity around a young child may be fine, but at a later age it could be confusing, intrusive, or overexciting.

6. *Beware of taking advantage of an HSC:*

- *Be especially careful about anyone using your HSC as a confidante or counselor.* HSCs are generally good listeners and very sympathetic, so their friends and even the adults around them may tell them their troubles, secrets, or fears. Teach your child that she can and should put a limit on this—changing the subject is often enough. Sharing should be equal and should not feel like a drain or burden. If people are truly troubled, they should seek help. Otherwise they can manage if she does not wish to listen. Tell her to come to you if someone becomes too much for her and she does not know what to do.

- *Do not show off your child's abilities* without receiving permission in private. Most HSCs will not like the high stimulation from so much attention. They will wonder if the audience is voluntary or was coerced. And if this involves any kind of performing, even just conversing with strangers nicely, the higher level of arousal means HSCs usually do not perform as well unless they have overrehearsed or become used to such settings. If she does poorly, you will be the reason, but of course she will not see it that way.

- *Household duties and unusual sacrifices should feel fair to your child.* Ask about it often and listen carefully. HSCs can be taken advantage of, and they can also, like anyone, *feel* taken advantage of when they are not. (Research shows that when it comes to household chores, even when they are divided equally, each person tends to feel they do about 70 percent!) But HSCs may not mention their dissatisfaction, and then its reality is never explored. Mulling it over, processing it thoroughly, they can develop a strong sense of being a victim. And sometimes the HSC, like a perfect Cinderella, really is doing too much. So avoid the temptation, especially when unusual sacrifices are needed, to ask more of the child who understands your need the most and wants to help. It may be the others in the family would benefit far more from some character-building sacrifices for the greater good.

When Your HSC Spots Your Weaknesses All Too Well

HSCs are, sad but true, very aware of others' flaws and subtle, unconscious "shadow" material—those things we all want to forget we are or can be. Highly sensitive parents know all too well about a sensitive individual's critical nature, being that way themselves. Less sensitive parents, being less aware of others' flaws, can see their HSC as too critical, uncanny, or just snoopy.

But your child's observations need to be expressed. When young, HSCs can feel deeply disillusioned and burdened with the growing awareness of their idealized parents' faults. Your HSC needs to talk about those that he has noticed without feeling it will damage your relationship. In fact, this is your chance to role model for your conscientious child how to handle criticism and how to live with being less than perfect.

Thus you must try not to become totally defensive or hurt by his close observations of you. "If the waiter made a mistake on the bill, why didn't you pay him what you owe him?" "I thought you said you were on a diet?" "The speed limit says thirty-five—why are you driving fifty?" They may be all too accurate for your comfort, and more astute than you're used to. Remember, your child will be noticing this sort of thing in everyone, and everyone has this sort of thing to notice. So, again, try not to be too defensive. If you can't stay cool, ask for a time out and go off and consider if there is any truth in what was said, then come back and own up to it, as well as refusing to accept what seems inaccurate. This is excellent role modeling for all your family members, if you are saintly enough to do it.

However, let your child know that it is a bad tactic to bring up observations about character during an argument—things like, "You're a liar; you lie on your income tax; I heard you say it on the phone." Or, "Maybe I cheated, but I've seen you cheat at games, too." It destroys trust to have one's weaknesses and vulnerabilities brought out at such times. In an argument, you stick to the issue.

I think every relationship needs times when each can speak freely of the areas in which each needs to grow, but this is especially true with an HSC because they truly need to learn how to give and receive criticism. Such times require all parties to be calm, eager to be helpful to each other, and desirous of feedback and self-knowledge. I find a day out in nature or a long car ride, perhaps late at night, are good times.

If these discussions do not happen informally, try the following activity, perhaps even in a family meeting—couples can do it, too: Each of you names three things you really enjoy about the other person (not "you're a good person" but "I like how kind you are to me") and one thing that does not work so well for you personally. ("I really feel angry when you walk into my room without knocking"— notice it is an "I" statement that begins with one of the basic emotions and gives a specific instance.)

When You Stop Being the One Who Does All the Adapting

So far I have emphasized your being patient, respectful, using a lower volume, and so forth. But your child is going to have to get along with nonsensitive types. They are most of the world. It is right and fair that when children are young, grown-ups do all the adapting to create the good fit. But eventually you will teach your child to adapt to you, too. This is one of the advantages of your not being so sensitive—you will be her first chance to practice. So as your child grows older and understands her temperament, she can also learn to understand yours and that of other family members.

Randall certainly understands Marilyn's different personality. For example, he says he is very aware of her lack of fear, and he is probably learning to tolerate her taking reasonable risks, even when he worries for her safety. He also speaks of being envious of her fearlessness. To help him control his envy, she can remind him of the package deal—as a nonsensitive person she has to watch her impulsiveness.

In order to adapt, your HSC will also need to learn to turn up the volume in a world of nonsensitive people. If you miss your child's hint about preferring a trip to the beach over a trip to the mountains, let her know gently that neither of you are at fault. Like throwing a ball so that it reaches the person trying to catch it, she simply needs to make her request stronger next time, so that the message reaches you.

Your HSC may need to learn to think ahead about his preferences so they don't get left out or so others don't become impatient waiting for a decision. As your child matures, a few displays of well-tempered impatience from you are fine. And if your HSC feels left out of conversations because there is not enough time to think of something to say, you can discuss planning topics of conversation ahead of time.

FINAL THOUGHTS

To know another reality—another temperament, culture, philosophy, or religion—can create deep respect for differences without any shame for who one is. It is perhaps the greatest gift of education, travel, and close relationships. One learns humility—no one has the total perspective. And all of this is the foundation of ethics. You gain a kind of wisdom that is irreplaceable. This is the ultimate gift you and your HSC have to offer each other simply because you have been born with a fundamental difference in how you face the world.

Are You Highly Sensitive?
A Self-test*

Answer each question according to the way you feel. Answer TRUE if it's at least moderately true for you. Answer FALSE if it is not very true or not at all true for you.

1. T F I seem to be aware of subtleties in my environment.
2. T F Other people's moods affect me.
3. T F I tend to be very sensitive to pain.
4. T F I find myself needing to withdraw during busy days, into bed or into a darkened room or any place where I can have some privacy and relief from stimulation.
5. T F I am particularly sensitive to the effects of caffeine.
6. T F I am easily overwhelmed by things like bright lights, strong smells, coarse fabrics, or sirens close by.
7. T F I have a rich, complex inner life.
8. T F I am made uncomfortable by loud noises.
9. T F I am deeply moved by the arts or music.
10. T F I am conscientious.
11. T F I startle easily.
12. T F I get rattled when I have a lot to do in a short amount of time.
13. T F When people are uncomfortable in a physical environment I tend to know what needs to be done to make it more comfortable (like changing the lighting or the seating).
14. T F I am annoyed when people try to get me to do too many things at once.
15. T F I try hard to avoid making mistakes or forgetting things.

16.   T   F   I make it a point of avoiding violent movies and TV shows.

17.   T   F   I become unpleasantly aroused when there's a lot going on around me.

18.   T   F   Changes in my life shake me up.

19.   T   F   I notice and enjoy delicate or fine scents, tastes, sounds, and works of art.

20.   T   F   I make it a high priority to arrange my life to avoid upsetting or overwhelming situations.

21.   T   F   When I must compete or be observed while performing a task, I become so nervous or shaky that I do much worse than I would otherwise.

22.   T   F   When I was a child, my parents or teachers seemed to see me as sensitive or shy.

Scoring

If you answered true to twelve or more of the questions, you are probably highly sensitive.

That said, no psychological test is so accurate that you should base your life on it. If only one or two questions are true of you, but they are extremely true, you might also be justified in calling yourself highly sensitive.

Chapter Four

When You and Your Child Are Both Highly Sensitive

And What About the Rest of Your Family's Temperament?

Non–highly sensitive parents should read this chapter, although you might choose to skip the first half, addressing the parent and child who are both highly sensitive—the advantages, the potential problems, and their solutions. But in the second half we look at the temperament of other family members (including your partner if you have one), how to optimize the effects they and your HSC have on one another, and how to use the temperament perspective to create postive change in your entire family.

Being highly sensitive myself, I now write as one HSP to another. Like our sensitive children, we have a useful trait, but we often have trouble in two situations: when we are being overwhelmed and when we have to stand up for ourselves as different but normal. Since this book is on sensitive children, not adults, we will not spend too long on these problems. But we must at least think about them, as how parents feel personally will always affect their children, HSCs in particular.

We should also acknowledge that we make excellent parents. For example, our trait makes us more able to sense a child's needs and ascertain what to do. And because we are sensitive to language, including body language, we can often communicate with children— all children—in a manner closer to their own way of thinking. We can understand their worries and their questions. This is not to say that other parents cannot do all this, too, but we are more likely to have these skills.

But we can also wake up dreading another day of being so totally responsible for such a demanding, needy other. And far from appreciating ourselves, we tend to compare ourselves to other, nonsensitive parents or to the models in parenting books. Those parents seem so much more energetic, patient, and full of clever resources. They never seem to need to retreat from their family life, or if they do, they do not seem to feel guilty about it.

Let's fully admit how difficult it is to be a parent and highly sensitive. We need our alone time, but there is no truly alone time with an infant, especially if you have more than one child and also a partner (or even more difficult, you are a single parent). And what if you have a career, aging parents, or other responsibilities? Forget finding time for the things you need, like a night of uninterrupted sleep, creative work done alone, time in nature, and meditation or prayer. Others can survive without these. We can for a while, but we eventually start to wither.

Soon after my son was born I was glancing through a magazine rack and saw an article titled something like "The Hell of Parenthood—What No One Ever Tells You Until It Is Too Late." I felt a sinking feeling that this was the awful truth—parenting *was* hell—and no one had warned me.

Fortunately, I had a husband eager to share the load and able to be at home about half the time. And every year was easier, from my viewpoint, partly because there were more chances to take time alone and to explain my needs to my child. My husband, not highly sensitive but awfully clever, was always finding solutions for me. My favorite was the one he came up with when he had to be away for a whole day and evening. In order for me to have some time alone, away from my fourteen-month-old, he arranged the kitchen so there were plenty of toys down below and a step stool for me so I could sit on top of the refrigerator, out of sight of my son. (Left alone with toys in a playpen or crib he would howl, but when he had the run of the kitchen, even though he could not see me, he tended to play happily.) Up on the refrigerator, I could read and write for several hours before he needed me. What a strange but clever solution! And what a relief.

WHAT HIGHLY SENSITIVE PARENTS IN PARTICULAR GAIN FROM PARENTING

On the other hand, I would not have missed parenting for anything. (Remembering that parenting-is-hell article, however, I always tell highly sensitive people contemplating parenthood that for those with our temperament, "It is *wonderful* to have children and *wonderful* not to—either is a wise choice.") The essence of why I am glad to have been a parent is that I love my son. I loved him the moment I saw him. I would not have wanted to miss knowing him. Children are seriously children for about a decade. But for five or more decades after that, they will be your friend—if you're fortunate to like each other. I always remember this when I meet an infant.

But there are other perks for highly sensitive parents: We gain both a deeper understanding of the meaning of life and a wider horizon. As one put it, "Before my first child, I was always tempted to withdraw. Having a child forced me to stay in the world, and it has been a life-transforming experience."

There is no doubt that with children we are forced to experience more, meet more people, and try many new experiences. What we might not risk on our own we will risk for our children.

Another sensitive parent, a mother of three HSCs, said, "It has been the single most significant lesson in my life—my children are my teachers."

FIRST PRIORITY—YOUR OWN STABILITY

Clearly, parenting when you and your child are both highly sensitive is a special situation. So let's get specific about what you need to know and do.

Since HSCs are so deeply affected by how their parents are feeling, it is important for sensitive parents to find ways to be calm, happy, and healthy in spite of their workload and other obligations. Your emotional stability depends on this, and therefore so does your child's. It is so much easier to raise a child right than try to fix an adult, believe me. So you are not being selfish when you take care of yourself. You are being very considerate of your child and those who will have to live with your child and possibly heal her if you are not healthy yourself. Again, this is not a book about sensitive adults, but I have much to say on the subject of self-care in *The Highly Sensitive Person* and *The Highly Sensitive Person's Workbook* if you need more encouragement.

The next thing you need to have is a full sense of the advantages for your child of your own sensitivity.

WHEN YOU AND YOUR CHILD ARE BOTH HIGHLY SENSITIVE

We will begin with the advantages to your situation:

1. *You understand your child's experience.* Remember from Chapter 2 the ways Estelle knew just how to raise Maria. There were no problems with food—Estelle had always cooked simply. There was no question about cutting the labels out of clothing because they itched—Estelle had always done that for herself. Estelle understood why Maria walked out of the movie showing how animals are butchered, and she knew how to respond when her teenage daughter was going to pass up a free trip to Sweden.

2. *You have real experience coping with the disadvantages of your trait.* You can report with realism and detail on how you coped with overarousal during a performance or what you felt and said when someone thoughtlessly commented, "Oh, you're just too sensitive." You can honestly say that things that really seemed difficult to you, too, did turn out to be okay.

3. *You can raise your child's self-esteem just by liking yourself.* As I will discuss in the next chapter, in this culture, self-esteem does not come easily for an HSC. But if you have gained respect for yourself as a sensitive person, your child will absorb the antidote from you easily, like the air he breathes.

4. *You have some answers to, or at least experience with, the questions HSCs tend to ponder.* You will listen and discuss these with the proper care, even reverence, when that is called for.

5. *You have the right "volume."* As I discussed in the last chapter, we all tend to communicate with the "volume"—the harshness, persistence, and so forth—that would best reach us if we were receiving the message. Sensitive people tend to communicate gently, at a low "volume," being careful about their tone of voice, questions, and use of silence. They understand gestures, nuances, and hints. Hence, for better and sometimes for worse, the two of you will communicate quite clearly what is on your minds. And neither of you will enjoy shouting matches very much, although some will happen, I assure you.

In general, your similar volume makes communication considerably easier for your HSC. When my son was twenty-seven, he finally decided to learn to drive. We decided I would teach him (although everyone predicted a mother teaching a grown son to drive would be a disaster). We did fine, because I was so aware of what he was dealing with, inside and all around him, that I knew intuitively when to speak up with a warning, instruction, or reassurance, and when to stay quiet so he could concentrate (which was most of the time). He also knew it was nerve-racking for me, the helpless passenger, and was supportive and grateful rather than critical of how I taught him.

6. *You share interests and tastes to some degree about food, aesthetics, and how to spend leisure time.* Each generation has its own fashions, but you and your HSC will probably agree on more than a nonsensitive parent would with the same child. Several sensitive parents commented on liking simple foods themselves and never having had problems with their HSCs around food, while nonsensitive parents mentioned it much more often.

A Home with Few Hassles

All these advantages are perhaps best conveyed by a description of Carin's home, which many of you could not imitate because your work takes you outside the home. But you might glean some ideas from her story.

Carin, a sensitive parent of two sensitive teenagers, shared with me that she "got pulled into parenting." She was near the end of medical school at the time (and also an accomplished professional musician) when she became pregnant with a child who died only fifteen months after he was born. She had worked through that experience, but the reality of parenting had convinced her that she wanted to be at home with her future children. "It had just become so obvious to me what children needed."

Part of what her sensitive children needed, Carin realized, was an orderly home. Carin is convinced that it helped her HSCs remain calm. Perhaps as a result, they tend to put things away themselves, preferring things neat as much as she does. Also, Carin decided when they were born that she would never yell, even from upstairs to downstairs or vice versa, since she herself does not like yelling, feeling it's rude. As a result, her children never yell at home either.

In addition, Carin has always respected their need for down time and a quieter social life, and has never called them "shy" or "timid" because they do not want to go to summer camp or prefer to read alone during recess. She also senses their subtle differences—Gretchen can take more hubbub, Larry has to have a more limited schedule.

Above all, Carin parents in a style that reduces stress for herself as well as her children. Rather than prepare scheduled meals, she keeps on hand the foods they like and lets them "graze." Or she does "short order" cooking when they want something. She has never pushed them to eat anything they do not like. They happen to like the same lunch every day, so she makes that: two apples, two peanut butter sandwiches with crusts off, cantaloupe balls, and water. No fuss.

At the same time, she aims as much as possible to put their needs first. (To do that, however, a sensitive parent must take excellent care of himself or herself when the children are not around.) When her children are tired, hungry, or upset, Carin sees to them and tries to put her own needs on hold for a little while. Her children know this is not because she feels inferior or that they deserve to be spoiled. She has her limits. But according to Carin, "That's just what it means to be a parent—being the grown-up, I am better able to wait." The result of this caring respect for them while they were vulnerable children? They respect their mother. Or as Carin says, "My kids are always nice to be around." This is a low-stress, low-volume house for certain.

You probably have a different style (I myself always wanted at least one meal a day seated as a family). But I found Carin a good example of using some of a highly sensitive person's best assets—creativity, conscientiousness, love of calm—to parent her HSCs. Her advice to you? "Entertain the notion that your child might be sensitive. Once you know it, you're all set. You just have to do parenting differently and question every 'should.' "

Where a Highly Sensitive Parent Has to Be Careful

1. *However you approach raising an HSC, it will probably be deeply affected by how you were raised.* Estelle, the sensitive mother in Chapter 2, definitely wanted to raise Maria, her sensitive daughter, in a way that was different from how her own parents raised her. But in trying to be their opposite, there is always the danger

of going too far the other way. Or we may be responding to our own needs at that age, projecting them onto our child and not seeing the child's actual situation. Perhaps as a child you had a particular fear of medical environments and no one appreciated your agony, so you give your daughter so much reassurance and treats before and after taking her to the doctor that, even though she has had only good experiences, she begins to wonder if there is some danger here that she has overlooked.

2. *Most likely, if you miss the mark, it will be in the direction of over-protection.* Many highly sensitive adults resent their parents' having pushed them so much that they always felt stressed and inadequate. (Of course others feel they were coddled too much, so that they grew up without important life experiences, and so push their own HSC too much.)

3. *You may not expose your child to enough new experiences.* Maybe you have tried roller coasters, chili dogs, and skiing, and you know they are not for you. In fact, you often spare yourself all kinds of unnecessary risks and stimulation, knowing the kinds of things you do and do not like. But all of this has been *your* choosing. If you limit your child's experiences as you have limited your own, your child will start out with your choices and perhaps never have a chance to learn for himself about roller coasters, chili dogs, and skiing.

4. *You will suffer when your child suffers, and that affects your child's handling of the pain.* It is quite likely that you are going to suffer more than nonsensitive parents when your child is in physical or emotional pain. But as I said in Chapter 2, what your child needs is a parent who can stay calm and "contain" these intense emotions. This may be more difficult for you.

5. *You may have trouble asserting yourself for your child's sake.* You may not be used to or comfortable with raising your volume so that nonsensitive types get the message: "No, she doesn't want to do that!" But your child will need you to, and to role model this firmness so that she can have it, too.

6. *You may have trouble asserting your own needs within the family.*

As parents, sensitive people often feel they cannot rest until they have met everyone else's needs perfectly plus having things neat and organized and everything on one's "to do" list crossed off. This provides other family members with a very dangerous temptation: When I do not want to do something, why not just leave it for the person who does everything? This is not good for your child's character.

7. *Whatever bad feelings you have about your trait or yourself, your child will learn these from you.* It happens by osmosis; by what we do, not what we say. You can't fake it. You have to like being a highly sensitive person.

8. *You can assume more similarities between you than there are.* Even if you do not relive your past with your HSC, you can be so aware of your sensitivity that you can think your child is almost your twin—liking and not liking the same things, for example. But sensitive people are highly variable in their likes and dislikes. I do not like movies containing horror or gratuitous violence. My son can watch any movie, liking those that are well done, however violent they are. He says, "It's just a movie." Put that way, this was a difference I could understand. But what follows is an example of a difference I did not initially understand.

A Personal Story of Overidentification

Both my son and I had difficulty making friends in elementary school. Neither of us played sports well (or wished to) and we were not relaxed and outgoing in groups of kids, which is, after all, most of what school is about. Instead, both of us had a few friends with whom we got along well enough in one-on-one play at home. So one day I said to him something that implied what I had been assuming for years—that he felt rejected and inferior to the other kids, as I had. He informed me that he did not like them, found them boring, and thought there was nothing wrong with him. They had the problem, for not appreciating his style of humor, for example.

My mind slid to a halt. I had been projecting my own low self-esteem onto him—and suffering through it all over again. His heroic stand with the kids at school was a better stance than my own (but Chapters 8 and 9 have even better solutions). True, as an adult my son looks back on fourth through eighth grades as the most painful part of his life. I certainly was not comfortable with an essay he wrote in fifth grade, for which the assigned topic was "Why We Need Friends." He changed the title and wrote his essay on "Why We Don't Need Friends." But he was somehow maintaining his self-esteem, and I had almost struck it a devastating blow by giving him the impression that I, like his peers, assumed he should believe there was something wrong with him.

What You Can Do

1. *To stay fresh in your approach and avoid overidentification, be familiar with all of your child's other qualities.* A good way to begin is to notice how your child is like her other parent. Have others who know the two of you point out how you are different.
2. *To avoid overprotection and to be sure your child is exposed to new experiences, rein in your anxieties.* Be realistic about dangers; look at the actual odds and weigh the danger of injury against the danger of your child living a life burdened with fears, limits, lack of skills, and regrets because of you. If your anxiety is very high, get some professional help. Do not share your exaggerated fears with your child.
3. *If your HSC shows an interest in something new, see that he tries it, even if you have no interest in it.* Of course the activity must be reasonably safe and appropriate for your child's age and abilities. And it should not be one in which you are almost certain he will come away feeling like a failure. Be careful here—short kids can succeed at basketball, awkward ones can still enjoy ballet lessons. A sense of success or failure usually depends on the teacher and, if there is a class, the level of mutual support (rather than com-

petition) established. Does your child want to learn to ski, ride a horse or a motorcycle, go to football camp, or try out for a play? Maybe these would give you shivers. In that case, find a competent, kind, soft-spoken instructor, coach, or family friend who shares your child's enthusiasm—anyone to take your place—and let it happen.

4. *If your child is not developing interests, see that the menu is broadened.* As a sensitive parent you must make an extra effort here. But perhaps you can turn any similar tendencies of yours to good use, by expressing any regrets you have about not having tried more things as a child. Or you can describe a point in your life when you changed (and are glad of it), feeling you needed to be better prepared for life, or that you would ultimately be happier once you were familiar with a few of the things other people seem to enjoy so much. Then the two of you might agree that a good personal goal would be to try one new thing a month—maybe you would like to have the same goal—and be very sympathetic about how difficult this may seem.

5. *When you are hurting because your child is, take a larger perspective—think about karma, or God's will, or whatever explanation you accept for the unfairness of our fates,* for fair it rarely is. Somehow we all come into life with certain difficulties to face and learn from, and your child has his own set. You can provide optimal conditions and some ideas on how you have maintained perspective through life's ups and downs, but you cannot remove the cup of fate from your child's lips. Being immersed in another's pain to the point of being overwhelmed by it does not help the other person. Not at all. Especially when the other is your child, who needs you to help him find a way to rise above it.

6. *Learn to assert yourself for your child* when it is appropriate and your child cannot or should not have to do so alone. It will be terrific practice for you and essential role modeling for your child. Take an assertiveness training course if you have to. When you fear you will not say it right, write it down and memorize it or

read it out loud. When you think of the right thing to say later, go back and say it. When you cannot do it face-to-face, send a letter or an e-mail. When you cannot do it yourself, get your spouse, another relative, or a sympathetic teacher to do it. Even an older sibling can face down a bully. But do not let your child feel that she is without support, that no one can help, and that highly sensitive people are by nature timid and easy victims.

7. *Learn to assert yourself with your child.* Sometimes your needs have to come first, so that you can take care of your child and your child learns that others have needs, too. Obviously you set these limits more as your child matures. But remember Carin's example: She put her children first, but not to their detriment. She kept an orderly house for their sake, but she was creative about what she let go—she does not cook regular meals. And her children have developed a sense of responsibility: they put things away, they do not yell at her, and as you will see in the chapter on adolescents, they are responsible for taking care of their clothes, going to bed on time, and doing their homework. For your child's sake as well as your own, give your child increasing responsibility for his behavior, his staying amused, and his home environment.

8. *When you are having trouble taking care of yourself, remember the lesson of the airplane oxygen mask:* Put yours on first, because an unconscious parent is a useless one. When my son was a toddler, he used to scream at dinnertime. I tried everything to please him. Then I took a course in meditation, and one instruction was to meditate twenty minutes in the evening before dinner. Twenty minutes all to myself that I "had" to take. His crying at that hour ceased; it seemed we had both been getting tense, and now we were both calming down. Self-care can be like that—it turns out to be good "family care" as well. And ignoring your needs will inadvertently convey that you see yourself as a second-class citizen, so naturally it would be easy for your child to also feel second-class.

9. *Try this for your own self-esteem:* Imagine that before you were

born you were able to choose your temperament and that you *chose* to be highly sensitive because of its advantages and what you could contribute to the world. Think about it.

9. *Try not to be excessively guilt-ridden and apologetic for every mistake you make in parenting,* request you must make, trouble you cause your child, or sacrifice that your child must endure because of being born as your child and sharing your fate. Just admit your mistakes and role model how one can live with making a few errors or flaws. Talk about a mistake you have made as soon as you are aware of it as well as later. Also, remember that if a few unavoidable sacrifices are required of your child, these can teach resilience and build character. Protection from all sacrifice and disappointment produces little tyrants and entitled monsters, at least with non-HSCs. HSCs who are protected from sacrifice are more likely to feel guilty for not suffering as much as other children and do not learn how to deal with future sacrifices that may be necessary.

A Personal Case of Getting Over Guilt

From the age of three until about twelve, my son had to put up with parents who were dedicated full-time to an important social cause. All of those involved who were parents felt very guilty about the time we took away from our children to do this work. A developmental psychologist who happened to visit us commented to me as she was leaving that we all seemed like excellent parents. Our only low mark was in setting limits. To her, it seemed as if our children (several of them HSCs) were making use of our guilt to blackmail us and run us ragged! For example, in our house, if our son wanted a story at bedtime, he got one, of course—even if we were exhausted. And then a second and a third, because we felt guilty about being so unavailable at other times.

She suggested that we look at our schedules to be sure we were available as much as parents in other careers (we were), and then describe better to our children the important work we were doing, and let them feel they were taking part in that, too, if they had to spend an afternoon in day care. Our son had no problem with that idea; indeed, he had always been proud of his parents' idealism.

WHAT ABOUT THE REST OF THE FAMILY?

Of course, there are more people in your child's life than you. Indeed, the triad of mother, father, and child—or a child and two mothers, two fathers, stepparents, or even a single parent and a grandparent, or any other additional family members (even a single parent and his or her job)—teach the HSC a great deal about social life as well as potentially providing great hope and resilience. "If one of you can't help me, maybe the other (or somebody) can." When both parents are highly sensitive, the HSC can receive substantial support from this little culture of three (or more) that values sensitivity and knows all about it. (Then the task would be to help any less sensitive children in the family feel normal!)

When One Parent Is Sensitive and the Other Is Not

When one parent is sensitive and the other is not, the sensitive parent and child may have the stronger bond, at least at times. Randall's mother, Marilyn, has noticed that Randall, at nine, now prefers his father's company over her own—Dad is also highly sensitive and Marilyn is not.

It is natural in families for birds of a feather to flock together. Gender is usually the bond, although what feathers matter can change over the years, changing the alliances. In our family, my son is at times closer to his father—they are both males, both love to talk, both Jewish (my son's decision). At other times my son and I have been closer, sharing a passion for writing, an artistic bent, an appreciation of Star Trek, and certain other, more sensitive qualities.

There are always joys and risks in very special parent-child bonds. The risks occur only when the bond begins to overshadow or threaten the adult partners' bond or becomes too special (or even romantic or sexualized) from the side of the parent, which overwhelms a child's own growth. A child may seem to welcome being intensely intimate with a parent, but a child cannot judge if it is too much, having no experience of the alternatives.

When one parent is sensitive and the other is not, there is also the question of what role each parent will play in deciding parenting strategies. Sometimes a sensitive parent will bow out, secretly feeling that sensitivity is a flaw and hoping the nonsensitive parent can raise a child without so much of it. Men feeling bad about their trait may do this—and sensitive fathers with busy work lives may find parenting difficult in any case, not realizing why family life seems so overwhelming. Similarly, a sensitive mother may decide to let a nonsensitive father raise their sensitive son to be "a real man," or their daughter to be tougher and more liberated than she is.

More often, however, the sensitive parent takes over the rearing of the sensitive child, playing the role of the true authority and protector, possibly leaving the less sensitive parent feeling left out, useless, and powerless—or just disgusted with both of them. This is bad for the child and the partnership. As we saw in the last chapter, nonsensitive parents have a great deal to contribute to the raising of HSCs—balance, groundedness, adventurousness, enthusiasm. Further, one must remember that a sensitive child with her biological parents still has 50 percent of her personality from the nonsensitive parent. In handling *these* traits, the nonsensitive parent is the expert.

How HSCs Can Impact the Parental Partnership

A child with an unusually strong temperament, such as an HSC, is often a source of intense conflict for the two parents over how to solve the unexpected problems that arise and the overall feeling that "Our kid isn't behaving like other kids." And then creeps in the question of what or who is to blame. "You always let her back out of anything hard." Or "He's scared to say anything at all now because you yell at him for speaking too softly."

Whoever is with the child more may develop routines and solutions that may seem like unnecessary catering or spoiling to the less involved parent. This is exacerbated if the child covers up the sensitivity around, or causes less trouble for, the less available or less accepting parent, who then thinks, or says, "What's the problem? I have no trouble with this child." Finally, the parent more involved in helping a young HSC cope may not have much energy left for the other parent, causing jealousy.

Just knowing these pitfalls should help you to sidestep them. Appreciate your partner's views and how they help balance your own. Be very gentle when you suggest a different way to do things. All parenting experts agree: You have to be a team (even more so if you are divorced). And an HSC especially requires the two of you to agree that he has a special trait, to know what about it is an asset, and to agree on what you will do to cope with any problems that arise. Otherwise, not only will your child feel like a flawed and hopeless case, but he may feel he is to blame for the discord.

Brothers and Sisters

Family compositions and dynamics are so complicated that I can only make some general points. When one child is more sensitive and free to express it, so that he receives special treatment, this is bound to create resentment among siblings with fewer or different special needs. For example (to use the traits described in Chapter 1), an active, approaching non-HSC who needs more limits and warnings will resent an HSC who can be trusted with more liberties and responsibilities. Or a "good" HSC may resent a slow-adapting, active, intense sibling who seems to get away with more because the parents have to choose their battles and let more go with that one.

Even when all the children in a family are HSCs, one may be more intense, active, or slow-to-adapt, causing the other to be "the good one" or "our mature child."

It always seems that siblings become as different as they possibly can be, splitting certain pairs of traits and developing them to opposite extremes. It is not so serious when both halves of the pair of traits, and therefore both siblings, are highly valued by at least one parent. But if one side of the pair of traits is devalued, then the child who assumes that trait carries what is devalued and feels demeaned, ignored, or overburdened.

For example, you may have heard parents say, "She's our genius and he's our champion athlete." Okay. But you have probably also heard something more like, "She's our genius, all honors classes, we're so proud of her. And he's still (sigh) more interested in sports."

Parents must be watchful not only to honor all types of siblings but to reduce these splits. In the above example, one would hope the parents want both children to fully develop both their intellectual and athletic abilities rather than specializing so completely. Society likes specialization because it is more efficient. Bakers should bake, dancers should dance, and we do not need any dancing bakers, thank you. But the individual is usually happier with a more well-rounded life.

Failing to honor both siblings' traits and develop balance in both is even more of an issue when one child is an HSC. In these cases innate temperament is involved rather than merely an interest or preference. It is easy to see how an HSC can become the good, wise, mature, helpful, brilliant child and the non-HSC the impulsive, overly dramatic, troubled problem child. Or the HSC is the cowardly, inhibited, shy, uptight, runt of the litter and the non-HSC is the heroic, outgoing, cheerful, fun-loving, "normal" child. In fact, both children are capable of being some of both if their parents see that and encourage it.

In a moment we will discuss other ways to talk about temperament so that opposites are equally attractive. But even when you have a secret preference about temperaments, abilities, interests, or whatever, honesty about that is not appropriate or necessary. And who knows, you and your less favorite child may be quite different people six months from now.

The Story of Jacques

Jacques was an HSC I knew who, at about five, became so jealous and sadistic toward his less sensitive brother, two years younger, that it was hard for anyone to be around Jacques. What happened? His little brother had learned to walk and talk and was being treated as a real family member whose needs had to be considered. Furthermore, the younger brother was receiving considerable attention now from his parents because he was an intense, active, persistent non-HSC—all having more impact now that he was three. He was getting into Jacques's belongings and into his space. He was also a big boy, so he was beginning to challenge Jacques's sense of physical superiority and receive more attention from their father, who saw the younger son as the potential athlete he had wanted. Then Jacques started school, which was difficult for him, especially the separation from his mother while his brother was staying home with her.

As a result of all this, Jacques seemed for a few years almost like the archetype of Hate. He was obsessed with everything his little brother did and criticized the little one's every move. Jacques fought for equal rights regarding each privilege given his brother and became irritable if his brother received a gift or display of affection from anyone. Jacques hit him if his parents turned their back, and if the younger one so much as touched Jacques or anything of his, he would launch into a detailed, hysterical tirade about the unfairness of it.

The parents understood at least some of the problems and were as patient, just, and loving as any two humans could be toward *both* boys. They tried to balance the attention they gave the two. Although the younger one still *required* more attention, Jacques was catching up on that score—he could be left alone, but not alone with his brother.

For a while Jacques was nobody's favorite. That, however, was never said, even in private, at least to me. And now, a few years later, the two boys, still elementary school age, are good pals and playmates. Jacques is a thoughtful, rational child, with hardly a drop of rancor or aggressiveness in him.

What happened? We might say that for a while Jacques was possessed by an attitude or energy of envious hatred to which any human can fall prey, although adults are sometimes better able to hide it. Since he could not hide it, to observers he became almost the embodiment of nastiness, while his rather adorable, innocent-at-three little brother/victim had become the embodiment of Goodness, even to Jacques, who must have hated himself all the worse for hating his brother. But his parents never lost faith that there was more to Jacques than hate—there was mostly goodness in both boys and a bit of "bad" impulses in both of them, too, just like the rest of us (the little brother, in self-defense perhaps, had developed quite a talent for crying and playing the victim and getting his brother into trouble). And so the whole of both boys was loved. This love, along with extra attention and praise toward Jacques (especially from dad), plus the passage of time, seemed to solve the problem. Time helped also, in that as Jacques's little brother matured he became a real playmate, and Jacques could teach him what he was learning in school and take pleasure in his little brother's successes.

What I want to emphasize is that his parents never fell into the all-or-nothing trap their son was in. They did not identify him with just one energy or attitude and then reject him for it. What a shame if a little child, still growing and vulnerable, becomes for a parent nothing but an example of cowardliness, stubbornness, weakness, or anything else.

By the way, even more than non-HSCs, many HSCs tend to genuinely love a new sibling (although one must never, ever underestimate the unconscious feelings of anger and hurt that are almost inevitable when the baby of the family is replaced by a new one). In fact, HSCs can benefit a great deal from a younger sibling, sensitive or not. The younger one allows the older HSC to lead, protect, counsel, and teach—building confidence in these natural proclivities of most HSCs.

Still, a young sibling can be terribly intrusive for an HSC, interrupting deep thoughts or complicated make believe, wanting to come into the older one's room, touching things that the HSC wants to keep just so. In the last chapter you met Randall. His younger sister, Jeannie, is his total opposite, according to their mother. "Jeannie loves playdates, loves to interact, would go home with anyone. No wonder Randall finds her irritating. She goes in to see him and he wants her to go away. But we're a family, this is what happens; it isn't personal." How well said.

Handling Conflicts

Especially when one child is an HSC and the other is not, siblings should not be forced to be together or even love each other. Tolerance and politeness is enough, but they are essential. The HSC in particular can be badly hurt by comments and teasing from a sibling, especially an older non-HSC. Nor should siblings be left to resolve their conflicts alone until you see they have the tools to do so: Simple conflict resolution skills such as taking equal turns speaking up and listening, knowing to take a time out when things are getting brutal, and knowing to look for a creative, fair compromise, plus whatever else they come up with on their own. And even with those skills, they need an adult eavesdropping to be sure the rules of good conduct are upheld—no name calling, physical blows, domination, or anything else intended to wound or kill the body or spirit. With practice, siblings really can resolve their own battles. With *practice*.

Talking About Temperament in Your Family

Every child has an inherited temperament of some sort, not just HSCs. So when sensitivity comes up as a topic, let the discussion move on to each member's temperament. Do not, however, become a total "reductionist," someone who attributes everything to one cause. Many times people act the way they do not because of temperament but because of their culture, upbringing, who's important to them, the present situation, or experiences with ones like it. For example, temperament has little or nothing to do with whether an adult stops at a red light, gives holiday gifts, or runs from a tornado.

With that warning, use the eight traits described in Chapter 1 and the books in the Resources to start the discussion. If your family is interested, use the seven traits at the end of Chapter 1 to rate everyone, and test their sensitivity, and consider their novelty seeking too (Chapter 3). With an older HSC, you can discuss each of the items on the adult sensitivity test in order to clarify how she feels about each and where others would give the same response and agree with her.

Then together you could make a simple graph of each member on each trait. But remember, the individual should be the final authority on how much he or she has of each trait. Still, it can be fun to have family members point out instances to encourage and praise the positive aspect of each trait. "You aren't persistent?! What about the time you would *not* quit until you learned to ride a bike?"

Keep It Positive

Keep it light and use positive terms for both poles of every trait (Mary Kurcinka's books help with this—see Resources). For example, for a high activity level you might use "active" or "energetic" rather than "wild." Its opposite is "calm," not "slow" or "lazy." For the intensity of an emotional response use "spirited" or "having strong feelings" rather than "explosive," "hysterical," or "overly dramatic." Its opposite is "mild" and "easygoing," not "dull." And so on.

The positive labels do not mean, however, that everyone has to always *enjoy* the company of someone who has strong views or is "always energetic" or "interestingly unpredictable." Explain to your family that one's temperament is not bad or wrong, and neither is another's emotional reactions to the resulting behaviors. The task is getting along with differences, which is one of the great human problems to be overcome, and families are on the front lines.

Finally, you may be thinking, "Isn't this too much labeling?" It could be if carried to an extreme or if labels are used as a putdown or as subtle name-calling during a conflict. ("You never give me a turn—that's because you're so *persistent.*" Teach children to stick to the issue—even persistent people can learn to share, so persistence is irrelevant, and name-calling only escalates the argument.) The reason for these "labels" is that it feels good to be seen for who one is. It is validating. It means others care enough to know who you are, fundamentally, and actually have noticed and do know what you are like.

When You First Bring Up Sensitivity

Funny things can happen in a family (or couple, for that matter) when you start speaking of high sensitivity in a positive or even neutral way. Everyone wants to be "sensitive," so it is important to begin by explaining what you or your HSC is sensitive to—loud noise, harsh speech, criticism, smells, touch, being surprised, or whatever. Go over the self-test. Make it specific.

Also explain that the word is being used in a special, technical way (and that it is hard to think up any better word for this trait—one neither too positive- nor too negative-sounding). In this case, "sensitive" does not mean being kind, empathic, artistic, or insightful. When sensitive people are at their best, they tend to display these assets, plus conscientiousness, spiritual inclinations, intuition, and many other virtues. But they have no monopoly on these, and when they are overwhelmed, they can cease to be all of these. This is a neutral trait best described as one of two basic survival strategies: one, which is sensitivity, means observing and reflecting before acting; the other means acting quickly and trying often. It is easy to see how each strategy succeeds in some situations and not in others.

It is often the case, however, that the sensitive person has been the "identified patient" in a family. That is, perhaps quite unconsciously everyone has agreed there is something wrong with this one, so there is nothing wrong with the rest of us (as if every family member did not have flaws). Or the HSC has been the scapegoat, the easy one to blame or criticize for every disappointment ("If she weren't so shy . . ." "If he only liked fireworks . . ."). Or the HSC has been the one everyone orders around, like Cinderella ("She's such a wimpy thing, she deserves it if she lets us boss her around").

When sensitivity begins to be seen in a more positive light, the HSC becomes empowered, and then the old roles and habits may be shaken up. All families have both love and "power trips" going on to varying degrees. But for a family in which power has been the main fuel for interactions, a shift in who is empowered can greatly impact everyone. Sometimes there is a fresh effort to keep the HSC in his place, or a new "problem member" is found.

It can be difficult for those within a family to see the kinds of family dynamics I have just described, but if you suspect these are entrenched in yours, you might want to consider getting the whole group of you to see an *experienced, highly recommended* family therapist for a little nudge in a new direction.

A FINAL WORD

In sum, whether you are a nonsensitive parent thinking through your relationship with an HSC or you are helping your family discuss each member's temperament, thinking about sensitivity will lead to change—a shift toward greater equality and appreciation of each member of the family. Talking about temperament can be wonderful "family therapy."

Chapter Five

Four Keys to Raising a Joyous HSC

Self-esteem, Shame Reduction, Wise Discipline, and Knowing How to Discuss Sensitivity

This chapter begins by discussing how to raise your child's self-esteem, along with why this is a special concern with HSCs. Then we discuss shame, a distinct emotion that HSCs are especially prone to feel. Third, you will learn the latest ideas about how to discipline HSCs so that they learn and change without being crushed. Finally, you will learn how to speak about your HSC's sensitivity to relatives, friends, teachers, and your own child, and how to help your child reframe any negative comments he hears.

THE FIRST KEY—SELF-ESTEEM

Children's self-esteem will fluctuate with life's ups and downs, but it is also true that a basic positive or negative attitude about themselves does develop. When the basic attitude is negative, the ups are hardly counted and the downs seem to be the truth. If you are reading this book, you probably care enough about your child that she already feels valued and has good, solid, realistic self-esteem. But there are some reasons that it may not be as solid as it could be.

First, HSCs need to be corrected and disciplined, but unless you know how to do it properly, your child is likely to take your corrections as global messages about his worth. (Remember my description of Star the beagle and Sam the border collie in Chapter 2.) HSCs usually want to follow the rules, and when they are told they have made a mistake, they process this feedback deeply in order to avoid that mistake in the future. Remember, getting it right the first time is the essence of the survival strategy they have encoded in their genes. With too much criticism, HSCs can arrive at the conclusion that it's best to assume they are usually wrong!

The second reason HSCs are vulnerable to low self-esteem is that they are such harsh self-critics. HSCs are acute observers and evaluators; they are born critics, in the sense of movie, book, or food critics. They are often compassionately free of judgment of those whom they perceive as needing love and acceptance. But they can be ruthless in their opinions of the human race in general, and also of themselves and those closest to them (who are almost a part of themselves and therefore expected to do their best).

Do not be confused by their ability to criticize accurately. HSCs cannot "take what they dish out." Because HSCs process their mistakes so thoroughly, they often need no criticism at all—they punish themselves.

Third, you cannot control what is said or done to your HSC when you are not around—you can only prepare your child's mind to interpret correctly whatever he may hear. And as I said in Chapter 2, your HSC is growing up in a larger culture that does not favor highly sensitive people. Boys in Western cultures have a particularly difficult time if they reveal their sensitivity to pain, criticism, overstimulation, or others' feelings. But even if your child only hears positive things about being highly sensitive, she has to notice that the world is not designed with her in mind. That this seems to be normal, "just the way things are," only adds to the unconscious sense that she is out of step. Thus HSCs need extra help in developing an inner answer or antidote to the general lack of enough acknowledgment of what they need and who they are.

Finally, I have to admit that I emphasize self-esteem and shame reduction because I know how difficult these are to alter in adulthood. Almost every adult coming to me for psychotherapy is a highly sensitive person who was raised by parents or enrolled in a school (usually both) that at best largely ignored them, so that they felt unimportant or, at worst (and more often), treated them as if there was something deeply wrong with them at their core. As adults, they continue to feel deep shame. Until faced and worked through, the shame and low self-esteem can cause excruciating pain every day—as much emotional pain as the worst sort of chronic physical pain. It also keeps them from finding friends or life partners and from fully using their talents (or else they overexploit those talents in an attempt to prove their worth). Trying to change those feelings in an adult is slow work and costly. Essentially, it involves rewiring the brain. So as a parent, you want to do everything you can to wire your child's brain right to begin with.

The Four Kinds of Self-esteem

Let's begin with a brief course in self-esteem. Children have at least four sources of it. The first is the most important. It is the sense of being loved by one or more people simply because you exist. It has nothing to do with accomplishments. For this feeling to be solid and stable, it probably has to begin at birth or soon after and continue throughout childhood, although children will of course encounter people who do not like them or days when their parents are not feeling full of love. But if the feeling is reasonably stable, by adulthood, even if those persons who love you are not around, you can carry that sense of your basic goodness with you your entire life. It is a kind of security that causes you to expect that generally most people you like will also like you, once they get to know you. It allows you to be dependent when necessary and loving when you feel it.

The other three kinds of self-esteem have to do with abilities. There is social self-esteem—a sense of being able to make friends, say interesting things that gain the respect of strangers, and lead or speak up in a group. It begins at home, spreads to close friends, then, with practice and success, it can extend to almost any social situation. There is also physical self-esteem, a confidence about appearance and abilities, about coordination and being able to trust one's body to learn a skill, play a game, accomplish a task, and look as good as other bodies do. And the last is intellectual self-esteem— a feeling of confidence in learning situations and that one is as good as others one's own age in at least some areas.

At times we meet people with too much self-esteem of one or all four kinds, in that they believe they can do things without any preparation or that they will be liked even if they are careless or obnoxious. But I have never met an HSC like this. HSCs are more prone to "depressive realism"—that is, when they estimate how they will perform or what others think of them, they are like depressed people in that they are quite accurate, while most people err on the positive side.

The realism of HSCs makes sense. Realism is very important to their innate strategy of trying once and getting it right. Further, they do not like the overarousal involved in surprises, like trying a behavior and finding they cannot do it or are not liked for it. They especially do not want to assume that they are liked or loved only to be shocked and hurt by what seems to be contrary evidence. So you are not aiming to give your HSC an unrealistic, grandiose level of self-esteem, just a positive realism.

Indeed, sooner or later your HSC will develop an overly keen sense of "shadow" parts—those all-too-human impulses and desires she has banished to her unconscious in order to be a good girl. For better and worse, sensitive people are a little more conscious than others of what's normally unconscious—the veil is thinner for them. So they rarely achieve an inflated sense of themselves for long. They know they would sometimes like to be horribly selfish or spiteful. It is your job to be sure your child can accept, and believes you can accept, those shadow parts. Your child will have to learn, very well, that having "bad" thoughts is different from doing "bad" things. To be aware of "bad" thoughts even has an advantage. It means we can keep an eye on them. They are right at the front door, knocking, not sneaking in the back.

The bottom line: Because HSCs are afraid to *over*estimate their abilities, virtues, or how much they are loved and lovable, you will have to be sure your child does not *under*estimate these either. Further, you can encourage her to overestimate just a little when it's safe to do so. It can be a reasonable strategy to tell yourself, "I can do it!" We all need a little grandiosity to make a fast break out of the gate.

I described Chuck in Chapter 1, the nine-year-old who skis and climbs trees, but carefully. He went to his first sleepover summer camp with great hesitation. Originally he planned to spend a weekend, then he decided to risk a week. But the camp insisted on two weeks. So he decided to try it, wanting to keep up with his older brother and cousin (not HSCs), and having been assured by the camp organizers they would all sleep in the same cabin. Upon arrival, Chuck learned that he would not be with his brother and cousin. His mother worried when her son's eyes filled with tears as he looked around the barren cabin, soon to be filled with strange boys. "Shall we go home then?" she asked him.

Suddenly his face toughened and the sensitive, realistic Chuck switched to one with more confidence, if not quite as much realism. "Nah. I only have to be in this cabin when I'm sleeping." And so he stayed.

How to Promote Self-esteem

1. *Look at yourself.* HSCs do not miss much. Actions—including posture, tone of voice, and facial expression—speak louder than words to these kids. If you feel bad about yourself or them, for being sensitive or anything else, they will know. If you or your child are highly sensitive, are you proud of it? Or do you still have subtle doubts, like a fear that your child will be unhappy as an adult

because of being sensitive? If you do not feel good about sensitivity, work on it. Change your views—today.

2. **Words count, too.** Speak admiringly of your child's sensitivity when it comes up (but be careful not to overdo it—you don't want to seem to "profess too much" to compensate for your secret worries). When your child needs to rest or take down time, you can connect this with something positive about the trait—"Of course you're tired from going to the zoo; you were noticing everything!" Especially praise your HSC's observation skills, ability to think things through, conscientiousness, creativity, intuition, and compassion. However, you want to make it clear that you do not expect these all the time. "You were noticing everything at the zoo," not "You're my little Sherlock Holmes, noticing everything everywhere we go."

3. **Spend time with your child.** Nothing says "I like you" like wanting to be with someone. Say it, yes, but show it, too, in this way in particular. Child psychiatrist Stanley Greenspan recommends a half hour of "floor time" with your child each day, with you just hanging out, following your child's lead. It heals all sorts of wounds, like a recent correction or moment of shame. With an HSC you will want to be sure he is ready for this much stimulating attention. A half hour might be too much, at least on some days, or a less stimulating way might be working in the same room or talking with him while you cook, clean, or drive. But when your intention is to spend time with him, let his needs decide how you do it, not yours.

4. **Show respect** for your child's feelings, needs, opinions, preferences, and decisions. This should start very early. Even if you must refuse a preference or set a limit, you can respect the impulse that came from within her. It can be as simple a matter as saying, "I know you really like ice cream, but you will have to eat some of your dinner first." Or "It makes good sense that you want to bake cookies—it sounds like fun and we would all enjoy them—but it's ten o'clock at night and I have to get up at six and

I know for a fact that it will keep me up, having you active in the kitchen until eleven or twelve." Such acknowledgments give the desire and desirer a sense of validity in the eyes of another.

5. *Help your HSC understand himself in relation to nonsensitive people.* Your HSC needs to learn that many people tend to think out loud, speak "off the cuff," and act impulsively without always meaning what they say or intending it to have such a strong effect. In doing this, you are teaching your child to mentally turn down the volume, to wear emotional earplugs. You can suggest, for example, "I wonder if he was just in a bad mood—you know how you can sometimes say things you don't mean." Or "Why don't you ask her tomorrow if she really meant that?" (Asking today may stir a defensive "Of course I did.")

At the same time, your HSC needs to know that nonsensitive people often do not "hear" very well. They do not immediately "get" hints or understand that expressions like "well . . . maybe . . . if it matters that much to you" really mean no. With non-HSCs, your child has to say things like "I want that," "It's my turn," "Let's do it my way now," or "Stop that, I don't like it." This will take considerable practice, one situation at a time, focusing on one person at a time who is not hearing her.

However, if he does not manage to turn up the volume or if he feels ignored, help him not to feel victimized. Some people just do not hear soft voices. (When I'm on Long Island, where my husband teaches, I can *never* order a bagel sandwich with enough volume, decisiveness, and speed to please the person taking my order. I try to take the glares philosophically.)

Most important, your child has to understand that there is nothing wrong with either the HSC or non-HSC; they simply have different styles. At the same time, he can have a personal preference and can even choose to express it: "To me it seems rude when you talk like that."

6. *Bring up strengths when your child mentions a weakness.* When your HSC brings up a weakness or failing, start, *please,* by honor-

ing the feeling: "I can see how you must be terribly disappointed with yourself for striking out twice today." But then mention a similar countering instance: "But I see it a bit differently, since just last week you hit a home run." Or "No, baseball does not seem to be your sport, but then, I know how much you enjoy gymnastics and how good you are at it." Or "No, sports are not your strong suit, but I do think you draw better than almost any kid your age. I wonder if Van Gogh could play soccer very well?"

Do not persist or get into an argument. Just mention it as your own view. And do *not* exaggerate abilities. This will only undermine the credibility of future praise.

This tactic of bringing up a success to match a failure is important for wiring your child's brain for self-esteem. Research finds that we can store our self-relevant memories using one of two "filing systems." People with low self-esteem and depression tend to have all their negative traits in the same file, so that when one memory of a failure or weakness comes to mind, they all do. In contrast, others have a value-neutral system. They have all their experiences and self-attitudes relevant to, say, sports in one file, academics in another, social life in another. Strengths and weaknesses are found together under a topic.

How do files develop that strong good-or-bad-me organization that we do not want? Partly it comes from parents and peers who make blanket-statement "filing labels." "You are a bad child." Now all the bad things your HSC has ever done can be reprocessed under that. Your child thinks, "Oh yes, I did that and that and that." Or "You are my little angel." All the good things go there. So you should try to avoid these kinds of valuing global statements and try to counteract them when your child uses them, as in the example of countering the strikeout experience with a reminder of last week's home run. Your child may say you are "just making excuses for me," but if the excuses are valid, they will be absorbed.

THE SECOND KEY—REDUCING SHAME

The second key to raising a joyous, confident HSC is avoiding shame-proneness. Shame is much more than the absence of self-esteem. Shame—and guilt, its gentler cousin—are powerful built-in "self-conscious" emotions (like pride). Psychologists distinguish them in this way: While guilt focuses on particular misdeeds and, often, on what can be done to amend them, shame is a feeling that the entire self is bad. Thus, when one feels guilty, one assumes an active self that can do something wrong and make it right; being shamed, one assumes one is passive or helpless. When feeling guilty, people tend to engage rather than withdraw, trying to make amends or at least defend themselves. When ashamed, people hang their head or avert their eyes, withdrawing, slumping, and looking small, indicating submission or just wishing they could disappear. It feels *terrible*.

No one feels shame or guilt all the time. But they can become almost like a personality trait, in that some people become shame or guilt prone, much as people become anxious or shy by nature. Shame, guilt, shyness, or anxiety are things anyone can feel sometimes, but some people feel them almost all the time.

A Word in Defense of Shame

I do not want to give a culturally biased view of shame, however. In more communal cultures, such as China and Japan, shame is a bit more common and expected. In these cultures, shame serves to keep people engaged with each other, doing the right thing. Interestingly, researchers have found that in Japan, shame, and also self-esteem and pride, depend more on what others think than they do in the United States, where it is considered a virtue to stick to one's view of oneself and not be overly swayed by others. Because others' views are not taken into account, people in the United States tend to have unrealistically high or low self-esteem. The Japanese have less variation in these feelings because they tend to carefully observe others' reactions, reflect, and then base their view of themselves on that—sound familiar? No wonder sensitive people tell me they feel at home in Japanese culture!

In cultures where children are raised to be highly independent, to feel shame is, in itself, shameful. So when HSCs feel ashamed, they also have to feel ashamed of feeling ashamed. Yet shame forces us to see the deeper implications of our actions. Moments of spontaneous shame—those not wrongly induced by others but arising from seeing the effect of how we have behaved—are those moments when we really see that we are way, way off-track. HSCs will feel this spontaneous shame very readily. It is part of how they learn, because shame is a powerful way to prevent transgressing in a similar way in the future. For example, once they feel ashamed of stealing from a store (something most kids try), they know they are not the sort of person who steals, and they can feel very virtuous and secure that they will never experience that particular shame again. HSCs love that feeling.

Having been fair to shame, I must now restate that the feeling of shame is just very, very distressing. A little goes a long way with an HSC. In its essence, the feeling is "I am no good." Shaming as a method of correcting an HSC is the sledgehammer method of putting in a thumbtack.

When very intense, shame can create a kind of frantic state of hostility—toward others or toward oneself. One time when you might find HSCs becoming explosively angry is when they feel shamed and cannot bear it. In most studies comparing the shame-prone and guilt-prone, the shame-prone were far more likely to be hostile, violent, and unempathic. They feel backed into a corner where, like Macbeth, they must live with a sense of unbearable badness. With HSCs, we can be certain that most of this shame-based, frantic attacking will be directed toward the self.

So here are ways to avoid shame.

Avoiding Shame-Proneness

Because shame is more than merely the opposite of high self-esteem, avoiding shame-proneness in your child requires a few extra cautions.

1. *Do not go to the other extreme and fail to correct your HSC.* First, a research study by psychologists Tamara Gerguson and Hedy Stegge looked at exactly what creates shame-proneness in children. They found that the worst cases were not caused by harsh discipline but by a total lack of discipline. In these families, parents had given the child the sense that nothing he or she did could ever be right, so discipline was not an issue. The child felt beyond redemption. We can imagine how having an HSC could be a disappointment to some parents, and if the parents decided it was innate and undesirable, they might not try to change anything in their "hopeless" child, so of course that child would feel deep shame. We will talk more about discipline in the next section, but the message here is, *even a fumbling style of trying to change and correct an HSC communicates more caring than something that would appear like you have given up.*

2. *Again, look at yourself.* Many people were raised by parents who used shaming as the method of discipline. "You idiot, look what you did!" "Can't you do anything right?" "You always spill your milk." "You disgust me." "What will people think?" It's amazing how often we find ourselves repeating the words of our parents even when we know how hurtful they were to us. Become as conscious as you can of your own proneness to feel shame and don't shame your children as you were shamed. Habits can be changed.

3. *Do not emphasize what you expect your HSC to achieve.* A little of this type of encouragement implies that you see your child as competent. But if you have a tendency to go overboard, it's best for you not to expect anything in particular. Try to enjoy your child from day to day, without thoughts of what he can do or bring you in the future. Help your child imagine a life that will be

successful on his terms. I often see sensitive adults who went out of their way to become what their parents wanted, only to find it was not what they wanted or what was right for their temperament. So they fail, or begin to anticipate failure, or see that they have to start all over at a later age in order to find their true vocation. Not "measuring up" leaves a deep sense of shame.

When the subject turns to "what will I be when I grow up," discuss what *she* would enjoy, what *she* would like to achieve, what would be the advantages and disadvantages for *her* of the different lifestyles—that is, discuss this topic as even-handedly as you can, putting your own hopes aside.

4. *Be careful of comparisons between kids.* As I said in the last chapter, siblings are often strikingly different. Unless you can fully convey that one is as good as the other in your eyes, be cautious about speaking in generalities about these differences. Focus on each child's strengths or do not compare them.

    Comparing your child with his friends can be validating or shaming. Shaming: "Why can't you just stand up and give a little talk to your class like Sean can?" Validating: "Sean can give a speech more easily than you can right now, but you're the one getting A's on all your written work."

5. *Look at your teasing behaviors.* Some people grew up in a family of teasers and claim that it was just their way of showing love and humor. But often teasing is a way to give covert hostile messages in a seemingly lighthearted way. These are almost always shaming characterizations, like "Oh good, John's cooking—the dogs will eat well, and then we get to order take-out after he goes to bed." HSCs will not be fooled. Do not tease unless you are sure your child will take it as gentle, loving, witty fun that he is free to return.

6. *Make sure your child doesn't feel as if she's the cause of any family troubles.* Young children in particular are known to use self-centered thinking, assuming "Mom and Dad fought and now they're divorcing because I'm such a difficult child," or "My sis-

ter got so sick because I was mad at her and wanted her to die."
In a weird way, children feel better and more in control of these
events by feeling they have caused them, especially when the only
alternative they can imagine is that bad things, like serious illness, can just happen, or people who say they love you can still
do something like divorcing, which hurts you terribly. So talk actively with your child about her understandings of what caused
any troubles that are happening, and be ready with a good explanation that is age appropriate and reasonably comforting.

THE THIRD KEY—WISE DISCIPLINE

Psychologists have studied with great interest the question of how
to raise children with a strong sense of right and wrong, since the
outcome greatly affects society. Graznya Kochanska at the University
of Iowa is one of the leaders in this work, and not surprisingly, she
has discovered that different methods work differently with different
temperaments. But first, let's take a look at some of the general principles.

The goal is for morals to be inner reasons for not doing something, not merely the fear of being caught. Morals that arise from inside are said to be internalized, as when a child does not steal
because "it is wrong." If asked why, he would say, "That's how I was
raised," or "my religion says so," or "it would be terrible if everyone
constantly took each other's things." (It would require a huge police
force and a lot of security alarms to stop thefts if morals were not internalized and most people were only afraid of being apprehended.)

Kochanska and others have noted that morals seem to begin
rather naturally in a loving child-caregiver relationship. Infants enjoy sharing and are bothered by making their caregiver unhappy—
there is a natural "mutual responsiveness" in us as social animals.
But eventually caregivers also start to prohibit certain behaviors.
These moments upset the child, disturbing the harmony between

child and caregiver and creating conflict between two motivations—to please the other and to have one's own way. So the child is aroused, distressed, and the conflict plays out in one way or another. If all goes well, around three years of age, children begin to accept their parent's point of view and make it their own. They both want to maintain the loving harmony and also now remember and make as their own the reasons why they should obey—for example, it's dangerous or upsets or displeases someone else. Their reason to not have their own way is now "internalized." A child may even say to herself, "I better not touch that, Mommy said it could break."

Now, here it becomes interesting. Research has found that values are internalized best when a child is neither over- nor underaroused. You need to have your child's attention, but not have her scared stiff. If children are underaroused when corrected, they more or less say "ho hum" and go on as before. We have all seen kids do this, especially when a parent repeats an order over and over without enforcing it. At the other extreme, when children are overaroused, they start to avoid the particular situation (and the person who punished them), but they will not be able to remember why they ought to obey, what was their parent's viewpoint. (For example, I recall very well the only time I was spanked as a child, but I have no memory of the moral lesson being taught, or even what I did to deserve it. I just remember the terror and humiliation.)

If a child is in a comfortable, alert state of arousal, he hears reasons for obeying that actually provide important information about how to live with others. "Don't yell or you'll wake Daddy." "When you kick Annie, it hurts her." "Kids don't like kids who bite." And with an older child, "I know some kids cheat, but besides damaging their own character and no longer being able to see themselves as honest, they are also harming things for everybody because grades become less meaningful and there is no way to know who needs more help and who should be advanced."

HSCs as Natural "Internalizers"

Armed with this research, Graznya Kochanska became interested in how *temperament* would affect moral learning. In experiments with very young HSCs, she found they were much more likely than non-HSCs to already have internalized morals. When alone, with no risk of any external punishment, they were significantly less likely to do things their parents had told them not to do. She suspected that this was partly due to their tendency to avoid risking criticism or punishment, but also their greater ability to notice what is happening, reflect, and inhibit their behavior.

For example, Kochanska observed which two- and three-year-olds simply *noticed*, when shown a flawed object, that it was in fact flawed. These children were also more interested in and concerned about the flaw. Then, on another occasion, she brought all the children back and found that these more observant, sensitive children were also the ones most upset when the situation was contrived so that while handling an object they damaged it—broke a doll, stained a shirt.

Kochanska also set up experiments with older children—five-year-olds—in which a child could break rules, cheat, and be selfish without risk of being caught. The HSCs were much less likely to do these, but at age five this was true *only* if they had had the gentle moral teaching described above, so that they had not been over-aroused when they were corrected.

The parents I interviewed seemed to have already done Kochanska's research on their own, given that they all made her recommendation: Keep it gentle! No spanking, no shaming, no withdrawal of love or isolating. Just a change in your tone of voice is noticed and distressing to an HSC.

Parents agreed that HSCs do make mistakes; they do break the rules (at home far more than at school). But they are usually very upset later, so they almost punish themselves with their regret. A talk about it is usually enough, parents said. Some did occasionally escalate the punishment to get their child's attention—they would impose a time out or take away a privilege. But they realized that when their HSC was tearful, trembling, or raging in a way that is clearly out of control, these are all ways of saying "I can't take anymore." The research we have reviewed as well as the experience of parents is that these are not times to escalate punishments, even though some authorities might say, "Stick to your guns and administer stronger punishment." That might work with non-HSCs, and even be important in order to gain their attention. But with HSCs, parents find that they win the battle but lose the war. The child finally stops due to being so frightened. You did get through. But he has now been truly distressed and is certainly not internalizing a lesson. Better to first calm an HSC and then decide on the right discipline. (We will talk about dealing with rages in Chapter 7.)

Parents also had other ideas for keeping overarousal around discipline to a minimum. Prevention was a large part of this: making your standards age-appropriate and clear, meeting needs before they are expressed inappropriately, and otherwise planning a bit. Let's consider each of these.

Preventing Discipline "Events"

Consider Your Standards

As a parent, you need to have a clear standard of behavior in your family for a given age in a given situation—standards for four-year-olds in restaurants, acceptable manners when ten-year-olds meet strangers, when an apology is required, and so forth. If standards have not been made clear, especially with older children, you might want to decide on them together, as a family—whether it is okay to yell in the house, swear, call each other bad names, hit, throw things, damage each other's property, throw food, be more than a half hour late without calling, slide down the banister, put feet on the furniture, or put the house keys anywhere but on the hook by the door! Standards arrived at together are often easier to enforce, because the child has already internalized them. But if your child is young, so that you need to be the one who sets the standards, or if that is simply your style, do be sure your standards are clear ahead of time.

It saves a lot of arguing when standards are clear in advance. You have already discussed your reasons (so the rules could be internalized while your child was calm). Hopefully you listened to whether your child found them reasonable and possible. If your child said she could wait politely for dinner if she had a snack and something to play with, you have a deal.

Do not, however, overestimate your child's ability to keep your standards, even if they were agreed upon. Especially with precocious little HSCs and first-time parents, the HSCs may be such angels in restaurants and so adult in their thoughtfulness and good intentions, even at three, that it comes as a complete surprise when they throw a tantrum and perhaps throw something that hits mother. Because it comes as such a surprise, everyone overreacts. Mother wonders if she has been too lax and becomes a powerful, morally correct adult who must discipline a little child who somehow "didn't know better" or "could not control herself." The little HSC feels ashamed and angry about falling from the proud place of a miniature adult into the depths of humiliation, the role of a powerless, stupid child.

If your child begins having frequent bouts of not obeying or of emotional outbreaks such as tantrums, you may just be asking too much of him, given his age and temperament. Lower your expectations, but in a consistent way—for example, if you no longer expect your child to sit still in the waiting room without a toy to play with, do not expect it when visiting in another home either.

Remember, standards save your child trouble as well as you. For example, Chuck's mistakes are usually things he says, especially his strong opinions. He is often right, but he has not been polite. His parents do not entirely squelch the expression of these insights, but their standards are such that they do require him to consider who is within earshot. This standard involves an important lesson for HSCs—that they cannot express everything they think and observe, but need to think whether it will be useful at that time, to that person. Otherwise, their comments will gain them enemies and little else.

Adjust the Expectations of Others, Too

If you leave your child with an adult caregiver, be certain that your standards and methods of discipline are similar. I learned the hard way to be very careful about leaving my HSC with any adult who lacked experience with children, might have forgotten what children are like, or was raised very strictly.

While I was teaching at a university, my sensitive and congenial son, then six, made a very positive impression on a reliable, pleasant college student I had had to the house several times. Since the feelings were mutual all around, I eventually asked the young man to baby-sit.

I came home to an uproar. The student declared my son was an incorrigible liar and would grow up to be a delinquent. Why? My son had not wanted to take a bath, but the student had insisted. So my son went into the bathroom, locked the door, ran the water, took off his clothes, put on his pajamas, drained the water, and came out. Not being very good at subterfuge, he did not leave a wet towel, so he was caught.

When I arrived, he was in misery, having been lectured relentlessly by the student, who had no idea about the moral loopholes that could be found by even the nicest six-year-old. From then on I made it a policy never to leave him with anyone who might expect adultlike behavior from him. I also never left him without all parties having agreed on all the details of what should happen while I was out.

Prevention Through Understanding and Good Planning

Some parents also pointed out that considering what caused your HSC to break a rule can be valuable, even if you have to be consistent and have some consequence for that particular episode. For example, Randall's mother noticed that most of his misbehaving was due to inequities he perceived between how he and his sister were treated. This drew his mother's attention to the fact that she sometimes understands and sympathizes more with her daughter, who has a temperament more like her own. As she worked on her role in the root cause of Randall's misbehaving, it decreased.

Melissa usually gets in trouble by being stubborn about what she needs. Her parents can often avoid these scenes by simply supplying a coat, a snack, or a break. Given what you know about your child, anticipating her needs is simply being polite—meeting one of your own standards. You know now that HSCs are troubled by discomforts sooner, "lose it" sooner, and cannot obey at such times because they are so uncomfortable or overwhelmed, hungry or tired, ashamed or frustrated. Preventing these states is not "caving in" but simply meeting needs that are reasonable for this child.

I also think it is fine to use humor and distractions to see that your standards are maintained. Put away the favorite toys before other children arrive. Sing a silly song when the walk back to the car is creating some whining. None of this diminishes the fact that your child can share with other children or walk quietly when that is required.

Finally, warnings help HSCs with transitions, the point where they are most likely to be difficult. Just see that your limit is maintained. "In five minutes it will be time to jump into bed!" (Do *not* add five more minutes after that.)

Transitions are also easier if they are steps in a routine, not sudden orders that are likely to be frustrating and disobeyed or countered with an argument. It is so easy and unhelpful to say, "So that's the end of the story—get into bed and put out the light." When you meet resistance, it is easy to say, "No arguments. You always try that and it isn't going to work"—all of which creates more bad feelings and soon escalates to the need for a punishment. Instead, try, "So let's see, you have put on your pajamas, brushed your teeth, I read a story, and now what do we do? I believe you get into bed and put out the light. That's our routine, isn't it?" If your child wants more reading, instead of giving an order, try saying, "Tomorrow afternoon we can read more stories, but it's only one story at bedtime."

The Basic Steps of Correcting an HSC

I make a distinction between correction and discipline. If a behavior changes when you correct it or your child seems to intend not to do the behavior again, perhaps there is no need for discipline or punishment. The following steps usually suffice when an HSC has broken a rule or failed to meet your standards of behavior.

1. *Consider the state of arousal of your child and yourself.* If one or both of you are overaroused, calm yourself, then calm the child. If you do not regain control of yourself first, you cannot help your child regain control. If your HSC is frightened of what you may do as punishment, be reassuring. "We'll work this out, don't worry." With an overaroused HSC, *do not* up the arousal with statements like "Wait until I get you home!"

   When children are quite overaroused, it may require twenty minutes or more for them to return to normal. To switch off your child's state of threat, go to another room together. Sit if you were standing, or lie down together on the bed. Or go outside and sit on the porch together. Take a walk together. You can even make going to this locale a ritual, as long as nothing too upsetting happens in your "talking place."

   In the example of my son's fake bath, he was so obviously upset by the baby-sitter's lectures that I first calmed him down, assuring him that I was interested in hearing what happened, not just punishing him. I did a few other chores first, watching to see if he was becoming more or less anxious because of this waiting. He did calm down.

2. *Listen and empathize.* HSCs need to feel heard, as they often have deep feelings or good reasons for what they were doing and they are unusually disillusioned by injustice. Getting an accurate

statement of your child's feelings and viewpoint will help both of you decide what to do at step four.

Returning to the fake-bath example, when my son had given me his version of the story, I let him know I had heard it. "I understand how unreasonable it seemed to you to be told to take a bath when you didn't think you needed one because you took one this morning. You and I should have decided on this before I left. I apologize for not doing that."

Remember, listening means refraining from oversimplifications such as "You just didn't want to take a bath, did you?"; simple, obvious conclusions such as "So you lied to the baby-sitter"; and global labels such as "Why are you always such a trouble-maker?"

What if I had heard a lame defense, such as "I was just having fun with him"? In such cases, you can probe further, or you can take that at face value and go on with setting your standards. But when a child is making excuses, it is being done to avoid being shamed and punished, so do not corner your child into any more lies.

If a child begins with what you think is a lie—"I didn't do it, I took the bath, he's the one who lied"—I would avoid trying to find out the "truth" and making him wrong. Perhaps say, "I guess I don't know whether to believe you or the baby-sitter. For us to trust each other, we need to tell each other the truth, and I know you do that as much as you can. When you can't, I hope you can tell me, at the time or later, what made it so difficult."

3. ***Restate your standards and, if your child is old enough, your reason for them.*** "When we are mad, we often feel like hitting. But we don't do it because we don't want to be afraid of each other or to give each other the idea that we really, really want to hurt anyone."

Returning to the bath example, I would say, "Whatever happened tonight, I do expect you to obey a baby-sitter and to be truthful. Even though I pay the person, the sitter is a guest in our house and should not have to deal with dishonesty or hassles. And I would worry if I thought you wouldn't follow this person's orders, because in an emergency a grown-up would usually know what to do better than you would."

4. *Decide whether there should be further consequences.* Is some reparation required, such as an apology? Is this a repeating problem with no good reason behind it, suggesting that your child has not been sufficiently aroused to internalize this behavior? Then you can decide together on a consequence for next time (and you must apply it consistently). Next time you can remind your child of this consequence and the thought of it should raise her arousal and remind her of your discussion.

In the case of the fake bath, I did not ask for an apology to the baby-sitter. I was too angry with him myself!

5. *State what your child can do in the future.* This leaves him with a sense of hope and a healthy alternative for the impulse. "When you're angry with me, you can tell me you want to hit me. Or you can hit something like this pillow and tell me it is supposed to be me."

In the bath example, these days I would probably suggest calling me on my cell phone if he and a sitter had a serious conflict. In those days I would have said, "We need to do it differently next time, don't we?" I would suggest that my son, myself, and the evening's baby-sitter all talk together about how the two should spend the evening and what is the bedtime routine for that night. Then I would listen to his ideas. I would also say, "If you really don't like what a baby-sitter has done, we'll discuss it when I come home and perhaps not invite that person again." If anything like this happens again, I can remind him of this agreement, and he can tell me why he did not stick to our plan.

I would end with a strong request that he let me know if a sitter upset him in any way. Obviously you don't want to encourage "telling tales," but one parent told me that her HSC had been hit by a baby-sitter and the little girl had not said anything because she wanted to be good.

Some Additional Points

Two other points to keep in mind when correcting your HSC. First, of course, you must adjust for the age of the child and situation. With younger children or when you must act quickly, you keep it simpler. *After* you have grabbed your child from the street, you say, "I know you like to run ahead, but you must stop when I shout 'stop' because I know when it is safe to cross. Now you can run." (Notice how even this includes most of the steps I described.)

To a young child you keep it very simple: "I know you would like to have all the toys, but you must let Jim have one toy because people share with their guests and friends." And to a ten-year-old in a tight spot you might whisper, "I know you're upset and don't want to, but you will now thank grandmother for the nice dinner. Then you can go to the car and we can discuss this on the way home if you want."

Second, do not forget our discussion of shame and that in even a very young HSC the idea of having to be corrected at all can bring shame. To ease the sense of being basically terrible, you can say something like, "Don't worry, Cindy, we all make mistakes." Or "I know you were tired and didn't like those kids much. I've often seen you share your toys, so this was just one of those days."

When You Finally Have to Use Real Discipline

1. *Keep "consequences" short, mild, and related to the behavior.* "If you kick again, you will have to sit over there in a chair farther from the rest of us." But watch for a shame or terror reaction and adjust the punishment accordingly. "All right, let's bring that chair closer—just a kick-length away. Okay?"

   One mother of an HSC sent her three-year-old to her room only once—"Never again, she was so hysterical." And in the year since then this little girl has never disobeyed enough to require any punishment at all. So remember, use discipline (punishment) sparingly. The aforementioned methods of correction—reminders and renegotiations of standards—is often enough.

2. *Be consistent—unpredictable punishment creates additional anxiety in HSCs.* If you have said no kicking and your child kicks again, you must remove him to the chair you have indicated. Do not keep repeating the warning. If he will not move, state a new consequence. "If you do not do what I ask, I will have to take you out of here." You go outside and do the steps above: listen and empathize, restate your standards (now it's obeying you) and reasons, decide on the consequences, and remind your child of what he can do instead.

If your child is still throwing a fit, it may be that she cannot help it—she's too overwhelmed by fatigue or some emotion. We will discuss this more in Chapter 7, but the basic idea is to connect with your child: hold her, calm her, try to put into words what's going on. Then try to reach a neutral solution, one in which neither you nor she wins, but your standards are restated and the resolution is delayed until later. And do discuss later what happened and what the two of you will do if it happens again. Do not let it go.

If you find yourself in "power plays" with your HSC, figure out why. HSCs can be clever, subtle adversaries. That does not mean they are "sly" or "evil." (It does mean that they can be good at chess.) You just have to find out what is really going on. For example, we found that our son would develop a real or feigned liking for any punishment we could devise. "Good, I want to go to my room." Or "Fine, I didn't want to see that movie anyway." We figured out that he was trying to regain some power and pride, since our punishment put us in the position of seeming to have all the power, all the mature authority. So we were consistent and carried out the "ineffective" punishment, then later on spent time with him in an intellectual discussion or board game in which he felt like an equal again—or even better than us. (This time we spent with him was the equivalent of Stanley Greenspan's "floor time." Greenspan recommends a half hour a day with a child doing whatever she wants. With a younger child especially, this should be down on the floor at her level, with her toys. Besides giving children the attention they need, it is an excellent way to restore security and self-esteem after a punishment.)

3. *With an older child, if the behavior is not going away, try to explore why with your child.* Do this at a time when it has not recently happened. Begin very gently. "You often have such interesting things to say, so I do understand somewhat, but why do you suppose you sometimes interrupt me when you want to speak?" In this case, you may hear that you never stop talking and decide to change your ways, not your child's. Or you may discuss the role of fatigue or overarousal in creating this behavior. After that, the two of you can decide together on the best way to change the behavior. Would it help to be reminded? What phrase would be best? Would it help to have consequences for forgetting?

When Your HSC Lies or Steals (It Will Happen)

Do not automatically use a major punishment. You want the lesson remembered, not the punishment. If your child is already overaroused and ashamed, take it easy. Thank him for telling the truth, whenever this finally happens, even after you caught him in the lie. Talk about how we all make mistakes, and a time you lied or stole as a child. When your child is feeling calmer, you can talk about how a family or society is deeply damaged when no one can trust each other. Tell about the temptations adults have, like hitting a parked car and not leaving a note or cheating on taxes, but that the money saved is nothing compared to the damage to your character and being able to think about yourself as a person with integrity.

Do not set up a situation where your child is forced to lie to avoid being punished or shamed. Do not ask, "Did you take the cookies?" Instead say, "Some cookies are missing since an hour ago and I think you're the only one who was in the kitchen. You know I didn't want you to have them, so what shall we do so that you are not tempted to take things I have asked you not to take?" With HSCs, it may be better not even to use the words *lie* or *steal*.

4. *And of course, none of this helps if you do not model truthfulness*

yourself. For example, do not encourage a child to lie about his or her age in order to receive a lower price or have your child lie when answering the phone, saying you're not there.

When Conflicts Escalate

Let's face it. Sometimes things get out of hand. We call it a tantrum at two (discussed in Chapter 7), but rages can happen at any age. Many HSCs are "explosive" in that they are easily overwhelmed, shamed, or outraged by the overarousal involved in being corrected or by what they see as unfairness. Even if they do not rage, they may defend themselves with a stream of subtle, good, and not-so-good reasons why you are wrong and they are right. What do you do?

First, read "Dealing with Intense Emotions" in Chapter 7—much of it applies to any age child. There I emphasize staying calm, empathizing, but sticking to your standards. To stay calm, you may need a time out as much as your HSC. Silence in the same room may be better than isolation, especially for a small child. Agree to speak or come back together in a certain amount of minutes—twenty is optimal. Emphasize that this is not a punishment; you can even put on the TV or radio to distract your child while one or both of you settle down. Just say you know things will go better when the two of you are calmer.

When things are less tense try to return to a respectful, rational discussion. Remember, feelings and preferences are never wrong—it is how we behave, express them, or always insist on our own way that can be wrong. Say, "I see that you don't like it. Can you tell me why?" "If you don't like going to guitar lessons, are there any lessons you would rather be taking?" Or "You used to like the lessons. Can you tell me what you don't like about them now? Has something changed? Maybe we can speak to the teacher or find another one."

And give options that signal equality. "I did not mean to offend you, so I would like you to tell me your likes and dislikes in a calm, grown-up way. I promise to listen and we'll find a solution."

Try to negotiate reasonable limits and duties that your child agrees upon and what the consequences will be when he crosses the line or fails to keep an agreement. Do *not* decide on a consequence on your own during a heated fight. Discuss it later, in the context of making a happier family, developing good character, and building a trust that each of you will keep agreements and not cross important boundaries. It is often an excellent strategy to bring up a behavior you want to change in yourself, or that your child would like you to change, such as no longer shouting when you are angry. Then ask your child to help you set limits on that and what consequences you will accept if you fail. Then it is not so much a child being punished by an adult as it is a method of behavior change any two people can employ.

Preventing the Reasons for Rage

The first rule is to respect your child's wishes when you can, so she will respect yours when you must insist. Deliberate the pros and cons from both of your perspectives, and do it out loud so she can hear how such conflicts ought to be resolved. For example, "I can see you don't want to play the piano for our company, and although I would like it, since you would not, I think that's all right with me."

Give your HSC responsibility for finding what works, since sometimes nothing will ever feel right. "I know you hate to shop, but I think you will probably agree that you need to come along so that when I exchange this shirt you can pick out one you like better. Would you get back to me soon about when we can have a shopping date?"

Finally, hand over responsibility at as early an age as possible, especially when real life will deliver the consequences anyway—for example, the consequences of not getting enough sleep, forgetting to hand in assignments, or not having lunch money or clean clothes ready for school.

Things to Avoid

As a reminder, here are a few mistakes to avoid when disciplining, dealing with lying or stealing, or involved in a heated conflict:

1. *Stay out of the heat of the fight.* You have to be gentle, strong, and firm. If you are in a public place or someone's home, remove yourselves to a quiet, private space. Again (I can't say it too often), calm yourself and then your child. Do *not* try to discuss the issue until the storm has passed.

2. *Do not threaten to withdraw love* ("Mommy and Daddy won't love you anymore if you do that").

3. *Do not make global, irreversible threats.* ("No one will like you if you do that"; "God will punish you by sending you to hell if you do that.") Such threats have ruined HSCs for life.

4. *Do not make threats of, or actually use, emotional or physical violence.* By violence I mean anything intended to hurt the child, such as "You stupid idiot" or a blow to the body.

5. *Do not give HSCs global instructions* like "be good when you visit their house" or "watch where you're going." They may take you literally and try to do these things *all* the time, or feel anxious because they cannot.

6. *Do not bring up temperament during conflicts.* Focus on the issue and the behavior. Do not say, "There you go being highly sensitive again," but rather "You really don't like that taste, do you? But I need you to take the medicine. Do you think it would help if we mixed it with something you like?"

7. *Do not let your HSC use his sensitivity as a way to manipulate others.* This is tricky. No one manipulates without a reason. And it's usually an attempt to avoid effort, punishment, guilt, powerlessness, or shame. But a feeling that is being feigned or exaggerated is different from a "real one," and you can usually sense it. What you want to uncover if you can is the feeling behind it. "All this nausea and disgust about your dinner when I'm leaving . . . are you afraid of something?"

If you can't find the underlying reason for the exaggeration or manipulation, stay focused on the behavior you want and the standards that have to be followed right now—standards that should already be familiar to your child. "I know you want that toy so badly that you think you're going to die, but we agreed we were only going to buy a gift for the birthday party. So right now we have to do that. You can be quiet and stay with me or return to the car and when I get there we can discuss how bad you are feeling."

If you are sympathetic and take your child's statement seriously, chances are he will admit later that the "disgusting" dinner or the "death threats" were only a way to express how bad he felt. Explain that there are other ways, and that it is your experience that these tactics (which you have used yourself at times) lead others to mistrust your words or to feel their sympathies preyed upon.

THE FOURTH KEY—KNOWING HOW TO DISCUSS SENSITIVITY

Many parents wonder whether to discuss with their HSC this trait of sensitivity with which their child was born. They often worry that a child will feel different or even flawed. My answer is that I believe all HSCs notice sooner or later that they are different. What you supply is a positive view of it and only the details that your child needs at the time. For example, you do not have to say it is innate unless your child is curious about that or it would help in explaining the trait to refer to sensitive relatives whom your child admires. You can minimize the importance of the trait in your child's life if she seems to see it as a huge problem, and expand on it if, for example, she is wrongly attributing her difficulties in certain situations to not being good enough or not trying hard enough when it is really a problem of being overaroused.

If you want, you can wait until the whole subject comes up naturally. The only problem with that approach is that you may want to discuss your child's trait with teachers or other caregivers. If you do this without talking it over first with your child, he will usually sense that you are having special discussions about him, even if these happen out of earshot. Those you have spoken to may mention it or simply change their behavior toward the child. Then he may imagine the worst—that you are trying to get him help because something is wrong with him. Or he may simply experience you as not trustworthy because you have discussed his private life behind his back.

How to Discuss Sensitivity with Your Child

Assuming you are going to discuss the trait someday, here are my suggestions.

1. *Any discussion of temperament has to be adjusted to a child's age.* Do not try to explain temperament in ways that might confuse or upset a young child, such as "You were born with a personality like Aunt Marilyn's." He may not like Aunt Marilyn, or even if he does, "personality" is not a word young children understand as you do—for example, that you mean some qualities are shared with her, some are not.

2. *Be clear that your child is not alone in being highly sensitive, that many others are, too.* "You like it quiet. You always did. You were just born that way. My brother, your uncle Joe, is the same way. Lot's of people are."

3. *Explain that everyone has a few temperament traits that stand out,* although it may be better to speak of people in general than to start labeling people you know. "Have you ever noticed how some people seem to have just been born with a hot temper? Others are always good-natured. You were born sensitive to things. Others just weren't."

4. *When a difficulty arises due to the trait, focus at the time on the solution, not the trait itself.* For example, you might say, "We should have brought along an extra sweater." But do not say at

this time "since the cold bothers you so much because you are highly sensitive." You do not want the trait associated with every problem or discomfort that comes up.

5. *When a crisis demands your child's best effort, do not bring up the trait as a reason for not succeeding.* Do not say, "Of course you're upset about this rejection—you're very sensitive." When in the thick of it, it is usually better to stick to relevant specifics so your child can learn to focus on the situation and self-regulate rather than having a global expectation that she cannot cope. Say, "I see you're angry about how they have treated you. What happened? What do you think you should do? What can you do next time to make things different?"

6. *Do not use the trait as a weapon during conflicts with your child.* "You can't go—you know you'll get too excited." Or worse, "There you go again, being overly sensitive."

7. *If your child complains about being too sensitive, bring up an example of a time it was an advantage.* "I know it annoys you that you can't yet play your violin in front of an audience as easily as Paul does, but remember how your teacher praises you for playing 'so sensitively.' It's that same sensitivity that makes you so aware of the audience."

8. *Be clear about the ways in which you think your child can change, the ways he probably cannot.* "I am sure that if you play in front of audiences more, you will relax more. You may never be as relaxed as Paul, but you may find you enjoy it sometimes, or even quite a bit, once the audience seems more like a group of friends you want to give your playing to."

9. *Identify people your child knows and admires who are or probably are highly sensitive.* It's always difficult to know for certain about famous people (but for starters, I suspect Tchaikovsky and Abraham Lincoln were highly sensitive). Look for cues in things you read—that someone was "thoughtful," "shy," or "sensitive" as a child. Collect these examples, especially those in fields your child likes, whether tennis, music, or horsemanship. Get to know who

is highly sensitive among your family's friends and relatives and point these out to your HSC, perhaps arranging conversations. An older child can benefit from a highly sensitive mentor.

Talking About Your Child's Sensitivity with Others

When you discuss your child's temperament with others—teachers, coaches, relatives, other parents—always think about the person you are addressing and the context in which you are speaking. Consider these questions:

- *How much time do you have to state your case?*
- *How open is the person to new information?* Are you dealing with someone who is rigid and already has "an ax to grind"?
- *Do you have a right to expect a good hearing?* For example, are you paying the person a fee for professional services?
- *Will you have to get along with this person in the future?* Are you dealing with a passing comment from a stranger? Are you in the process of deciding whether to develop the relationship?
- *Does this person have any power over you or your child?*
- *To whom might this person repeat what you say and would it be distorted?* Do you want to ask the person to keep what you say confidential, and could this person do that, given his or her own nature and professional responsibilities? (Is a school counselor obliged to tell a teacher what you say about your child?)
- *Who else is present?* Is there anyone there your child knows? Anyone who might misunderstand what you say or repeat it in a distorted way?

Of course, most people will be on your side and want to help. So usually your task is to tell them enough about your child, especially what works with your HSC in the situations they may encounter if they are, for example, baby-sitters, parents of your child's friends, or relatives wanting to get to know your child better. With an older child, discuss together what information you would both like conveyed—food preferences or allergies, bedtime, quiet times, and so forth, as well as what to say, if anything, about the trait itself.

Besides telling, listen—that is, ask those who teach or care for your child how he or she solves problems that come up. People experienced with children and also experienced with your child can give you fresh ideas, as well as give you a glimpse of how your child behaves when away from you.

Your Sound Bite

When you do not know what reception you may get, but you know you have to say something about your child's sensitivity, you need a brief statement, a "sound bite," containing all the vital information in one sentence. You can create your own, but have it thought out in advance. Or you can use this one: "It may help you to know that my child is one of those 15 to 20 percent born with a very sensitive nervous system. He notices every subtlety, but is also easily overwhelmed when a lot is going on." (Or "by change," or "by pain," or whatever might be most relevant. For even more brevity, you can leave out the percentages, but they do establish that this is relatively common and normal.)

If the person shows interest, give more details.

Your Quick Responses

You also need to think out your preferred responses to specific comments. Here are a few of the most common, along with examples of how you might handle them.

1. "Your child is so shy." "That's interesting. I don't think of her as shy at all. I guess if by shy you mean afraid of what others may think, she may seem that way, but often she's just watching, or she's getting used to things. When she's ready, she warms up quite nicely. I think of her as being highly sensitive, attuned to everything, not shy."

If your child truly is shy, but also sensitive, you can say, "Yes, he's very aware of what others may be thinking about him, but once he feels at home with you (or here) and knows you (others) like him, he will be fine." (In other words, "your judgment will not help the situation.")

2. "Your child is so sensitive" or "overly sensitive." "I rather like her sensitivity. Is there a specific thing she's doing that is a problem for you?"

3. "What's the matter with him? All children (ought to) like . . . " "Actually, research finds" (use that phrase only if it seems helpful) "that children vary considerably in what they like to eat" (or "wear," "do for fun," "do during the summer," "in how stimulating and busy they like things to be," or whatever applies). "It all depends on their innate personalities."

4. General rude pushiness. Keep the following phrases handy: "No, my child does not wish to do that." "This is not helping her/us." "That does not work for him/us." Do not offer any further explanation. Nothing more is required. You have set your boundary. Stick to it.

Handling Bigger Conflicts Around Sensitivity

If someone insists that your child is behaving "abnormally," speak of the assessments you have done or professional opinions you have received. For example, "Her pediatrician says her personality is quite within the normal range. She's simply highly sensitive." Mention the knowledge you have gained. "I have read quite a bit about the research on this and he is perfectly normal for his temperament type." If the person pursues it, state that you're sure he or she means well, but in fact this discussion is not helpful. Then change the subject.

If someone says one child cannot receive special treatment, ask if that is really true. Often there is special treatment, and even laws demanding it, if a child has, for example, Attention Deficit Disorder, dyslexia, disabilities such as blindness or deafness, and so forth. Using these examples may help the person see the situation in a familiar way. Be sure to point out that your child has no disorder, but does have an innate normal variation in temperament, which means that things go smoother for everyone if your child receives just a little special treatment at first. A pediatrician or temperament counselor might even supply you with a letter or a phone call to verify your child's trait. Also, make it clear that you are only trying to be helpful, so that the person or institution and your child will have a good experience in the long run. Mention the person or institution's goals very specifically, not just your goal that your child not be uncomfortable. But again, make it clear that your child does not suffer from any kind of disorder or syndrome. If that assumption is likely to be made, I would avoid asking for special treatment for your HSC; it's not worth it.

If You Don't Speak Up

If you choose to stay quiet when someone makes an inaccurate or disparaging comment about sensitivity, be sure to explain to your child why you took that approach. For example, you might point out that some people are so opinionated on a subject they will not listen or you have another plan for handling this situation.

HEALTHY BOUNDARIES: ANOTHER WAY TO THINK ABOUT THESE FOUR KEYS TO RAISING A JOYOUS HSC

So now you have the four essentials: ways to build self-esteem, reduce shame, correct appropriately, and discuss sensitivity anywhere. Another perspective on these is to think of them as helping your child develop healthy boundaries. All HSCs need more help with boundaries than other children because they take in so much and are so sensitive to what others think, feel, and say that their own self can be overwhelmed and overlooked. Thus the idea of personal boundaries is a good metaphor to have at hand.

This metaphor comes from systems theory, which is an attempt to create ways to talk about and compare the workings of almost anything—things as different as one-celled animals, cities, computers, plants, organizations, bodies, or selves. Systems theory points out that basic to all of these is an outer boundary, marking the one system off from others like it. That boundary must let in what the system needs but keep out what would harm it.

A child needs to do the same—to feel her boundaries, to take in what is good for her and keep out what is bad for her. What is good for her is love and useful feedback, which you now know how to be certain she receives. These build self-esteem. Things bad for her are messages that something is terribly wrong with her—you now know quite a bit about avoiding chronic shame and speaking positively about sensitivity. Also bad for her are experiences that are too overwhelming for her to learn from—the kind of discipline you now know how to avoid.

All of this self-esteem, low shame-proneness, appropriate discipline, and positive understanding of sensitivity will facilitate healthy boundaries in your HSC. Your child will be comfortable being who he is, and he will be able to let in people and messages that are good for him without undo fear of being hurt, rejected, or shamed. He can keep out the bad because he will not be easily persuaded that he is wrong or does not deserve to have his own boundaries, his own opinions and needs. He will be confident in his judgment. He will feel he has the right, even the duty, to keep out the bad.

We all know children with poor boundaries, even if we have not thought of them in these terms. We can sense their poor self-esteem, because they act as if they have decided that "if no one likes me, I will have to do whatever others want to try to please them." They will let in or do anything no matter how bad it is for them. We see children who feel so much shame that they seem to have decided "I'll do *anything* to stop this pain," even if it means letting in something bad like drugs or keeping out help because it would seem to validate their shame. Or "I would just as soon disappear, die, or become one with this other person I admire." They would prefer to blur or obliterate entirely the boundary making them distinct from others. In all these ways, they tend to take in what is bad and keep out what is good.

But your HSC will be different. Beginning with this chapter, you are learning to help her identify what to keep in, what to keep out, guided by her pride in her unique preferences, needs, and abilities rather than shame about them. You will listen to your child's side of the story before disciplining. You will help her say what *she* thinks about being highly sensitive. In all of this she will be learning how to stand up to others, even those who seem bigger and stronger. This is the kind of HSC the world needs and who can enjoy being in that world.

APPLYING WHAT YOU HAVE LEARNED

1. Discuss your child's trait with your child and your partner. Decide together with whom you would like to share this information and how. Ideally, it would only be with your child present. Respect her wishes but explore the reasons if she wants her sensitivity cloaked in silence. This could be an opportunity to note and remove any shame surrounding the trait. (Remember, it is neutral, with advantages and disadvantages.) Thus, in time, your child should not mind *trusted* others knowing about it.
2. With your child's permission, prepare your "sound bite," the brief statement about sensitivity, and run it by your child.
3. Think about three situations you have been in when your child's trait came up and you wished you had had a better response; think through that response now.

PART II

FROM INFANCY TO YOUNG ADULTHOOD

Chapter Six

Off to the Right Start

Soothing and Attuning to Highly Sensitive Infants

This chapter begins with how to recognize and care for a sensitive infant, including what to do if your baby seems to cry a great deal. You will also understand your newborn's instinctive awareness and memory of you, especially acute because of his sensitivity. Then we turn to issues that arise with the two- to six-month-old, discussing overstimulation and sleep problems. With the six-month- to one-year-old sensitive infant, we discuss three processes that are especially important for them: attachment, attunement, and self-regulation.

NEWBORNS—HOW TO RECOGNIZE THE SENSITIVE ONES

There is not as yet an infallible way to know whether a newborn is going to grow up to be highly sensitive. Some, but not all, start out "reactive" and stay that way. Reactive infants are those who cry easily if they experience strong stimulation, presumably because they are startled or overstimulated. Then there are "colicky" babies—those who are eating all right, gaining weight, not sick, yet during the first four months are crying more than three hours a day at least four days a week. Pediatricians have long known that this type of crying has nothing to do with chronic indigestion or colic. It is often the result of a reactive infant who is getting no relief from overstimulation, which we will discuss in greater detail later on.

A newborn's tendency to cry easily (that is, be "reactive") or for long periods (that is, be "colicky") can be due to many things besides innate temperament. Sometimes it seems that a newborn's body is simply not working quite right yet, or the baby is reacting to a parent's anxiety or a family's general high level of stress. (At this age, anger and fear are not differentiated; the cries are simply a distress reaction, a signal to the caregiver.) Even if a baby's crying reaction is due to temperament, it can be due to other traits besides sensitivity—for example, of those traits described in Chapter 1, crying may result from high intensity, high activity, or low adaptability.

One particular reason not to assume a frequently distressed baby is sensitive is that many parents I talked to said that their HSC cried very little the first year. Often it was clear that these parents kept everything just right for their baby, so there was rarely a reason for their sensitive child to cry. For example, Alice was the perfect infant—until the electricity went out one night, which eliminated the night-light and soft music she was used to while she slept. Then she let her parents know just how sensitive she was. And you remember Randall, who had the wonderful nanny and only showed his sensitivity at two years, when his mother tried to take him to play groups.

Even though some sensitive newborns do not cry, thanks to attentive parents, do not assume that parents with sensitive babies who do cry more are necessarily mishandling them. Some babies simply cry more, no matter what parents do for them.

So, if we cannot recognize a sensitive child from the amount of crying alone, what else can we look for? Maria's mother knew her daughter was sensitive because of the subtleties she noticed and the way she maintained eye contact at two weeks of age, following her mother's movements around a room. Several other parents mentioned similar attentiveness in their newborns. I suspect this is a better indicator of sensitivity, although if you have not been around other infants, you would not necessarily know that your child was unusual. I feel confident, however, that most parents will be able to tell if their baby is highly sensitive, especially once they understand the trait and especially if one or both are highly sensitive themselves, which, of course, greatly increases the odds of their child having the trait.

Having established that your newborn may be highly sensitive, what especially do you need to know? The fact is, there are not many special instructions for the care of very young sensitive infants—unless your child is crying a great deal. If that is the case, this chapter may help considerably. Otherwise, my goal is to help you appreciate how much is happening in this new, particularly sensitive human being.

Responsiveness—The Solution to Everything at This Age

All newborns need one quality in a parent: responsiveness. Those who study infants agree that it is the most important factor at this age in developing later mental health. A responsive parent of a new baby means one who tries to take care of the baby's needs and to respond to the baby's cues and emotions—her desire for contact and for more stimulation, and also for protection and for less stimulation.

Being right about what an infant needs and wants can be difficult with newborns, especially when the parents are new, too. Newborns cannot talk or even signal much except general distress. Parents at first have to intuit what the problem is, and sometimes that seems impossible, even for the most highly sensitive parent. But with experience, parents do usually learn to be responsive, out of pure self-defense—a crying baby riles up everyone in the vicinity. Guessing the reason for an HSC's crying, however, requires learning some of the finer points about the causes of infant tears.

All babies cry when they are over- or understimulated, over- or underaroused. Indeed, you could say that is all they cry about in the first weeks. They cry to generate some activity and attention because they are underaroused. Or they cry because of the stimulation created by some pain or discomfort. The feelings created by, for example, too much heat, cold, hunger, noise, or a wet diaper—at this age it is all merely undifferentiated high stimulation. Later, there are specific reactions to specific stimuli, but there remains also a general reaction to the level of arousal.

As you have already learned, sensitive people of any age reach a state of overarousal much sooner than others. And before that, they usually show signs of trying to regulate their own arousal. In infancy, they try to turn their face away or they fuss and cry in order to try to end their overarousal. But if you are used to babies who can "take more," you might not notice these signs or guess their cause. You might even think your baby needs to be picked up, fed, played with, or rocked—adding to his overstimulation. You would be trying to be responsive yet have no idea that the real message being sent is "no more—I'm overstimulated!"

How to Reduce an Infant's General Stimulation

If your baby seems otherwise healthy but is crying too much, you can find out if the problem is overstimulation by making some of the following changes and seeing if the crying decreases (if it doesn't, or you make too many of these changes, your baby may be understimulated, or perhaps something else is needed—more on that in the next section).

1. *Be careful not to "jazz up" your child* with rough games and an excited voice.
2. *Eliminate most of the toys,* mobiles, pictures, and other cute baby paraphernalia from her crib and other areas.
3. *Reduce the sounds your infant hears,* all day as well as during sleep times. Install rugs and drapes, keep music soft or off, keep voices calm and quiet. Remember, the best stimulation for newborns is whatever resembles life in the womb—rocking, being held snugly, hearing mother's voice.
4. *Establish routines your baby seems to like.* Do regular activities like bathing and feeding in the same way each time and at the

same time of day if possible, so there are fewer surprises. Some newborns establish their own routines, while others seem rather disorganized in their first weeks and need help with this.

5. *Cut down or eliminate excursions* and visitors for a while.
6. *Use only the softest all-cotton clothing,* outfits that are simple and identical every day.
7. *Attend more to adjusting the temperature* of the room and of food and bathwater so that it's just right for your child.
8. *Make bedtime particularly soothing* by having a bedtime routine and being sure your baby sleeps enough by keeping the house quiet, the room darkened, and whatever else it requires (more about sleep in a moment).
9. *Carry your baby on your body.* If your back can handle it, I highly recommend using one of the many styles of baby carriers. A study assigned new mothers to either carry their infants an extra two hours a day or to increase visual stimulation every day (a control group). At six weeks of age, the carried babies cried an hour less a day than the stimulated babies. Being near you certainly reassures your HSC, reducing overstimulation due to fear. Above all, if you must take your baby into a highly stimulating situation, hold her against your body.
10. *Get your baby outdoors* for part of each day, preferably just to sleep. Frankly, this is merely a hunch of mine, because the outdoors always helps me to calm down. European babies seem to cry less, and unless the weather is awful they are always set outdoors in their carriages to nap. Indeed, our first pediatrician, a Parisian, formally prescribed a daily time outdoors for our son, as if we obviously ignorant American parents might not know to do this.
11. *Avoid a move or travel during this first year if you can.*
12. *Keep yourself calm.* Avoid stress if you can. Do not become angry around your baby. Protect him from the aggression of a brother or sister. If you must leave your infant with another caregiver, be sure this person is warm and responsive.

What to Do While Your Baby Cries

Even if your baby is not crying excessively, you probably do all you can to stop his tears. Aletha Solter, a child psychologist originally from Switzerland, develops her view in *Tears and Tantrums* that babies and children should be *allowed* to cry—once you are sure there is no pain or problem you can correct. Crying can be a signal of distress, but at other times it is a way to release tension from physical or emotional stress, especially for very active or intense babies. It's important to encourage this kind of release.

So, what *do* you do when your infant cries? First, Solter emphatically advises not to leave your infant to cry alone. But once all the immediate physical needs are ruled out, your goal is not to stop the crying but to pay attention to your baby and allow her to howl. Sit in a comfortable chair, hold your baby, and look into her face. If she arches away from you, try to be reassuring with gentle touch. Do not bounce or jiggle her, but take some deep breaths, try to relax, and think about your love for her. Talk to her: "I love you. You are safe. It's okay to cry." Talk about what might be the problem and how you imagine she feels. Cry with her if you feel like it.

Are there times when you should not use this approach with an HSC? Perhaps. Some sensitive babies do seem to need to be left alone because they are so terribly overstimulated. You will probably know when this is the case—his day has simply been too long, too stressful. In these situations, it may be better to get both of you into a quiet room, preferably your baby's own. Put your baby down to rest and sit with your hand on his body. Pressure is especially reassuring to sensitive children. While it is a small additional source of stimulation, it is also a source of reassurance that you are still there. I would probably not hold or talk to a child who is obviously this overstimulated. But you can try whatever works for your baby and you.

Finally, I like the advice of Tracy Hogg, author of *Secrets of the Baby Whisperer: How to Calm, Connect, and Communicate with Your Baby:* Treat an infant like a human being! No rattles in the face, rough jiggling, or putting her legs over her head. Talk to your baby. Tell her what you are going to do and why. She is human; she understands more than you think.

If Your Baby Is Still Crying Too Much

First, what is too much? The average baby cries two hours a day during the first two weeks, three hours a day at six weeks of age, one hour a day by twelve weeks. A sensitive infant might cry a bit more during a period of overstimulation. But if your infant is over four months and crying for longer than two hours at a time or more than three hours in an entire day, and doing either of these more than three days a week, the situation definitely needs attention.

Ninety percent of the time reducing stimulation as described above solves even these cases. But if it has not, you will need to learn how to help your baby in other ways. One study looked at babies who were extremely irritable soon after birth, following them closely over the first six months. Later, at age one, these infants were still very irritable and much more likely to be insecurely attached to their mothers. But the study also found that these mothers were less responsive and involved than the mothers of less irritable babies. It seems that there was a kind of mutual dance that was leading mother and child farther and farther apart. However, as part of the study, fifty mothers of such babies were given specific training in how to soothe and play with their infants. Their babies were much more responsive and crying less when observed at one year. They were also more sociable and smart, and far more likely to be securely attached. In sum, if the information in this chapter does not help you with your irritable baby, you may benefit from professional help. (See Resources at the end of this book for a temperament counselor, or ask your pediatrician for a referral.) The point is, newborns really notice and care how they are treated, and HSCs will do so even more.

The rest of this chapter is designed to help you appreciate this amazing baby you have. You will sense that most of what you do is automatically fine—at this age, parenting is physically tiring but usually not mentally taxing. Your instincts and the subtle communications between the two of you will be enough to handle most matters easily. Yet your impact on your child, especially his preverbal mind, may be at its greatest.

Do Not Underestimate Sensitive Newborns—They Know Your Every Mood; They Learn and Remember

Because we do not remember our own infancy, we tend to assume that newborns will not remember what happens to them and are generally not very aware of what is going on. Nothing could be further from the truth.

Here is a fine example of a newborn's exquisite awareness. When I left the hospital as a new mother, we went straight to the home of two older friends, a pediatrician and a pediatric nurse who had six children of their own. They had invited us to stay because my husband and I were living rustically in the backwoods of British Columbia at that time, and I had had a cesarean. My doctor did not want me to go back to hauling water and wood too quickly, so he would not release me from the hospital unless I had a more comfortable place to stay temporarily.

The first evening in my friends' home, I rocked and soothed my HSC in every way I could think of (not many), but he would not stop crying. After a long polite interval, our friend who was the experienced mother and baby nurse asked if she could hold him. The moment she took him into her arms, he stopped crying and his body relaxed. She was doing what I had been doing! But the difference was at a deeper level: Emotionally, she was at ease while I was not.

A newborn's ability to learn and remember is perhaps even more contrary to our image of passive, unaware newborns until you think about it. Given how much infants need their caregivers to ensure their survival, it makes sense that they would have ways to remember from birth who these people are and how to get along with them. Indeed, using clever experiments and measures of bodily reactions, infants have been shown to have excellent "implicit" memories—the kind of memory that allows both infants and adults to learn lessons and form ideas without being conscious of any of it or having words for it. And since sensitive adults evidence more implicit learning, no doubt sensitive infants do, too.

From these studies of implicit memory, it is clear that newborns recognize and prefer their parents' voice and face as well as their native language, even when spoken by a stranger. Since newborns do not usually recognize their father's voice quite as readily, this learning probably starts before birth, in the womb. This ability to learn— for example, to recognize what is familiar and what is new—only increases with age, becoming quite keen by seven months.

Among the most important details for infants to learn are the cues about various emotional states, since these indicate how the caregiver is feeling about the helpless newborn. This is why making and understanding the meaning of facial emotional expressions are a specialty of primates (the "monkeylike" subset of mammals that includes humans). All primates possess muscles attached to the skin of the face and special areas of the brain for detecting subtle expressions. Not surprisingly, human infants are able to recognize faces and emotional expressions very early, and actually much prefer looking at faces. But your child likes your face best of all, and desperately needs the reassurance and information he learns from your expressions. Is that noise okay? Do you like me to coo?

During experiments in which mothers are told to show no expression on their faces, this is found to be highly distressing to infants. And if you separate babies and their mothers and have video cameras trained on them so they can see each other, they will make faces and respond to each other's expressions in that familiar way that all primate mother-child pairs do. But if you put this out of synch, so that the baby is watching an instant replay, he becomes frantic. When the predictable does not happen, the baby *knows* it is "wrong." He is designed to gain from you all the knowledge, soothing, and sense of protection that he possibly can. It is how he survives.

No wonder responsiveness is the single most important ingredient in caring for newborns. Your sensitive baby in particular knows what you feel and needs to know that you know what he feels. Besides this being a common experience for parents of HSCs, evidence for this extra emotional awareness comes from the fact that HSCs are generally born with more active right hemispheres, which is associated with emotional and social knowledge. Your sensitive newborn's right hemisphere is probably very active right now, noticing, learning, and remembering all about *you*. So express yourselves. Let your face and words tell him what you think he feels and what you feel in response.

TWO TO SIX MONTHS—HOW TO BE RESPONSIVE BUT NOT OVERSTIMULATING

From two months on, your infant will be more obviously responsive to you and in need of feedback. At this age your HSC has positive emotions like joy and curiosity, and the single negative emotion of distress can also now be anger at not getting what her positive emotions tell her she wants. At this point, too, she notices better what is new around her. And she is becoming highly social; even when alone, she is responding to an imagined you. For example, if she succeeds at playing with a toy she previously enjoyed with you, she will express the same delight as she did with you. She imagines you there.

At this age, however, your sensitive baby is still using you mostly as a "self-regulating other," as the person who regulates emotional and bodily life by soothing or exciting, by labeling experiences as good or bad, by initiating or stopping play, feeding, and other events that are pleasant or unpleasant. You do most of it and so your presence is essential. In particular, your sensitive infant is still very prone to overstimulation and must rely on you to control what reaches him. That can be tough when you are being told that at this age infants *need* plenty of toys, music, and socializing. So let's give you another culture's perspective on the level of stimulation infants require.

Oh, to Be a Dutch Baby

Because cultures vary in what temperament traits they admire and encourage, we are better able to understand what our own culture encourages by comparing it to others. If you see that yours does not promote sensitivity, you will have to think carefully about the parenting advice you read or receive from other parents and decide whether to do as other parents around you do, or to do things differently.

A good example of a different culture comes from the research of Charles Super and Sarah Harkness from the University of Connecticut. They spent a year in Holland, noting interesting differences in how the Dutch raise children, view temperament, and hence affect how their children display their individual temperaments.

The Dutch, first of all, see temperament as less of an issue because they believe everything is pretty well resolved by emphasizing the three Rs: rest, regularity, and cleanliness (all three start with *R* in Dutch). Thanks to the emphasis on the first two, the Dutch infants Harkness studied slept *two* more hours out of twenty-four than a comparison group of U.S. infants. And the Dutch group were far quieter when awake, not as restless and active as the U.S. infants.

The U.S. infants were more active, Super and Harkness believe, because their mothers kept them more stimulated. These infants were talked to, touched, and generally "jazzed up" if they were being quiet or if they were upset. And their cortisol levels were higher. (Some cortisol is necessary for life, but too much too often is not good, and a frequent problem for HSCs.)

Super and Harkness concluded that the U.S. infants were being accustomed to a higher level of activity that permanently changed their nervous system. This change became set at about sixteen to twenty-four weeks, as did a pattern of more calm in the morning, less in the evening, probably explaining why they slept less and why U.S. babies (and adults) have so many sleep problems. In contrast, the Dutch children tended to become more restful as the day wore on and were ready for a long sleep at night. (You can imagine how much the U.S. approach is contrary to an HSC's nervous system.)

The researchers also observed that babies and small children in the United States were encouraged or at least allowed to entertain adults and show some will, make demands, be independent. In Holland, babies and children were expected to be calm, quiet, and well mannered—part of a conversation but not the subject of it or the center of attention. How much easier for a sensitive child.

Finally, Dutch parents were not out after seven at night. No one expected them to be—parents of infants and small children were not asked to dinner parties, for example. The Dutch believe that parents should be at home to put children to bed. And if a school ever had an event in the evening (rare), classes started later the next day so children could sleep late. Again, all of this would make it easier to meet the needs of an HSC, almost automatically, and easier for HSCs to feel normal.

While we certainly do not want to idealize the Dutch, it is important to remember that your culturally programmed response is not the only one possible.

Don't Be a Parent Who Overstimulates

Sometimes it is easy for parents to realize they are overstimulating their infant with things to see, but do not notice when they themselves are the source of stimulation. But especially at this age, when your child is sitting up and being so adorably responsive, you may be doing it unintentionally. Daniel Stern, a specialist in the infant-mother bond, based on his years of infant observation and research, is well aware of the potential for the overstimulation of infants. He describes a baby whose mother was constantly "in his face," trying to play games such as peekaboo that anyone except the mother could see were overexciting and distressing her son. The baby learned to cope by avoiding eye contact or even looking toward her face. He turned or hung his head and closed his eyes. Later, when he could walk, he just left the room. But unfortunately, such early lessons become quickly generalized: Stern reports that later this infant became "avoidant," choosing to avoid most forms of intimacy with most people. Stern also described another baby of this age who, instead of avoiding her mother's overstimulation, became overly compliant. She would gaze into space and accept whatever was done to her—a different type of reaction that a sensitive infant might have to constant overstimulation.

Stern suggests that a parent might be overstimulating for many reasons: "hostility, need for control, insensitivity, or an unusual sensitivity to rejection [by the infant]." I would add that simple ignorance of an infant's sensitivity might also be the cause, especially if you have raised other children who liked or needed more stimulation.

You can easily avoid overstimulating your baby now that you know the typical signs of distress—crying, turning the head, looking down, closing the eyes tight, staring into space, or any other expression of misery. Think of your baby as a sensitive individual who needs to balance her need for some space around her with her need to feel secure through being close to others. She has to learn to shift from meeting one need to meeting the other, and you can help by matching her shifts.

Keep in mind that you do not want to overprotect either. Sensitive infants should not be swathed in cotton and kept in a sensory bubble. There is some evidence that exposing infants to a little stress may reduce their reactions to further mild stressors. The only exceptions are infants who are already highly stressed. So the key to developing resiliency is to offer the *right* amount of stimulation and challenge. Again, knowing the right amount requires your being responsive, alert to what your child can take in and find useful. There might be some discomfort for a moment, but it should be followed by your infant enjoying the experience and being calmer next time.

Sleep Problems Around Six Months

Around six months of age, many more sensitive infants have difficulty falling or staying asleep compared to other babies. I suspect this is because of their increased awareness, causing them to draw the attention of others to play with them. One pediatrician found that in his practice about 25 percent of the babies of this age were not sleeping through the night and almost all of these were highly sensitive.

What is normal sleeping? It varies with age, of course, and actually becomes worse before it becomes better. At five months, only 10 percent of children are waking between midnight and five in the morning on three or more nights a week. But at nine months that percentage actually increases, to 20 percent. After nine months, the percentage sleeping through the night steadily increases again.

Since overstimulation is often the cause of sleeplessness, you need to consider whether it is occurring during the day, leaving your baby too excited at night, or whether the problem is too much noise and stimulation just before bed or in the rest of the house after bedtime. I tend to believe now that infants should not be left alone to cry themselves to sleep—after all, they are probably expressing their normal, built-in, instinctive response to the danger inherent in being left alone. Suppressing that must be quite a task for an infant. But sometimes you can sense that even your soothing is too much stimulation, and a dark room and crying is the only way your baby will fall asleep. It may all depend on the child and the evening. In fact, on one particular evening in Paris in 1971, I set out to enforce the let-'em-cry strategy and discovered something else that worked even better.

At about six months, my son became very difficult to get to sleep and keep asleep, and we were getting desperate from lack of sleep ourselves. So on this night we put him to bed and let him howl. On that very night our wealthy Parisian landlady was having a garden party and climbed the many stairs to our tiny loft to tell us that our usually good baby's screams were disrupting her party.

What to do? Ruin the party or interrupt our attempt and have him learn, after all his screams, that enough crying always "gets results"? In spite of the possible handicap to practical thinking created by having several graduate degrees between us, we found a very simple if weird solution: We threw blankets over his crib to muffle the sound, leaving a tiny hole for air. He went right to sleep.

After that night, we constructed a little sleeping tent—four aluminum poles, with their ends squashed flat, drilled through, and bolted together at the top. At the bottom, we stretched them out to create an area underneath of about three by four feet. We attached netting around the bottom and up about a foot and put a covered foam mattress inside. When our baby went in (which he liked to do), we covered the entire contraption with more blankets—always the same ones so he would see the same patterns when he looked up, and always with a gap left so he had plenty of air. Under this tent he heard little noise, saw no light, and must have felt sheltered and secure because in there he would always go right to sleep.

The tent went with us everywhere we traveled (all around Europe that year), so that he was always in the same little cave. This made an enormous difference in hotel rooms, where previously he had always cried. It was his crib every night until he slept in a regular bed, around three. As an interesting aside, when he went off to college and had the chance to design his own room, he created a sleeping tent.

Other Sleep Solutions

When sleeping problems persist, pediatricians occasionally recommend a mild sleeping medication. If that option is given to you, ask about using lukewarm chamomile tea instead. But *do* ask your doctor before trying this. Emilio (the boy who set up home in his playpen) was very difficult to get to sleep, and his mother often found it helpful.

Dr. Solter, whose ideas about crying I already described, recommends letting your baby cry herself to sleep, but in your arms. Again, some babies may be temperamentally too highly active or intense, or momentarily too overstimulated, so they only become more "revved up" by being held, especially when smelling mother's milk or seeing the chance to interact with you. But for some babies it may be that letting them cry in a parent's arms is all they need and will increase their chance of sleeping through the night. Because mothers may be associated with nursing, fathers are great candidates for this task of holding the baby while she cries herself to sleep. And if she cries more with him rather than less, according to Solter, this just means she feels secure enough to express her feelings.

SIX MONTHS TO ONE YEAR—ATTACHMENT, ATTUNEMENT, AND SELF-REGULATION

At about six to ten months, your baby may suddenly not like to be held by or even to see strangers (although some HSCs are like this from the start). This is because the pause-to-check system has switched on, and your highly sensitive baby's system is super sharp. Now she can really compare a new situation or person to past memories and decide if this one is familiar and safe, or similar enough to something familiar and safe, that she can relax and get to know it. Naturally, more than ever your baby will look to you, needing to know for sure how to respond.

Since your baby is probably crawling or even starting to walk, your facial expression is now the main contact between you. For example, infants crawling along Plexiglas to the edge of a "visual cliff"—a seeming drop-off that is made obvious by a large pattern on the floor under the Plexiglas—will typically look to their mother for guidance. If she smiles, they continue to crawl. If she frowns, they do not. Obviously, they know to look to their mother, not to just anyone in the room. They know who matters, who is looking out for them. Your baby is attached to *you,* her parents.

In short, this is the age when your baby becomes quite bonded to a few trusted caregivers and, again, is far more cautious with everyone else. He has a very clear mental model of what to expect, good or bad, in various situations from his caregivers. Even if caregivers are not responsive, they are at least predictable, familiar, and the only source of care that he knows.

This capacity of infants to stick with a particular caregiver has been termed "attachment," and variations in the infant-caregiver relationship are called "attachment styles."

Attachment and Your Sensitive Infant

Attachment style refers, again, to the fact that all children develop a mental model of what to expect from close others. It begins in infancy, of course, but once formed, it is very difficult to change. It becomes a style in that it controls an individual's expectations throughout life, affecting friendships and marriage of course, but also deciding how optimistic or pessimistic will be one's view of the world, and in subtle ways determining much of one's overall mental and physical health.

The reason for discussing your child's attachment to you and others is that the level of security of the attachment bond affects HSCs more than other children. About 40 percent of all children, and therefore of adults as well, have an *insecure attachment style.* My research indicates that it is not more common among sensitive adults, but this insecurity does affect them more adversely when it occurs.

As I discussed in Chapter 3, studies have found that if an HSC feels secure in his attachment to an adult, in a new and highly stimulating situation he will have the typical HSC's initial startle reaction, but after that he will be no more threatened than a non-HSC. But an insecure HSC will go from being startled to being threatened. This makes good sense. Attachment seems to be especially designed to tell us who to turn to for safety and good judgment when we are faced with something new that might be dangerous. Since sensing subtleties that might spell danger is one of the HSC's specialties, of course he in particular needs to feel secure. One can imagine that insecure HSCs go through the world meeting every new event with a sense that they are on their own and therefore probably cannot manage. Everything becomes frightening and hopeless, which explains my finding that adults with good-enough childhoods are no more anxious or depressed than nonsensitive people, but with rough childhoods, they are much more so. Secure attachment in infancy is essential for a sensitive person to grow up normal and happy.

The Attachment Styles

Predictably, but unfortunately, parents with an insecure style tend to raise children who are also insecure. Their own parents are their main role models. But awareness helps. So, to know your own attachment style, try on these descriptions and see which one fits.

The securely attached person expects to be liked and cared for. You feel safe being close to others, safe going about in the world. It is as if there is a loving calmness available, either nearby or in the back of your mind, that has its origins in being connected and close to another person. (Obviously, for some, this is not unrelated to a religious feeling, and attachment style does have some interesting relationships to spiritual beliefs.)

As for insecure attachment styles, there are two. One is *anxious preoccupation*. In childhood, this style makes one clingy and afraid of being left alone, and in adulthood it makes one fear being unloved or abandoned, so that one ruminates about one's close relationships almost constantly. The anxiously preoccupied are usually the product of unreliable parents. Sometimes they received what they needed, sometimes not, so they became continually concerned with how to maintain a caring response.

The other insecure style is *avoidant* and develops when parents do not want a child around, are neglectful, abusive, or terribly intrusive and overstimulating. Avoidant infants minimize contact with their parents and cannot explore in a relaxed way because they have to stay vigilant for signs of trouble and ways to get the care they need in spite of their caregiver's attitude. Naturally, they try to manage on their own as much as possible and to reveal very little emotion; as adults, they try to avoid being close or depending on others.

Promoting Secure Attachment in an HSC

Because HSCs are so aware of everything and so easily put on the alert due to their pause-to-check skills, the environment in which a sensitive infant can be secure is a bit more constrained. Sensitive children need unusually responsive, alert parenting, based on their needs and not their parent's fears and stresses. In contrast, nonsensitive children can manage with a broader range of behaviors from their caregivers.

You have probably been making your HSC secure all along, through your moment-to-moment natural attunement to him. Indeed, most parents of HSCs seem to manage to supply this extra attentiveness quite automatically, given that HSCs are no less likely to be "securely attached" than other children. But here are a few trouble spots to look out for.

First, try to avoid separating your young HSC for more than a few hours from her main caregivers, especially in the first year or two. If you employ a caregiver, aim to keep the same good person throughout these early years. Humans—all mammals, in fact—do not thrive if separated from their primary caregiver, even if they are fed and kept warm. In an extreme example, studies of monkeys who were isolated soon after birth have found that as adults they were not able to mate or rear offspring and they often fought others to the death rather than merely making a display of anger as mammals generally do. They self-mutilated by cutting themselves or banging their heads, and overate. Monkeys separated from mothers for briefer periods grew up behaving normally except under stress—then they became biologically and behaviorally anxious.

To raise a secure HSC, you also want to do all you can to keep down your own stress level and that of the others to whom your child is attached. Studies of monkeys raised with a mother stressed by an unreliable food supply found that the young monkeys seemed normal while around their stressed mother, but as adults they were submissive, timid, and quick to cling to anyone available, plus, like the monkeys separated from their mothers, they showed the behaviors and neurochemistry of anxiety and depression, and a permanently altered brain. They did have a mental model of attachment—they expected to be miserable.

Finally, studies of HSCs in particular make it clear that they need caregivers who display sufficient flexibility, warmth, and supportiveness—here we are back to the idea of responsiveness. They are not secure with mothers who are angry, punishing, withdrawn, or inflexible. All of this makes less difference with non-HSCs. So let's talk about being attuned to your attentive infant.

ATTUNEMENT

Attunement is the second important influence on infants six months to one year old and is probably what contributes most to attachment. Moments of attunement and misattunement have been a focus of considerable research. Attunements are those subtle interactions when your infant displays emotion—excitement, fear, delight, or whatever—and you express it back, communicating that you understand and can feel the same. This can happen between parent and baby as often as about once a minute, both during quiet times and when an infant is exploring new people or places and looking to the parent for a second opinion.

Attunements are important at all ages, but take on a new significance between six months and a year. Before about nine months, when your baby expressed an emotion, you were likely to express it back in exactly the same way—a squeal gets a squeal, a coo gets a coo. After about nine months, you are far more likely to use a different *mode* of expression than what your baby uses. If your baby makes a face, you make a sound, but one that matches the intensity and type of emotion expressed by her face. Your HSC rises up a bit, waving and laughing. You say, *"Yes,* isn't it great?" Your strong "yes" matches your child's physical energy. If she squeals, you might nod your head vigorously. In other words, your attunements tend to match in intensity, duration, "shape" (the energy rising at the beginning, middle, or end), and any sense of rhythm or pulsation rather than being straight imitations. Attunements tell your infant whether you are really "there" or not, which is why they affect attachment. Being with an unattuned caregiver feels less safe—someone unattuned is less likely to respond quickly to expressions of fear or distress.

The attunements that start at this age, in which you express back the emotion in a new modality, also lets your baby know that you have the same *feeling* inside, not just that you are imitating a *behavior.* "Mother is now feeling what I feel." Baby researcher Daniel Stern calls these brief but significant moments "interpersonal communion"—that is, you are "sharing in another's experience with no attempt to change what the person is doing or believing." To Stern, these moments are crucial for developing an infant's sense of the shareable emotional world; "feeling states that are never attuned to will be experienced only alone, isolated from the interpersonal context of shareable experience."

Learning from Your Misattunements
Normally, attunements go on quite unconsciously and unnoticed—neither baby nor mother act as if anything has happened. But if a researcher asks a mother to respond with less or more intensity than her infant, her baby immediately stops and looks at her as if to say *"What's* going on?" Most parents found these "off" responses ac-

tually quite difficult to make, and this is definitely an uncomfortable moment for an infant.

Researchers have also observed that all parents are occasionally misattuned. No one is perfect at understanding and reflecting another's experience. And sometimes parents deliberately misattune to alter a baby's level of arousal—to calm an infant or excite him. Further, all parents selectively attune, in this way communicating their fears, dislikes, and fantasies for their child. One way they do this is by not matching their infant's excitement over, for example, getting dirty, banging a toy, or masturbating. In these ways parents let their children know which emotions are approved and can be shared and which ones cannot be.

As the parent of an HSC, you could be prone to particular misattunements. First, you might not fully reflect your HSC's distress or fears because of wanting your baby to be tougher or happier. But remember that such a strategy will make fear and distress become emotions that cannot be expressed and shared with others (this often happens to little boys). These become "unacceptable" feelings and, for a sensitive child, very difficult to cope with alone.

Second, because even in infancy sensitive children are so attuned to disappointing or doing wrong, HSCs can become extremely compliant if you attune to only quiet, obedient behaviors. Do not squelch their enthusiasms too harshly, even if you do not want some of them acted on. When you deny your infant something she desires, leave room for some protest and anger, perhaps even encourage its expression.

All of this is *not* meant to suggest that you are not properly attuning to your baby. You almost surely are, and when you are not, you are probably "good enough." But an awareness of these subtle interactions will make you an even more sensitive, responsive parent to your HSC. If you feel you are having some trouble attuning, seek help with whatever is distracting you or compelling you to try to mold your baby's reaction rather than merely responding to her.

The Role of Solitude

It is important not to conclude from all of this talk of attachment and attunement that infants should never be without social interaction. Research indicates that solitude allows the brain to reorganize itself, reestablishing balance. Sensitive infants, like sensitive adults, need more such reorganization time because it is their nature to prefer to process everything deeply and thoroughly. Sensitive infants often signal that they want to disengage, so the trick is having that attunement to your infant that allows you to provide her with needed solitude as well. Security of attachment is not determined by the amount of time spent in the bond, but the responsiveness of that bond to the infant's needs. Leaving her alone when she wants to be alone also adds to her security.

Solitude reinforces security in another way as well: It allows your child to think of you when you are not there and know that you still exist. And by crying out to you when she feels the need to, your baby learns to know these feelings and that she can act on them and gain a response from others. If you supply everything before your baby feels these needs, you take that experience away.

Self-regulation

The third important influence on six-month- to one-year-old HSCs is self-regulation, which begins around ten months and can continue to develop throughout the life span. It refers to a growing sense of choice about what emotion to act on. From noticing what works and being attuned to your reactions, your baby is beginning to discover that he may not want to respond immediately to his hunger and eat anything he is handed, or hide in fear when facing something big and noisy. Perhaps he has found that he does not like some foods, or some big, noisy things turn out to be fun.

All of this matters for HSCs because it means that from now on they can override the orders from their active pause-to-check system, and from the go-for-it system, too. They can feel cautious because something is unfamiliar but choose to go ahead. Or they can want to go ahead but decide to be cautious. This adds tremendous flexibility to their lives, so the more of it the better. In particular, when HSCs are self-regulated, their natural caution is under their control and can be only caution, not true fearfulness.

Sources of Self-regulation

Some of the capacity for this sort of self-control or willpower is inborn, and there is some evidence that it is stronger in HSCs since it is stronger in children with high "perceptual sensitivity." But your HSC also learns self-regulation from you. You are teaching her how to control arousal through your own coping methods, and through selective misattunement you indicate the kind of reactions you approve of—in particular, when you want her to control her pause-to-check or go-for-it systems. For example, she can learn from you to cover her ears when a sound is too loud or match your smile of delight as she touches the rabbit just a little bit to see that it doesn't bite.

Now is when you begin to see the effects of your attunements. If you encouraged through attunement your child's spontaneity and exploration, which I urge you to do with a sensitive infant, your child will be less reined in by his strong pause-to-check system. But if you discouraged spontaneity and exploration, your HSC will probably be overcontrolling these by ten months, unless his genes have created a very strong go-for-it activation system.

Attachment also affects self-regulation. An insecure HSC, who seldom feels a parent's attunement or only feels misattunement, will not be able to self-regulate as well. In particular he will not be able to override his strong pause-to-check system because he will sense a lack of support when he faces new challenges.

A FINAL WORD

Remember, no parent is always responsive and a source of perfect security. Sometimes we just cannot figure out how to help our HSC sleep or why she is crying constantly. But when you do finally "get it," the relief is especially sweet for both of you. Besides, infants also want and need to respond to their caretakers, to have it be mutual.

Likewise, no parent attunes perfectly all the time. Sometimes we do not see what our child feels, sometimes we do but are tired and must "fake it," and sometimes our values and culture may dictate that we not attune to and thereby encourage certain emotional reactions. Indeed, perfect attunement would create a sense of near merger—a child with no sense of a personal, private world of unique emotions separate from what you and he feel together.

Finally, no parent is a perfect role model of coping and self-regulation. The parents of HSCs in particular can feel quite helpless in the face of their reactions to an overstimulated child.

A baby can be a lot of trouble. And at times your HSC will need even more from you than other babies would. But remember, in ten short years this little infant will be nearly an adult and hopefully a good friend. So treat him like your good friend now. And expect to look back on this first year with fondness and longing (and the desire to hold every baby that comes your way). There is a kind of sweetness and closeness possible at this age that will affect both of you for a lifetime. Enjoy it as much as you can.

Chapter Seven

Toddlers and Preschoolers at Home

Adapting to Change and Dealing with Overstimulation

This chapter focuses on the sensitive one- to five-year-old and helps with (a) coping with change, (b) reducing your HSC's unnecessary experiences of overstimulation, and (c) handling moments of intense emotions. This chapter also has a special section on one- and two-year-olds, and offers issue-by-issue help with the simple, specific things that can pose special problems with the highly sensitive preschooler, such as choosing clothing and food, getting dressed, going to sleep, and riding in the car.

As you know so well, your HSC's main difficulties result from overstimulation and overarousal, and the greatest source of overarousal at home is change. This difficulty with change can manifest in many ways, but the end result is resistance and misery, whether it is about facing unfamiliar foods, changes in the daily routine, being asked to wait longer than expected, shifting from play to eating or sleeping, making the transition from being with you to being with another caregiver, or having a new baby sister. As you probably know all too well, a surprise or sudden change in plans can be particularly distressing for an HSC. So are new experiences and demands.

COPING WITH CHANGE

Your HSC's difficulty is perfectly understandable if you consider that every change involves processing stimulation that was not there before. Put yourself in your child's place: All the thinking you did preparing for and doing *A* must be sorted through and altered for doing *B*, and if *B* is new, that means even more processing and planning.

Notice that one type of change involves *shifting* from one familiar person, place, activity, or object to another that is also familiar— what I call a transition. The other involves becoming used to something entirely new or unexpected—what I call adapting or coping with a change in circumstances. Remember, even if your HSC is also a high novelty seeker who is generally enthusiastic about new experiences, adapting to the new experience can still be a challenge. It may be more overstimulating when it is actually happening than when it was imagined, and in any case, this type of HSC still has to figure out whether it is safe and how he personally, given his nature, can be successful and happy in it.

Meet Alice

Alice is three, and even at this young age she is not "shy" about letting others know what she likes and dislikes. She does not like changes. She likes the same chair, the same clothes, the same food. She does not like new people coming to her house, especially if they try to touch her. She does not like new people to look her in the eyes. Her mother insists she must acknowledge the other person, so she is allowed to put up her hands as if they are spectacles—that's her way to signal her feelings and also to hide from prying eyes.

When Alice started preschool she refused to talk for the first four months. But at home with a cousin or a neighborhood friend or her own family, she talks "all the time" and likes to make jokes and even to sing and perform.

Alice has learned to watch out for sudden, unpleasant surprises; she anticipates others' reactions. If another child is being punished for stepping out of the line, that is enough to keep her in line. If another child is offered a lap to sit on, she announces that she does not want to do that. She never throws tantrums; she is very "mature." But she knows what she wants and insists on it. As her mother says, "She is wise beyond her years."

Alice is one of many kinds of "typical" highly sensitive preschoolers. Some are less strong willed, some are more outgoing, but there is a thread of not liking change that runs through each of their stories and matches the sensitive nerves running through each of their bodies. Consider how much change they have faced already. They have been catapulted from infancy into family life and possibly preschool as well. They can suddenly walk and talk like little adults, sometimes better than other children. But they are not at all adults when it comes to experience handling a highly stimulating world.

General Pointers for Helping Your Child Adapt to Changes (Both Transitions and New Circumstances)

Even though your HSC has difficulty with change, she will have to learn to manage it. We could say that life is a constant round of making smooth transitions among the familiar—getting up and facing the day, going to school or work, coming home, going to bed. And life's greatest challenges are about facing the unexpected in other people and in one's circumstances. Let's begin by considering some general points about coping with change.

1. *Accept and absorb what you have just learned: Your HSC finds most changes very challenging.* Your child is not alone or abnormal. Randall, for example, was slow to give up wearing diapers and drinking from a bottle. He had to be coaxed. Remember how Emilio would not leave his playpen. Alice does not like new

clothes. Again, every change involves new stimulation, and because HSCs pick up on more, they pick up on more that is new. A new food is not just a new food, but full of odd flavors, scents, and textures. Reading a story is very different from lying in bed alone in the dark and trying to go to sleep.

2. *Trust that your HSC will make most changes eventually,* given enough time. You can lay out the new clothes on the bed and let her grow used to them. In a few days she will probably be wearing them. Of course some adaptations may take years! Alice likes vanilla ice cream and hot fudge, but not touching each other. It is a safe bet that she will not change in a few days, but it is equally likely that she will eat them together by the time she is ten.

3. *When you know a change is coming, be sure your child is physically ready for it.* That means he is healthy, physically fit, well-rested, and fed. Almost every behavioral problem at this age has some roots in the body—it is tired, hungry, coming down with a cold, having an earache or an allergic reaction, or too hot, cold, or thirsty. These states can come upon a child rapidly and affect sensitive children more than others. Adjust your expectations accordingly.

   To maintain health and fitness, be sure to include time in nature and exercise. Some experts recommend exercises involving joint compression—jumping rope or jumping on a mattress or low trampoline. It seems to help a child be more in touch with her body.

4. *Do not expect your child to cope with change or stressors when already in a negative mood.* Wait for a better mood or try to create one with humor, a game, a walk, or whatever usually works.

5. *Do not overestimate your child's capacities.* HSCs very often seem "mature" and "wise beyond their years." Their parents can easily forget how really young their bodies and minds actually are. For example, children at this age do not always understand the real reason behind a change in circumstances and the assumptions they make can add to their stress. For example, they can easily

think that they are the reason daddy went away for a week or the dog died. Children at this age also have trouble distinguishing between a thought or dream and reality. Given their reflective natures, all of these errors can affect HSCs more. Finally, children at this age have trouble keeping in mind that changes and their resulting emotions may not be permanent. When they feel bad that you have gone, it seems to them you are gone forever and this feeling will always be there. HSCs, again, will experience more intensely the feelings resulting from the fear that "this is forever."

6. *Generally, the less you can make an issue of a change you want your HSC to make, the sooner he will make it.* He already knows you want him to, but this way he doesn't have to deal with your feelings about the change, too. And he doesn't feel he is in a power struggle in which he might lose, which is my next point.

7. *Try to avoid making your HSC feel powerless.* Often the problem of overstimulation is being augmented by a sense of being powerless. "This is being done to me without my permission and I cannot stop it." To feel powerless is never comfortable for a preschooler's budding self, so eager to feel effective. In addition, the HSC may also feel, "I will be out of control because this is going to overwhelm me."

One way to restore power is by offering some choices about how and when the change will take place. "Before we put out the light, would you like me to read a story or sing a song?" "Would you like to put away the game before you eat, or leave it out and play with it again later?" Beware, however, of offering too many choices. In general, it is probably best at this age to offer two at a time. "Would you like to wear a skirt or pants?" Then, "This skirt or this one?"

Remember, too, that new foods and clothing raise other issues about being out of control. They are put into or on the body, making their impact highly personal, physical, and potentially intrusive. So in these cases, and in all cases when it is possible, reassure your HSC that he will not be forced to eat, wear, or do something he finds truly distasteful or unbearable. Just point out that you personally have found a particular choice or change worked out well (without implying he ought to).

8. *Prioritize.* Do not try to institute changes or introduce new elements into an HSC's life all at once. This month work on adjusting to sleeping in a bed, not a crib. Next month you can try introducing life without the pacifier.

9. *Loosen your child up through play.* If your HSC seems to obsess *too* much over every change and its consequences—"What if I don't like it" or "I can't do that; I might make a mistake"—try to play your child out of some of her desire for certainty. Create make-believe stories or games involving fantastic choices and unpredictable, funny outcomes. Encourage playfulness of all sorts, including games that require quick decisions, making a mess, or letting things be undecided, confusing, or chaotic for a while. Help her get wet and dirty frequently, without worrying about getting clean and dry again. Make all of this humorous and creative, but *do not* make fun of your child's difficulty or compare her to other children.

Making Smooth Transitions

Transitions from one familiar activity to another happen all day long, and your HSC will probably need your skillful help. Thus, it is worth giving special attention to this art form!

Remember, transitions involve complicated sensory input for a young HSC—things are the same each time, but also different. It is dinnertime, but maybe the smells from the kitchen are unfamiliar. Meanwhile, the game that has to be abandoned was particularly compelling, drawing your reflective and creative HSC into a deep state of involvement. The following suggestions may seem as if you are doing all the work and making it "too easy," but your HSC will be able to do each of them for himself with time, so you are really teaching coping skills.

1. *Give advance warning.* "Five minutes now." "One minute now." Or set a timer or a wind-up toy so the child can see the time ending. And do not say it's time to get out of the water or go to bed until you mean it. At that time, make it happen.

2. *Keep what you can the same.* "You can bring your truck to the dinner table if you want." Be creative in highlighting the nonchanging: Some smells from the kitchen may be unfamiliar, but you can mention the foods you have made that are familiar. You can also point out that the game will be there when dinner is over.

3. *Offer an inviting "when-then."* "When you get out, then we'll dry off and have some cocoa before bed."

4. *Make it humorous or fun.* Try crawling into the bedroom, mooing, and announce you are the "bedtime cow."

5. *Play out the transition.* Use a dollhouse and dolls or stuffed animals. "Patty is playing, but now dinner is ready. What does Patty feel? What should Patty do?"

6. *Again, give choices.* "Do you want me to dry you off or do you want to do it yourself?" "Do you want me to read a story before bed or sing a song?" I repeat this advice because, while it can seem to complicate matters for you, it reduces your child's resistance due to feeling powerless, and so it can save time for you in the long run as well as strengthening your child's sense of self.

DEALING WITH OVERSTIMULATION

Our next subject, overstimulation, can arise from change, but also from a long or exciting day or too much noise or too many things to see. Think of your child as starting the day with a full gas tank—probably the neurotransmitter serotonin—and every experience processed, like every mile driven, drains a little. (Or your child may not be starting with a full tank, if she did not sleep well or is ill.) Think about how you will use that fuel and what you will do when you hit empty. Here are some suggestions:

1. *Learn to recognize quickly the first signs of overstimulation.* These will differ from child to child, but usually involve overexcitement, irritability, eye rubbing, balking, whining, or refusing to eat when he ought to be hungry.

2. *Pace yourselves.* Often your child can recover for a while and go on if given a break, but without a break she cannot.

3. *Reduce unnecessary stimulation,* especially when your child will be exposed to more later—for example, on days you will take him on errands later or he will be in preschool. Also, use the ideas in the previous chapter for reducing stimulation for infants.

4. *Provide buffers whenever you can.* Bug repellant for out in the country, earplugs for fireworks, dry clothes for a trip to the beach, or a playdate in the snow.

5. *Ask others to help* by keeping in mind your child's stimulus load for the total day, especially if you are leaving your child in another's care. Otherwise, when the two of you are reunited, you will be the one dealing with a child running on empty while you still need to take her to the dentist. And when you ask what your child has been doing, think about how much energy will be left.

DEALING WITH INTENSE EMOTIONS

Sensitive souls take in everything and ponder. Part of pondering an experience is having an emotional reaction to it. The more you ponder, the stronger the reaction, and also the more complex. First maybe you fear the thing. Then you hate it. Maybe then you are angry with it. Then you fear how others will feel about your feelings. Then you consider its good aspects. You start to want it, too. And so forth.

As a parent of an HSC, your task is to try to keep up with all of this when you and your child are interacting. You need to try to guess the feelings and *name them:* Fear, love, joy, curiosity, pride, guilt, anger, sadness, despair. The latest thinking on emotional intelligence says this naming is very important. You also might do well to watch for the emotions you are likely to handle awkwardly or miss entirely due to your own family history. (Most families have emotions they deal well with—for example, joy, pride, anger—some they deal with poorly—maybe expressing love—and some they try to deny entirely—perhaps fear and sadness.)

When your child is sobbing, screaming, and trembling with fear, it may be hard to listen and reflect calmly: "I see you're very, very upset—very angry and afraid." But this is what is needed, so that your child does not have to feel all of this alone.

Good "containing" of your HSC's intense emotions, so your child does not feel that she and her entire universe is just falling to pieces, involves a paradox. You must communicate that you understand exactly how she feels, but you are not being "infected"—you are not becoming frightened, angry, or overwhelmingly sad yourself. Even if you are totally exasperated, the less you show it, the better off *you* will be as well as your child. When you are melting down, too, your child becomes more upset, not less.

As you state the feeling and try to contain it, you can also remind your child that the situation will not last forever and can be resolved. "I know your foot must feel awful; I hate stones in my shoe, too. As soon as we get out of this muddy place, over to that bench, we'll take it out." Or perhaps it cannot be solved. "I know you wanted the pasta shaped like bow ties, but it is still pasta, made from the same stuff, and we have to use up this kind before we get another kind." This accepts the feelings as being real, but also puts them in the context of time and other realities.

When your HSC seems to be "manipulating" you with exaggerated or feigned emotions, remember that this is still a small child, not a member of the Mafia. You are always in control. If your child is really feigning an emotion, it is still for an emotional reason. Find out the reason—or the reason you are reacting with disbelief.

Remember, too, that it is easy for a child of this age to feel intense emotions because of your own reactions. Suppose you are in an elevator with your arms full of groceries and your two-year-old has insisted on carrying the car keys. Suddenly you see that he has noticed the gap between the elevator and the floor. He looks at it, at you, at the keys. You shout "No!" He grins and drops the keys down that interesting hole.

At this age this is *not* a hostile act, no matter how much trouble it will cause you. It was an experiment for him, and part of living with a two-year-old for you. Two is very young. Do not attribute adult motives to a child, or expect adult empathy. You can be upset about the problem you now have to face, but try to contain your anger—that is, try to be a saint. Otherwise, your HSC will soon be overcome with guilt and shame. The trouble that he sees this act cause should be enough punishment.

Next time your child gets ink on the new couch, remember the saying of my aunt, who raised many children of her own and others', and who gave me the best rule of my parenting life: *People are more important than things.*

Now, What to Do

1. *Remember, your child is out of control, so you must stay in control.* This is contrary to what your body is saying, which is having its own reaction. It wants to strike back, give in, shut down, break down, or get out. But you are older and you can control your reactions, or rather select among them, which is what you want your child to learn to do. So take a few seconds, maybe draw a few deep breaths, then focus on your goal.

2. *Focus on your goal: to connect and get through to your child,* to return her to a calm state of mind. Threatening, isolating, and punishing will not connect the two of you. It will only upset her more, since you are now giving into the same forces that have overwhelmed her.

3. *Try to touch your child gently* (rather than jerk) if you have to control or move your child.

4. *Speak calmly.* No yelling. In other words, in everything you do, be gently firm and do not overreact. As for what you say, this is not the time to argue or even discuss much. Nothing will get through. It is the reasonableness in your voice that will help more than what you say. Just name what seems to be happening. "You are really angry right now. We are going to go someplace to talk about it."

5. *Try to get the two of you to a private place.* You need a quiet room with the lights low. You can give your child the choice of staying alone to calm down or having you there, too. Stay if you are wanted.

6. *Hold your child* if he is willing. Whatever seems to dispel the tantrum better. Let the screaming and tears go on for a while. If it is about something he cannot have or do, say that. "I know you are angry about . . ."

7. *If this seems to be much ado about nothing, try to find out what else is going on.* Is this all due to overstimulation? It often is. Has your own emotional state caused this situation? That, after all, is the most potent source of stimulation for your child at this age. Has your child learned that these tantrums get your attention? Or is anger covering up for upset over a loss or fright that happened earlier? Get down to eye level and start guessing. "Do you want me to listen to you more? Are you upset because you can't have that toy? Was George hitting you? Are you worried about something I have said? Or are you just ready to go home?" Ask one at a time, about three guesses at most and very slowly to give your child time to think. Wait for a nod. If you are not getting a response, stop. And remember, getting the right answer may not matter as much as getting one that your child is satisfied with. She has now started thinking, not screaming.

8. *Remember, prevention is the best cure.* Watch for the signs of a coming meltdown and try to forestall it. Know what triggers your child—not being taken along on a walk, having to wait, not having food served right, not getting to unlock the door himself—and

avoid it if you can without becoming a slave. Older children are able to control their tantrums and should be expected to endure some frustrations; younger children are just learning that skill. After all, not so long ago they were babies for whom you did everything they wanted.

If the Meltdown Continues

1. *If things are not getting better, keep controlling your own feelings.* This little child is not rejecting you, controlling you, or really wanting to hurt you. He is just overwhelmed. If you cannot calm down, take a break, especially if your child would be better off without you there for a little while. Get another adult to help you out if possible.
2. *Try alternatives to talking.* A drink of water, a walk, a chance to run around outside and play, a nap. Try a total sensory change: a bubble bath, listening to music, playing with clay or warm water, getting a back rub, repetitive physical motion like swinging or rocking, or deep breathing from the belly—even toddlers can learn to do it. This is not spoiling, but bringing down the intensity. Later you can discuss what happened and what is not acceptable behavior.
3. *Keep to your standards—it is reassuring that you have not changed.* Mention them, and find flexible ways to enforce them. Say, "I know you are angry but you cannot hit. You can yell that you don't like me." If your child does hit you, calm down. Then catch her hand and hold it gently but firmly, saying "You may not hit."
4. *Think carefully before you discipline a small HSC for a tantrum.* Wait until both of you are calm. If this was all due to overstimulation, you will sense that your child is as dismayed with this outburst as you are, and there is no need for discipline, too. Rather, you can discuss how the two of you can prevent it happening again. Even if the behavior has been repeating, it may not be something your child can be expected to control yet.

5. *Use time outs but not as punishments.* Several parents have found them to be too stressful for HSCs, even though they work well with other kids. It is usually better to stay near or hold your young HSC. But sometimes an HSC will be better off entirely alone. Be sure your child understands that this is *not* a punishment; it is a way for him to calm down. "Let's have a cool down on the sofa." Or "Why don't you take some time out? You can stay with me here or go to your room and play."

6. *Keep the longer view.* Research finds that children allowed to have their tears and tantrums at this age tend to be more confident and less trouble when they are older.

7. *In all of this, remain your child's ally.* She does not want to have these exhausting tantrums, but she does want *something*. Discuss how she can express herself in other ways and what she wants you to do if it does happen, including what to do at home versus at the supermarket.

Emotional Outbursts That Become Aggression Toward Other Children

Aggression and anger toward other children are not common in HSCs, but a few parents I interviewed mentioned them. Some children are just born intense, slow to adapt, persistent, active, or easily frustrated (or all of these) yet sensitive, too. Others have witnessed violent exchanges, or have discovered the power of anger to stop others from overstimulating them or otherwise crossing their boundaries.

Sometimes it seems that children are so overwhelmed by social situations, including perhaps parents' expectations that they be more mature and thoughtful than they are able to be, that they just snap. Others have been so overprotected from all frustration that they can't handle it when it happens. A parent's fearfulness for a child can reinforce a child's sense of not being able to cope with unpleasant feelings, so exploding is the only option left, especially for an active child. Again, it seems that the only coping mechanism they have is aggression.

Finally, children can be affected by seeing violence on TV. They may come to expect that this is the way to solve problems. If they are full of pent-up energy and bored, they may simply act out what has been entertaining them on Saturday mornings.

One way or another, most or all of these reasons come down to goodness of fit, which was described in Chapter 2. A child is angry when his temperament, his natural way of being, is not working well with his environment.

Here are some things that can help:

1. *Teach your child how to warn everyone when he is reaching this point.* If you can see it coming, say, "Sean, if you are getting irritated because of something, tell us what is the matter." If you have some ideas you can name a few. "Are you hungry? Are you mad at Jimmy for having that toy? Do you want to go home?" After it happens you can remind him: "Sean, next time tell us you want to go home before you are so angry."

2. *Teach how to prevent that point from arriving* by self-calming tactics (walking away, counting to ten, asking for support from others), or asking to leave a situation, or telling others "You're bothering me."

3. *Teach all the ways anger can be expressed* so your child can choose. Some ways of doing it are quite acceptable while others are not or depend on the situation. We have a form of anger for every body part—giving 'em the eye, turning a deaf ear, spitting it out, turning up your nose, giving the cold shoulder, getting it off your chest, sockin' it to 'em, kickin' 'em out, giving 'em the boot, and so forth. Expand your child's repertoire by going over these, perhaps as a game you both act out, and talk about which ones are okay to use with another child.

4. *Consider where she's observing violence* and learning that it's a way to resolve problems. At home? From peers? On TV? You may not be able to avoid this exposure, but you can begin to discuss it as wrong in real life.

REGARDING ONE- AND TWO-YEAR-OLDS

Having explored these three general issues of dealing with change, reducing unnecessary overstimulation, and handling intense emotions, and before going into very specific matters like nightmares or car trips, we should consider the highly sensitive toddler specifically.

Around the age of one, your baby is starting to walk and is also beginning to understand language—long before speaking, she understands you. Although I have no data to prove it, I suspect HSCs understand their parents earlier because they pick up on all the subtle clues to the meaning of the words, such as tone of voice or gestures. (When children start to talk will depend on many factors.)

Language makes possible whole new worlds of shared experience—and whole new complexities, especially for HSCs. For example, adults know that people often do not always say what they are feeling or what they really mean. Sometimes even you will say "no" but your voice and expression will say "yes." Your HSC will need to learn how to handle this, and you will be challenged in all new ways to be an honest, thoughtful human being.

You will also now have to consult with your sensitive child before making decisions, and you will be more aware that you cannot talk about just anything without your child understanding you.

Many of the good things your child can acquire—security, confidence, compassion—are seeds already planted and sprouting by this age. If these are not planted, however, there is still time. Everyday life, of course, determines the condition of these sprouts. So now let's look at the typical issues that arise with one- to two-year-olds.

Eating problems. Breast feeding is obviously the best way to feed any baby. Most infants indicate when they want to stop nursing, so do not rush weaning unless you have a child who adapts very slowly to all changes, so that you suspect he will never get the idea on his own, or another baby is on the way. When you do introduce other food, do it slowly and do not be surprised if there is some resistance.

At first, our son would not eat any food, including meat, unless it was mixed with mashed banana. We were living in Paris at the time and bought quite a few bananas *bien mur* (well ripened).

Meal time is an ideal opportunity to show your attunement to and respect for another's feelings (ask the French). If your infant does not like a particular food or even a particular brand of it, respond to that! Eating problems are usually the parents' problem—they want their child to eat what the child does not like. Babies have control over so little in their lives, surely their likes and dislikes about food can be respected.

Still, you want your child to have variety, so you need to introduce new foods. Show your child your enthusiasm for the food. Present it several times. And wait and see.

Your first separations. How an HSC will react to being separated from you is rather unpredictable. As we said in the last chapter, very young children instinctively protest being left entirely alone or with someone not responsive to them. But if there is a responsive, capable person around whom your child already knows and trusts, chances are she will be fine. If she protests fervently, or you call to check in after an hour and she is still crying, I would "give in" and avoid the separation if possible. In my opinion, separations from familiar caretakers should be minimized before three years of age, at least. Stick it out that long, and a few years later you will have a child who is more independent, not less.

The reason for taking such care regarding separations is that very young children, especially young HSCs, seem to remember them as traumas. I have encountered a number of sensitive adults with intense separation anxiety who had in their early history a long separation from their mother. Emilio, the child so fond of his playpen, was left with his father and grandmother for ten days when his baby brother was born. As a result, he developed a fear of his mother leaving him again that is still strong at six years of age.

If you leave your child with a good caregiver for long periods, expect to see your child bond with this person. When my son was almost three, we left him for an entire month with his grandmother. When I returned, he clearly adored her—she is a wonderful and skilled mother and had devoted the month to her grandson's care; they had thoroughly enjoyed each other. To my chagrin, when we were reunited at her house he did not know who to run to, her or me, when he was hurt or needed something. To this day, they have a strong physical and emotional bond.

Learning to use the toilet. Try to avoid showing signs of disgust when changing diapers. It is easy for a sensitive child to feel "dirty" and disgusting all over from your reaction or terms. Enemas, too, should be avoided if possible, as this loss of control and bodily invasion is hard on HSCs. It all complicates an HSC's learning to use the toilet in a relaxed way.

It is tempting to teach HSCs grown-up practices early, as they are often so willing to please. On the other hand, some parents have said that use of the toilet became a lengthy problem involving one step per week for months once their HSC became overly focused and anxious about it. So waiting until your HSC is a little older, or shows real insistence on doing it the way you do, may save trouble in the long run. No matter how long you put it off, your child will not be wearing diapers at twenty. Or even at five. So relax.

It helps to be aware of some of the problems HSCs may have in this area so that you will not be surprised and convey that to your child. For example, HSCs tend to find wet and dirty diapers distressing, which should make things easier. On the other hand, underpants can feel strange to them after being used to diapers; the toilet or potty may feel hard or cold; the sound or mere concept of flushing may seem threatening. Feeling the need for privacy, HSCs may go behind something or away from the caregiver, especially when having a bowel movement, making it harder to teach them. They may be embarrassed to say they need to use the toilet when they are not at home. Thanks to all of this, they may become constipated as a result of trying to delay, and if a bowel movement hurts, they may try to avoid it all the more.

One of the best toilet learning methods for an HSC seems to be leaving the potty in a prominent place and letting the child go naked. Keep the atmosphere casual, sociable, private—just you and your child.

If you feel as if you and your HSC are in some kind of a power struggle around toilet training, back off and consider how you might give your child more power in other areas. This is an area where a child will sense that she can exert some control, and she will if this is the only area where she can.

Genital play. Most infants discover their genitals around ten months and begin to play with them, not so much for the sexual-sensual pleasure as for satisfying their curiosity and need for comfort from their body. They may stroke themselves as they would their mother's breasts. By around eighteen months, some babies seem to begin to feel genuine sexual-sensual excitation from masturbating—that is, they are clearly intentionally arousing themselves and self-absorbed.

If you choose simply to ignore your child's masturbating, showing no attunement to this particular pleasure but plenty of it to others, a sensitive child will almost surely realize it is not approved. But you may not want to give that message. Remember, self-exploration of everything, including the genitals and the pleasure they give, is a natural part of development. And lessons about sexuality are lifelong. Hopefully, your child will learn to associate sexuality with secure attachment and general intimacy, not with stony silence. You will want to take your own views and cultural values into account, but in my opinion the best approach is to be more positive than "neutral," since neutral generally translates as negative. Perhaps the best plan is to communicate that masturbating is fine, but something done in private.

As for tantrums and the "terrible twos," I have not seen evidence that sensitive children are more difficult than other children at two years. In fact, I think they are easier. However, sensitive children of two years of age, and sometimes much older, can become hysterical or furious when pushed too hard by a long day or a difficult interaction, so do apply what we have already discussed in this chapter about overstimulation and intense emotions.

DEALING WITH ALL THOSE EVERYDAY PROBLEMS

Returning to suggestions that apply to all one- to five-year-olds, let's consider the day-to-day issues that are likely to arise.

Nightmares. Nightmares are normal at this age, even for non-HSCs. Most small children dream of being abandoned or being attacked, the two biggest dangers they face. You simply reassure them that they are safe and loved, and that it was a dream, not reality.

Throughout their lives, however, sensitive people have more intense dreams, so at some point (closer to five than one, of course), you can start helping your child to accept them and even make use of them. Discussing a bad dream in the morning helps to dispel the shadow it can cast. Perhaps you can even explain why the dream may have happened—perhaps something frightening happened the day before the dream. You can start to teach your child, too, that she can learn from dreams, even nightmares. Nightmares are attempts to get our attention about something troubling us, or to help us rehearse how we will face what we fear.

If a dream is not frightening but interesting, you can apply some of the simple ideas of dream interpretation, such as "I wonder why Bear came to you in your dream?" (That is, "what qualities of a bear might you need right now?") Or "I wonder why that fairy is trying to get your attention? What do you suppose her message would be if you could talk to her?"

I know one family that gathers on the parents' bed each morning to hear each member's dreams before going on with the day. They do not "analyze" them, but merely witness what is happening in each other's psyche.

Fear from watching scary movies or TV. Most HSCs are greatly bothered by scary or sad scenes in stories, movies, or TV. But since many non-HSCs have no trouble with these, indeed seem to need them to find a story interesting, much of the media are not designed with your child in mind. You may think you can protect him, but he will see these scenes when visiting others or even at school. Or you may want your child to be able to watch *Bambi* or see *The Nutcracker*, but what about the scary parts?

Teach your HSC that she can stay in control. She can leave the room for those scenes—you can even tell her when they are coming. She can close her eyes and cover her ears. She can ask others to warn her about the scary parts, describe them in detail to take away the shock, and tell her the happy ending.

Eating problems. As I have already said and many parents of HSCs emphasized, let your child decide what to eat. Then there are no eating problems. There may be some serving gymnastics—seeing there is no spaghetti sauce on one portion of pasta or no broccoli touches the potatoes—but you can manage. Be careful about becoming a short-order cook for a demanding little HSC, but you may not mind scrambling an egg for this one when the rest of the family wants a meal the HSC cannot abide. If you do not bring junk food into the house, he will choose a good-enough balanced diet over the long haul.

You can also discuss upcoming meal menus with your child so she's not surprised, but instead is happy to come to the table and eat what she helped plan, perhaps even helped prepare, and now anticipates. Eating is usually a social time, so keep it pleasant. By not rushing and keeping meals happy, you also give her a chance to see others eating foods she has rejected, and perhaps, while in her good mood, she might try them. And do teach your HSC how to decline a food politely; she will not be polite at another's table if she did not have to be polite with you.

Which raises the issue of manners. Too much emphasis on table manners in these early years can make your HSC tense, angry, or ashamed during meals. But lacking them will make him even more tense and embarrassed in future years in other company. So make a list for yourself of what has to be taught (chewing with mouth closed, using a napkin, elbows off the table, and so forth). The list will convince you that you *will* teach it all eventually. Then tackle one habit at a time. Perhaps make it a game for everyone. And remember that imitation works best. HSCs usually notice what others do and want to do that, too, without needing to be chastised—just a reminder now and then.

Eating out. Before you're at the restaurant, help your child plan what he will order, given your knowledge of the menu. Role-play ordering, or explain that you will order for him, once you know what he prefers. Use new restaurants as ways to introduce novelty and new foods gradually. Go back to the old standbys when your child is not feeling strong.

As for restaurant manners, I have seen some very young children able to sit still for several hours at a restaurant with just a little consideration of their needs—a snack right away, something to look at or play with quietly. It helps, too, if they see eating out as an exciting privilege with certain expectations attached, just as you have to wait in line at the carousel. But for some it will be a few years before they can sit still; they are simply too restless or active by nature. Adjust your expectations to your child's age and temperament. If some in your party are willing (they often are but do not think of it), let them take a turn going out with your child or carrying her around to look at interesting things in the restaurant. A child should be able to have a good time, too, when everyone goes out.

Getting dressed and clothing issues. Again, as much as possible follow your child's needs and preferences. At three, Alice chooses her own clothing. So can your HSC. Many parents mentioned the problem of scratchy labels and fabrics or socks and shoes that rub. This is absolutely normal for HSCs. Take your child shopping with you so that the two of you can learn what is comfortable, and expect some purchases will be mistakes and have to be given away unused.

To soothe yourself (you should *not* become angry), discuss with your child how the two of you made the mistake and how to avoid it in the future.

When you have to insist on your child wearing a certain type of clothing for the sake of appearances, make deals: "Wear the dress to the wedding, but we'll bring some comfortable clothes and at the reception afterward you can change."

Allow extra time for deciding what to wear and dressing. Select clothing the night before if you expect any problem.

Organize closets and dressers so it is easy to find things. Label drawers or baskets with pictures of what is inside. Perhaps put whole outfits together (shirt, pants, underclothes, and socks in one bundle).

Bedtime and sleeping. Going to sleep and waking up are major transitions. Making a routine of it helps. Post a "list" of pictures of what needs to be done to get ready for bed and let your child lead you through it. Have a routine of quieting activities before bed—bath, story, prayers, or whatever you both decide. Let your child wear whatever he wants to bed. If he keeps popping out of bed, try making some get-out-of bed cards. He can use them for any reason, but when he runs out of cards, that's it.

Make the room dark, covering windows with curtains if there is light outside at night or in the morning. Use a night-light if your child prefers a cozy glow rather than pitch blackness. Provide quiet, with carpets and drapes in the room and a quiet time throughout the house. At this age, you can also let your child fall asleep with you. But be sure you sleep well, too.

If your child wakes in the night, of course find out what the problem is. Fear? Loneliness? Thirst? Too hot? Trouble settling down due to overstimulation? Sometimes, as Dr. Solter says, a good cry is all that's called for. If she just wants to stay up, try using the get-out-of-bed cards again. And tell her that she can stay awake, but you need to sleep so you will feel good in the morning. Doesn't she need to as well?

Shopping and errands. One parent gave me the best advice I have heard on the subject: the rule of two, or "never take an HSC on more than two errands a day." Period. Shopping and errands are exhausting for them—the getting in and out, the jarring of turns and stops, the rapidly changing scene out of the car window, whatever is going on inside the car, and the different environments in each place, most designed to assault the senses as well as occasionally having "bad vibes" (grumpy employees, dingy surroundings, pollutants). You may be used to auto garages and convenience stores, but HSCs are encountering them for the first time. HSCs need to be exposed to some of this—it's the world they were born into—but in small doses.

It also helps to tell your child where you are going and how long it will take, and consider that an agreement that cannot be broken lightly. (You do not want your child breaking agreements with you, and one way to see to that is to keep your own.)

Car travel. Develop a routine for getting in and out—for example, you do not move until seat belts are fastened, so there is nothing to fuss about there. Stick to a seating plan for who sits where. Take breaks every half hour to an hour on long trips. That may seem often, especially to the driver who is eager to "cover some miles," but the more breaks, the farther you can go ultimately.

Breaks should involve being out of doors if possible, away from the tumult of cars and businesses. Have a picnic, not a fast-food break.

In the car, seek the optimal level of arousal for your child. Is your child bored or overstimulated right now? You can shift the level by varying what is going on—conversation, games, music, singing, looking out the window, and complete quiet times.

Your HSC's room. If possible, HSCs should really have their own room. They need the privacy, a place to go and be still, the chance to control their environment. If they must share, try to avoid having your child in a room with a nonsensitive child, especially an older one, and especially if they do not get along. The differences and potential for domination are too great. If all else fails, consider erecting partitions that make the boundaries clear.

What we said about room furnishings for infants still applies: Keep it simple, with carpets and drapes to muffle sound. But at this age you also want a room easy to keep orderly and clean, especially to keep dust-free, since HSCs tend to have allergies, so aim for rugs and curtains that can be washed. There will be toys, so stimulation may be reduced best by having plenty of storage for hiding clutter (boxes or baskets rather than shelves), and not hanging too many posters and pictures. But more and more, this will be up to your child.

LESS-OFTEN-THAN-DAILY ISSUES

Doctor Visits. The choice of doctors and other health care providers is important with an HSC, starting from birth. Most of your HSC's reaction to doctor visits will be determined by the doctors and nurses he encounters (plus some interesting toys or books in the waiting room or that you have bought and bring out just for this occasion). From three months to a year and three months our son had a world-renowned and nasty pediatrician (the Parisian who wrote out all of his instructions, including taking our infant out of doors every day). This guy admitted he hated babies and all people, and handled babies in a way that made you believe it. In spite of having a wonderful doctor after that, and only good ones in the years that followed, our son had a fear of doctors that lingers a bit to this day. I am absolutely certain he remembers being handled during his first inoculations by this angry, unfeeling man.

Tell your pediatrician about your child's temperament and listen for whether this professional "gets it." There should be no pathologizing of it, or dismissing of it. A good book to loan your child's doctor, besides this one, is Jan Kristal's *The Temperament Perspective* or William Carey and Sean McDevitt's *Coping with Children's Tempera-*

ments. They are explicitly written for professionals who treat children.

You and your child's health care providers need to know the following facts:

- HSCs feel pain more.
- As a result, HSCs may complain more and then receive more tests and medications than they should.
- On the other hand, some may underreport their symptoms if these have been dismissed so that they feel ashamed, or if they have had bad examination or treatment experiences. It is important to know if your child underreports or overreports.
- They experience more headaches.
- They are more distressed by injections.
- They do less well during hospitalizations.
- They have more allergies.

Having said all of that, you can also mention that children with this temperament are on the average *healthier*—fewer illnesses and injuries—than non-HSCs, provided they are not under stress. But when conditions are stressful, they have more of these than non-HSCs.

You may also have to explain that the behaviors that sometimes result from this temperament—shyness, not talking in school, sadness, anxiety—generally do not need to be treated with antidepressants or other medications. Rather, these children need to learn to gravitate to those environments (and people) where their trait is an advantage.

"Where babies come from," sexual play, issues around masturbation, and nudity all deserve careful reactions from you, since HSCs cannot help but be aware that sexuality is a highly charged issue. Answer questions thoroughly and encourage your child to ask and talk about it often, but keep your child's age and likely exposure to this subject in mind. You do not want to say more than is needed.

Look at your own views and what you want to pass on and what you will need to be careful not to pass on. Explain about appropriate public behavior so your child will know if an adult is not behaving properly. Explain why sex is so private and what private parts are (those hidden by a bathing suit) and who may and may not see or touch these. Mention the family doctor as a special exception, since that is often confusing.

Again, your child's age and exposure to these subjects from elsewhere is the question. Two-year-olds and five-year-olds have very different needs, but age is perhaps less important than realizing what your child is learning elsewhere: Does she have the chance to watch television freely or converse alone with other children? What about Internet access to pornography (a very real and serious problem)? Remember, she may not ask questions because she is shocked by what she has learned and wants to deny it, thinks she already knows it all, or is embarrassed that she knows too much.

Parties and playdates at home. Parents and child educators all note how much birthday parties have become a major event and stressor for children. Going to parties is discussed in the next chapter, but when it is time to plan a party for your HSC, plan it in light of *his* temperament, not that of the guests.

The usual suggestion for the size of a birthday party is one to one and a half guests for every year of age, but even that may be too much for an HSC. Consider having a family party, or family plus one special friend. Keep it simple. Be a leader in your community in this regard—quality of interaction is more important than quantity or ostentatiousness or high stimulation.

Involve your child in the planning and preparations, including the amount of time allotted for each activity, so she will be better prepared for these transitions and help you stay on schedule. When the party is over, there will be a letdown and many leftover emotions and events to process. Make this a priority for you over cleaning up. A walk out of doors or a quiet bath may help her calm down while she digests all the experiences.

Do not have a surprise party for a young HSC. I have heard too many stories from sensitive adults about being surprised at this age by a roomful of shouting children. The ungracious, ungrateful birthday child ran crying to his or her room, and the parents, understandably frustrated, added shouting, shaming, and punishments to an already miserable moment.

During the party, remember that this is another learning experience. Your child does not know about parties and party behaviors, so do not expect a flawless performance. Take time-outs during the party if he becomes upset or overwhelmed (go to another room and help him regroup).

Opening presents is a real minefield. Before the party, you can practice smiling and saying thank you. Perhaps make it a game, imagining absurd gifts, and your child having to respond with a polite "thank you" every time, and some appropriate comment that is not a lie. "What a charming boa constrictor, Grandpa. It will look so nice around my neck." Still, as with non-HSCs, when he opens presents he may not react "properly"—that is, hide his disappointment, glee, or consternation ("What *is* this thing?"). Adjust your expectations to your child's age and think back on how it has improved each year.

Compared to parties, playdates are much simpler, of course. Having a child to your house is ideal for an HSC in many ways—everything is familiar, your child feels more in control and has more status, and you can keep an eye on things. But keep playdates short and not too frequent—one a week may be all your HSC wants or needs, even though other young children may be in a social whirl and you are overhearing considerable "who-is-seeing-whom" talk among parents.

A FINAL WORD ABOUT HSCs AT THIS AGE

There is something innocent, trusting, fresh, and funny about this age. Your HSC will make observations that will make you proud, happy, and filled with laughter. Your HSC will love you at this age in a way that never happens again. (I remember the exact moment my son climbed onto my lap to be held for the last time—he was six, actually. I knew it would be the last time and savored it.) Young HSCs are admittedly a great deal of work. But they are so wonderful, too. So embrace these precious years and enjoy yourselves.

Chapter Eight

Toddlers and Preschoolers
Out in the World

Helping Them Feel Successful in New Situations

This chapter offers ways to support your sensitive one- to five-year-old as she enters the world, so she can use her innate wisdom of pausing to check, but then trust life enough to go ahead when the odds are in favor of safety and success. We will consider hesitancy in the face of trying new things, social shyness, going to a preschool, and dealing with realistic fears, all with the goal of preventing discouragement and fearfulness in your sensitive child. In the process, we also discuss choosing a preschool and how the two of you manage your good-byes there.

Y ou may recall Walt, who as an infant crawled to the edge of a blanket, encountered grass, and cried. Not surprisingly, Walt was also vigilant as a toddler when trying new things. At Gymboree, he would watch. In fact, he loved to watch. About when time was up, *then* he wanted to participate. He was not exactly afraid; he just wanted to observe before joining in. If he had witnessed something that scared him, we can guess that he would not have *ever* joined in.

This chapter aims, above all, to help you prevent a child like Walt from becoming fearful of new people and experiences like those encountered at Gymboree at two, other children's birthday parties at three, preschool at four, and kindergarten at five. Then later Cub Scouts, dating, taking one's first job, or going to college.

You will recall from earlier chapters, however, that some HSCs are bold and outgoing—their sensitivity is more sensory, around food, clothing, or noise, or more emotional, in that they can sense what others are feeling. Those with this boldness are probably high in novelty seeking, as discussed in Chapter 3. They are also probably very secure in their attachment to whoever takes care of them, as discussed in Chapter 6. Yet, by definition, all HSCs pause to check to some degree, so this chapter will apply even to this type of child at times, if not always.

THE DIFFERENCES AMONG FEAR OF NOVELTY, FEAR OF STRANGERS, SHYNESS, AND PLAYING ALONE

People used to speak of "shy" children in a very generic way, referring to all timidity or fearfulness, but those studying shy children now see that the fear of novelty and of strangers are quite independent. Thus we will treat them separately in this chapter, as different kinds of fears.

You should also remember that pausing to check before proceeding, the hallmark of the HSC, does not necessarily mean there is any kind of fear, of novelty, strangers, or anything at all. And children who like to play alone at this age are not necessarily shy either. If your HSC is warm and loving with you and involved in active make-believe play, no problem. (If your child is not, I recommend reading Stanley Greenspan's chapter on the self-absorbed child in *The Challenging Child*. If his advice does not help, talk to your pediatrician or seek some professional counseling.) It is true that if children pursue this preference for solitary play past five, they may be seen as odd and then begin to feel truly shy. By truly shy, I mean a tendency to fear being judged and rejected. But this is less common in children under six, so we will not even discuss true shyness until later chapters.

THE NATURE OF FEAR IN NEW SITUATIONS AND HOW TO PREVENT IT

In anyone, fear begets fear—the research on this is clear. Whenever we are faced with a new situation, our evaluating systems decide whether we ought to be afraid. We are more likely to feel fear if our body is already flooded with stress hormones or we have been exposed to frightening things in the past, especially in childhood, before we developed an array of coping skills. When fear goes on too long, a person becomes "hyperexcitable." Then fear can easily develop a life of its own, existing as anxiety without any current threat, and attaching itself to almost every experience that comes along. That kind of anxiety is very difficult to overcome. The prevention of fearfulness is much easier, and prevention in childhood in particular.

Every new situation raises at least three types of questions for the HSC:

1. *"Is it safe to go ahead?"* Will I be hurt or happy? Will I succeed at this or fail? Your child's answer depends on his past experience with similar situations.

2. *"Do I have what it takes to handle it today?"* Is there anyone around to support me? Am I feeling strong and rested? Your child's inner state at the moment and past experiences with encouragement and support from you and others will decide this one.

3. *"Do things usually work out?"* Do I generally succeed in new situations? Is it fun to explore new things, meet new people? The answer here depends on the global impression of life that your child has been building.

How can you influence the answers to these questions? When your HSC pauses to check, as she will do, you want your child to be realistic about the first question, the safety of a given situation, and her likelihood of success. You hope that the facts will dictate here; that she will respond to the situation rather than categorize everything as dangerous. But she may need reassurance about the *mean-*

ing of the situation. If you see a rope and think it is a snake, of course you are afraid. If she sees a dog larger than she is and thinks it is like the wolves and lions she has heard about in stories, of course she needs reassurance. She will need even more reassurance if she is insecure because of a recent separation from you or a frightening experience.

Her answer to the second question—Am I ready?—you can influence more. Give your child every reason to feel secure about your responsiveness to her needs and feelings, in a new situation and at all times. See that your child enters new situations feeling maximally supported by you, and also prepared and fit. When those are not the facts of the situation, realism is also important. She needs to know when she is not ready and wait until she is.

Finally, when answering the third question, how he generally views the world, you want your child to be able to draw on a reservoir of memories of success and pleasure in new situations. Here you can maximally control the reality in which your child lives. Yes, there are some dangers in the world, but there is also an abundance of joy, adventure, and kindness from others waiting for him.

Building Confidence in Preschoolers

The task of building this reservoir of success and pleasure is trickier with an HSC because everyone is likely to be uncomfortable and to fail when overaroused, and for HSCs, at this age especially, new situations are often *very* new—exciting, stimulating, strange, and therefore overarousing. Thus, besides helping your child feel secure and supported, which you do with any child, when your HSC goes out into the world, you have the additional task of making an experience a good one by doing all you can to keep things within her optimal level of arousal.

Of course, not-so-great experiences are bound to happen and are even valuable—from these, with your help, your child learns how to handle adversity and overcome fear of what has upset her. But your

HSC will, by nature, imagine plenty of bad outcomes without there being a large dose of them having actually happened.

It is important to protect your HSC, at this age especially, from truly frightening experiences. This is *not* the age to "throw 'em in and let 'em sink or swim." If a bad experience happens, discuss it *together* and even play it out together, so that you can reassure him this time through or at least bear part of the burden of what happened to frighten him. This will help keep your child from developing a constant state of hyperexcitability by trying to process over and over, on his own, the bad experience, as HSCs can do.

Finally, you will have to balance pushing and protecting. In studies comparing the coping abilities of secure and insecure HSCs (toddler age), the secure HSCs who scored high on competent coping had mothers who were less pushy than the average mom. The mothers of insecure HSCs were intrusive, not allowing their toddlers to use their natural coping style of avoiding overstimulation at first, then approaching slowly. My guess is that all the mothers wanted their children to look competent in front of the experimenters, so they pushed a bit, but the insecure children had insecure, insensitive mothers who really pushed, and the mothers of the secure HSCs pushed about right. In a study of what causes fear in children in general, temperament played a definite role in predicting who would become fearful, but another good predictor was an insensitive, over-controlling parent.

As the parent of an HSC facing a new situation, you will have to walk a fine line between overprotecting and pushing too hard. How do you do it? Use your intuition from your child's body movements, words, tone of voice, and facial expression. Encourage your child when you can tell she really wants to do this thing—that is, wanted to until it was about to happen. We all do that: We are eager for the opportunities provided by taking a trip or giving a talk until it is about to happen. Then we wish we had never agreed to it. But if we do not go ahead, we know we would regret it later. Your child just does not know that yet.

You back off, however, if your child is so nervous, reluctant, over-aroused, or beyond his competence that he is sure to refuse or fail.

When Fear Is Not About Fear, but Anger

Not all fear is straightforward, however. HSCs are usually "internalizers"—their sadness and anger as well as fears go inside, out of sight, rather than being displayed directly. Anger is not as often "acted out" by HSCs through shouting, hitting, lying, or stealing. For example, an HSC may feel angry about a new sibling or being left out of something, and want to do something spiteful. But HSCs can also be afraid of their anger, afraid of doing something mean as well as the punishment for it. So the feelings are buried.

The parents of such a good child feel great. Their child is handling the situation so well—no anger, no trouble at all. Meanwhile, deep inside, perhaps so far in that it is unconscious, their child is preoccupied with badness: "I hate the bad thing that was done to me, I am bad for hating people, I must fight this badness in me. It is *so* dangerous."

Suddenly fears erupt—irrational fears of all kinds of things, like shadows or pinecones or a certain shape or pattern. Neither the parents nor the child have any idea about the connection.

When you suspect your child is being too good, and at the same time is too afraid, encourage the expression of anger. Explore with her why she might be angry—for instance a time when you were angry with her, set limits, or had to leave her. Look for sibling rivalry, too. Encourage your child to talk about these feelings. Sometimes it works magic.

Helping Children Enter New Settings—Planning Ahead

Having discussed fearfulness in a general way, we turn first to avoiding being afraid in new settings, then with new people.

There are many ways to help your HSC enter new situations successfully, without fear. Some involve planning, others involve your response in the moment. We'll begin with planning.

1. *Enlist help.* If there is an adult in charge, consider discussing your child's hesitancy and what role each of you can play in overcoming it. Or bring along a child your child knows, or find out the names of other children involved and have your child meet one of them a few days before, preferably at your home.

2. *Discuss the setting with your child beforehand.* Do not assume your child knows what the beach is like or what happens at an Easter egg hunt. This way your child has no surprises.

3. *Discuss some of the less desirable possible outcomes so that you can discuss how you both will cope.* "How will you feel if you don't find any eggs?"

4. *Mention an easy way to exit or stop the experience.* "If you don't like it, we can just leave."

5. *If it fits the situation, say often, "Maybe it won't work, but who cares?"* In other words, role model risk-taking yourself. Another example of that sort of talk: "Shall we try it? Do we have anything to lose? I don't think so." Or "Sometimes I get pretty scared, too, but then I think, What's the worst that could happen? If it's not much, I go for it."

6. *Try to familiarize your child with some part of the experience ahead of time.* Going on a pony ride? Hang around some horses or ponies a week before, then pet them. Try out the mechanical pony at the market—first just the saddle and stirrups, then the movement. Going to start playing ball? Buy a ball and let your child sleep with it first.

7. *Acknowledge and discuss all of your child's feelings.* "I want to do it." "I'm afraid to do it." "Will you be angry if I don't do it?" "I will be sorry if I don't do it." "I'm so excited and curious." "I do not want all this excitement." Remember, all of these feelings could be present. Do not stop with one.

8. *Again, be sure your child is rested, well fed, and ready to go.* Otherwise, postpone new experiences until he is.

9. *Fan every flicker of enthusiasm,* any interest or eager anticipa-

tion. This is your child's go-for-it system, which works in opposition to the pause-to-check system. Do not exaggerate or try to create such feelings when they are not there; that leads you to being the one always speaking for doing the new experience and your child always being the one against it, when in reality your child has both feelings. In other words, don't be the one saying, "Look, a slide! Won't that be fun?" A cautious child's automatic first response is likely to be, "No way are you going to make me climb that thing."

To avoid this kind of "splitting," you can gently point out whatever enthusiasm your child has shown. "Sounds like you want to try the slide." But if she comes back with her fears, acknowledge those as equally valid. "Yes, it does seem pretty high from down here, doesn't it?" You can also mention similar experiences that your child has liked or aspects of the experience she already knows she likes. "I know you like slides. This one looks a little harder to climb and be up on top of. Then again, a tall slide means a better slide down." Just avoid a debate about it in which you represent "go for it."

10. *Role model enthusiasm for life.* Having things that matter, things to look forward to, small- and medium-size pleasures—these are what make happiness more than huge events. And an important source of these small joys are new experiences, like trying a new restaurant or walking a different street home. The go-for-it system is what makes these fun, and your child has that one, too. Show how to turn it on and use it.

ABOVE ALL, MAKE USE OF BEING ABLE TO TALK

Several parents of HSCs mentioned how much easier it was to deal with their child's hesitations in new situations once their child was old enough to talk about it. Here is an excellent model dialogue that one parent shared with me:

Her son said, "Mom, I'm scared about this swimming lesson."

"Yes, of course you are," she replied. "It's a brand new thing for you." (She acknowledged his fear without shaming him for it.)

"Do you get scared?" he asked.

"All the time." (She explained that fear is normal.)

"What do you do?"

"Well, if I'm afraid of something, but I really know I want to do it, too, or I don't want to be left out, I just try to go ahead and do it." (She role modeled self-regulation.)

She went on to say, "Maybe I can make it easier for myself, like asking somebody else what it was like for them the first time." (She taught coping through sharing feelings, talking to others.)

She added, "If I were having my first lesson, I might even tell the teacher I was nervous." (She taught that there is nothing wrong with asking for help sometimes.) "But even if I couldn't do that, I would try to go ahead, see if I liked it. 'Nothing ventured, nothing gained.' " (She encouraged risk taking.)

Step-by-Step Help for Your Child in a New Situation

1. *Go with your child into the new situation.* Draw her into it. Stay near until your child's mood has changed from caution to pleasure, then step back.

2. *Try to have another child interact with and involve yours*—one who seems kind and friendly, compatible in other ways, or a bit like yours.

3. *Remain available, but do not hover as if expecting to be needed.* If your child calls out for you, match your response to the intensity of the cry for help. Do not rush in. Start with a calm, "Yes?" See if that is enough.

4. *Let your child become involved in small steps,* and protect him from being teased about this. You can remind others that they were probably the same way about something at first.

5. *Talk about mixed feelings being normal.* Maybe describe the first

time you dove off a high board or galloped a horse. If she does refuse to proceed, let her, without shaming her—it will make her less anxious about your reaction next time she is deciding.

6. *Point out that he often does not want to do something at first,* then decides to later—maybe it was like that the first time he entered a pool or got to know a cat. You are helping him find the path back to that happy place of having gone ahead and being glad he did.

7. *Do not become impatient.* Yes, frightened or conflicted children can become demanding, clingy, and irritable, but getting angry back will not help. Focus on your child's fear underneath the annoying behavior. Remember, you are trying to tame a wild thing—a wild, instinctive impulse to flee. A false move now will only add to your child's arousal and ultimately lengthen the time it takes to accomplish what you hope for. And do not force your child or allow anyone else to. You may win that battle but lose the war. How can she feel respected for who she is, or trust you, if you do this? And when children are overwhelmed by fear, that memory is all they will take from an experience anyway.

Following Up on an Excursion into a New Situation

Your goal, of course, is to raise a child who will check out a new situation, as is his nature, but see it realistically, and if it is safe, then to go ahead, anticipating pleasure or success. So after your child's foray, highlight what was positive.

1. *Be sure to point out any success.* Do not exaggerate, gush, or brag in front of others. But be sure she recognizes the fact that she had a successful, enjoyable experience if it was that way. "Did you like the slide? Yes, I thought you did. You were having so much fun it was hard to stop."

2. *Point out progress,* how he was a year ago or a month ago in similar situations. Change is a process, neither an impossibility nor an overnight miracle. "You used to look at slides like that with

such longing, but you never wanted to try one. Today you did. That was great."

3. **Reward the attempt,** not the success or failure. "It's great that you tried going up partway."

4. **Put your child into the role of mentor or teacher,** for a stuffed animal or a younger child. Let her act out how she did what she did, overcame some or all of her fear, and the fun that resulted, so that the whole process is well remembered.

5. **Use this opportunity to encourage fantasies of being in charge,** strong, and confident—hero or heroine fantasies.

FEAR OR HESITATION WITH OTHER CHILDREN AND ADULTS

Now we turn to the second type of fear, that of strangers and new social situations.

Janet would hide her head when strangers came up to her even when she was six months, before she was "supposed to" according to developmental charts. Even when she had not seen her grandparents for a few days, she needed time to get to know them again.

At two, her mother sent her to nursery school, hoping it would help. "It was awfully traumatic," her mother remembers. By Halloween Janet still had not spoken to her teacher. She was allowed to come in costume to school and dressed up as a bunny. From behind her mask, she finally began speaking. Yet her teacher, and all her subsequent teachers, reported that she had high self-esteem and seemed happy. After nursery school she liked kindergarten. She still had trouble talking to her teacher, but she made a close friend that year, one she still has, at nineteen.

It is completely normal for toddler HSCs to be reluctant around unfamiliar people. What you actually see is an ambivalence—the pause-to-check system says "Be careful, this is a new person," but hopefully the go-for-it system says "But people are usually nice to little kids so I will try smiling and see what happens." Some of my best exchanges with strangers have been with children of this age across an airplane aisle.

What you do not want your toddler to be learning from you or others is that most people are dangerous. At the same time, you want to honor your sensitive child's need, if it occurs, to go slowly with some or all strangers. Tell visitors that your child will be friendlier soon if they wait and do not push themselves on him. If he still does not warm up, make some excuse and allow your child to be "shy" with this particular person—he may know more about this person than you do!

Do not allow even close relatives to force themselves on your child before your child is ready. One of my earliest and worst memories is of being used in a skit at a family reunion as the "patty-cake" passed from one relative to another. I felt terrified, powerless, and betrayed by all these adults who did this in spite of my protests.

Can a child be "too" friendly? Not at this age. There is so much concern about kidnapping and child abuse that many parents tense every time their child interacts with a stranger, all in an effort to avoid what is statistically quite unlikely to happen. Your little HSC can sense very well what you think the odds are of strangers being dangerous, so do not communicate higher odds than there are. When she is older, you can teach her not to get into cars with strangers and what boundaries adults should not cross. At this age, you are the one who should be keeping an eye out for dangers, not her. But try not to make your watchfulness noticeable to her. When you or other trusted adults are around, your friendly child should be able to go on assuming that interacting with strangers is safe.

Social Hesitancy May Be Normal, but Do Not Ignore It

All the research I have read on preventing shyness at later ages makes the same point: help a socially hesitant child join in at this age, when not doing so is less of a stigma. At later ages, being a loner will create real reasons for shyness. While these researchers may be biased because of an interest in "curing" shyness or a belief that everyone should be outgoing, they are right that social confidence is highly admired in our culture. A small dose of sociability, or at least the ability to turn it on when needed, is invaluable. It gives you choices.

Further, it is important to remember that we are all social beings. All children are calmer and more secure in the presence of the *right* others, even if it is just one person they play quietly beside. And even if one's preference is to have a few close friends, one still has to meet a large number of people in order to select out those special few.

Megan Gunnar, a child psychologist at the University of Minnesota, studied the cortisol level of schoolchildren over a year's time. The children who plunged in, including those who were quite reluctant but did anyway, had high levels at first, while those who held back were clearly less stressed. But by the end of the year, the ones who had gone ahead had lower levels of cortisol, and those who had persisted in playing alone now had higher levels, never having overcome their fears, so that they were now isolated and without social support.

The bottom line: To prevent your child from suffering later, you may have to cause a *little* "trauma" now. You need to help your socially hesitant child enter a social group and join in. Or again, you can let a savvy preschool teacher help you with this task—some of them are quite good at it. These first social experiences are important. And again, do not worry: Social hesitancy at this age is normal and not at all a sign of trouble, unless it is allowed to continue and develop at a later age into persistent, active withdrawal.

What to Do in Order to Prevent or Reduce a Fear of Strangers

First, if you yourself are cautious around others, your child will imitate that. So once again, you will have to be the role model. Work on your own shyness a little by bringing people into your home; try to speak with strangers in a relaxed way.

Now, let's look at what not to do, which is exactly what I did. When our son was born, we lived on a remote island in British Columbia. We were in Paris from the time he was three months old to when he was one year and three months, then returned to the island. He was healthy and had had most of his shots, so we did not have to go to town with him again—two ferries and two car rides away—until he was almost three. On that trip to the pediatrician, he saw another child and asked me nervously, "What's that? Why is that person so short?"

"Gee," I innocently mused, "I wonder if we should have tried to get him to the homes of some other children?"

All this was before anyone realized small children need others of their kind to play beside. When we left the island and he started preschool, you can be sure he watched a long, long time before joining in.

But you can do better. It can be especially important with HSCs to begin social experiences with other children early, but to make them HSC-friendly, which means calm and brief. And be choosy. Select the right children (and accompanying adults). I am sure you would not spend time with just any adult because he or she happened to be your age. Why should your child? Keep searching for the right children and settings for your particular HSC.

You might begin by getting together with one other parent who has a child your child's age. (The child can be a little younger if this will give your child confidence, or older if the child is nurturing toward younger children.) If the two children play well together, bring them together often. Then you can expand to play groups in which mothers and toddlers are together in the same room. In that setting you can see how your child is doing and he has you nearby.

Next, try other activities—perhaps a music, art, or tumbling class—with parents on the sidelines. But again, be sure the group has a nice feeling to it. Even one bully or distressed child can make a group unpleasant, so expect to be selective.

Of course, some of you will be sending your HSC to child care or preschool very early out of necessity. So let's consider the advantages to your situation.

The Importance of Some Preschool Experience

Preschool is an excellent way to help a child enter the social world outside the home and prepare for the major transition of going to kindergarten. Janet's mother always wondered if she was right to send her daughter to nursery school so soon. While two might be a little young, the teachers I interviewed emphasized that parents should definitely send HSCs to a preschool, *as long as it's one that works well with such children.* The reason they all gave was that, without preschool, kindergarten is just too difficult for HSCs. Further, while parents may feel a sensitive child should only go two days a week, the teachers find HSCs do better going every day, even if for a short time, so that they have a routine and do not have to make the transition between whole days at home and at school, losing some of the advantage of habit and familiarity.

Step-by-Step Help for Your Child in a New Social Setting or with Strangers

As with other new experiences, you want your child looking forward to being with others. Therefore, when your HSC does not do well with a particular child, do not try to push it—HSCs do not always mix well with extreme non-HSCs or those who are very stressed. He will have to get along with them later, but why start with the toughest cases?

When entering new situations, like the ubiquitous birthday parties, adapt all the points mentioned above for entering other kinds of new settings and situations. Discuss ahead of time the social setting, who will be there; when your child likes another child, be sure to encourage that relationship; mention the good times she has had with another child when introducing a new playmate—"it could be that much fun again." And remember those steps: go with your child, then step back, stay available, then disappear when everything is fine. And again, keep these social times brief so that when they end your child is still wanting more and will want to go back. In addition:

1. *Plan.* Think about how to make a given social situation easier for your child. Perhaps you and your child can go early and help set up. Feeling like an "insider" when others arrive can help a great deal. Plan to leave early, too, before he's tired and drops out of things, then feels left out.

2. *Practice.* Role-play, do some make-believe, about how to enter, what to say in response to questions, what to ask or talk about. Start with a clever response to what *every* adult asks. "I'm five and I'm in kindergarten. What was your favorite grade?" Try to make this fun and funny, not heavy. If your child has an unusual interest or pet, she will probably relax when she gets a laugh for asking, "Would you like to know what brontosauruses ate for breakfast?" Or when she says, "This is a nice cat. I have a dog named Pippie and he eats snails."

3. *Enlist the help of your friends.* Encourage your adult friends to talk alone with your child. Nothing gives a child confidence like holding the attention of an adult. But coach them not to ask too many questions. A study of reticent children during kindergarten show-and-tell found that when adults ask children questions, children actually talk less. It seems that questions are a bit of a power issue, at least for a child—an adult's question decides the topic and often implies the answer as well. Teachers think asking questions saves time, but it actually takes more time to coax a few words out through questions than to be patient.

Adults are not to blame; it's how we talk. In adult conversations, silences of more than two seconds are infrequent and awkward. But when teachers were trained to stay silent with children for longer than they would with adults, the children talked more.

Comments that do help are personal ones, such as "I once had a cat, too. It was black so we called her Mystery." Then wait. And use any nonverbal means you can to show you are listening and interested.

4. *Enlist the help of other children.* Sometimes it's possible to encourage a kind, socially confident child to initiate a conversation and help your child in. Pairing your child with a younger one and letting your child be the social leader can also build confidence.

5. *Be social yourself.* Invite your friends over and express enthusiasm about your friendships.

6. *Find just the right setting to launch your child alone into social life,* which leads to our next topic.

CHOOSING AN HSC-FRIENDLY PRESCHOOL, DAY CARE, OR NURSERY SCHOOL

All day care centers and preschools are not created equal, obviously. Remember Alice from the last chapter? Hers understood sensitivity. Others won't. So you have to ask questions; you have to go and observe. Your first criteria is a setting that is not too noisy or crowded, that is soothing rather than highly stimulating (and, of course, one that promotes values similar to yours or those you admire). Such a setting will help your child stay in his optimal level of arousal while tackling social life. Groups should be small and the facilities well-kept.

After considering the environment and resources, mention your child's sensitivity to the teachers. Some will think your child must be a problem, others will think, "Yeah, yeah, all parents think their kid is special and different." Watch for the teacher who *gets it,* or at least seems willing to listen. Be sure at this point that almost everything you say about the trait is positive.

Especially if your child is socially hesitant, ask how the teachers would handle a child who does not join structured groups or does not play with other children. You should hear an attitude of letting the child take some time, then initiating small steps to help the child join as he feels ready. Perhaps he will be allowed to play first only with the teacher or with one child, then the teacher adds another. Perhaps a group of two can be formed, then of three, then of four.

Observe for the first thirty minutes to two hours, and do this for several days. If your enroll your child, you may still want to stay in the car or somewhere nearby for a few days, so the teachers can find you if she is not adjusting well.

Separating at Preschool

Preschool, nursery school, or day care is usually when your child first experiences daily separations from you. You want these, also, to be successful and routine and *not* memorable. Leaving him at a preschool loaded with toys he has never seen before, a place both of you have observed together for a while, is a good place to begin—after some previous trial stays with grandparents, other relatives, or good friends who are experienced with children and fond of yours.

1. *Talk about the separation,* so it does not come as a surprise. But match your emotional tone to your child's, being matter of fact unless she expresses sadness or dismay. Then indicate you will feel some of the same, and how you will cope.

2. *Talk about what you will be doing while you are separated* (nothing too exciting—"I'll be talking on the phone" or "cleaning the kitchen") and what you will do when you are back together, so your child can experience your continuing existence and relationship.

3. *Let your child take something from home as comfort,* maybe something of yours or a picture of you to keep in his pocket or "cubby."

4. *Come back early the first time, keep the time short.* Point out often that you will come back, that you did come back.

5. *Say exactly when you will be back, in terms of her schedule*—"after your rest time."

6. *Have a special good-bye routine or ritual.* Maybe invent a special

handshake or hug and a comforting or funny saying you leave each other with: "Don't eat any slugs" or "Keep your grin on."

7. *Check to see if your child is crying for more than five minutes after you leave.* Call when you get to work, or have another parent who came later call you. If the crying continues for more than fifteen minutes or happens throughout the day for several weeks, it may be too soon for your child to be left. But crying can also be part of the good-bye ritual, especially for slow-to-adapt kids. Follow your instincts. Is the child who cried in the morning coming home thrilled and happy? If not, you might want to keep her at home a little longer or shorten the stay, or look at the school. Are there too many children or too much noise for an HSC? Give it at least a week, provided you feel the school is warm and nurturing.

8. *Once your child is used to your leaving, keep your departures firm, cheerful, and short.* You do not want your child picking up on any ambivalence in you. And make the coming-and-going times regular.

9. *Do not rush a separation either.* A well-paced departure from home and departure by you at school keeps the arousal low and leaves enough time for the adjustment.

10. *Remember, returning home is another transition.* Make coming home enjoyable. Have your child use the toilet before leaving— he may not have been aware of the need. Talk in the car about what happened at preschool. Have a snack waiting if your child could be hungry or thirsty—again, HSCs may not be aware of their needs until they are back in a quieter environment. And a snack is a nice transition ritual.

11. *Spend time at the school now and then,* letting your child show you what she does there so that both of you can talk about it at home. This helps to integrate the two worlds.

WHEN YOUR PRESCHOOL-AGED CHILD
ENCOUNTERS SOMETHING WORTH FEARING

While caution about new places and people is easily soothed, in-evitably your child will hear about or experience something truly frightening. When this occurs, you must face your child's fear. Do not just hope it will go away by not talking about it, even if you feel afraid, too, or guilty that you could not prevent your child's anxiety. If you have feelings about what happened, work them through with another adult first. Then talk with your child.

1. *During your discussion of what frightened your child, do not say more than is needed.* This is one reason why you want to deal with your feelings first, so you are not sharing your own worries with your child. On the other hand, she may already be imagining what happens during an airplane crash, or when calves are slaughtered, or to a child who was kidnapped, and if these fantasies are pro-ceeding, better to get them into the open. So start by asking what she knows, believes, or imagines about the feared thing.

2. *Let your child express his emotions thoroughly.* Once the images are out, you still need to hear how all of that makes him *feel*. You want fear to be something your child can share with you so he doesn't have to bear it alone. Do not minimize fear or shame your child for feeling it.

3. *Explain how you handle this fear.* If there are precautions you have taken to be prepared for a disaster or to keep out intruders, de-scribe these—this teaches active coping. Explain what you do about fear you can't control—this teaches self-soothing and self-regulating. For example, "I tell myself I can't control everything, but the chances of that happening are so small that I will not worry about it." Or "When the airplane shakes like this in the air pockets so much that it scares me, I tell myself I am feeling God's hands, and whatever God wants to do with the plane, I accept." Speak of the fear of the uncontrollable as something everyone must either face down or be shackled by.

4. *Clear up misconceptions about what can happen and the odds of it happening.* Explain why there are no tornados or earthquakes in your area. If your child is old enough to understand, give her a lesson in odds—flip a coin over and over, looking for eight heads in a row. Explain those are the odds of the feared thing happening.

5. *If the fear is one that can be reasonably overcome, plan a gradual exposure and desensitization.* Your child does not have to overcome *every* fear, but learning how to do it with some fears is a good idea. First, you might read books about the feared things— airplanes, spiders, snakes, dogs. Then tell cheerful stories about them, gradually adding more of the elements your child fears. Then imagine experiencing these things together. Then go look at some. Then touch them. (However, extreme fear of spiders, snakes, and heights is probably inherited and harder to modify, although not impossible. For snakes, when you begin seeing the actual animal, obviously you start at the reptile section of a zoo or pet store, not in the wild.)

6. *Watch for fears your child is embarrassed to mention.* Try saying, "A lot of people fear . . ." Or "At your age, I feared . . . How about you?"

7. *Neutralize the fear of violence from others with the goodness that others can do.* Perhaps you can introduce your child to a kindly police officer or school security person and let him learn how hard these people work to keep children safe. Protect your child from hearing frightening news stories in particular, but if he does, discuss it right away. Role model a balanced, rational response: "This is rare, this is not what people are usually like."

8. *If you worry about criminal violence, take a course or study up on how to keep you and your children from being victims* so that you can feel you have done all you can. Then try to relax. Your HSC will sense your fears.

9. *If your child does witness an upsetting event such as an automobile accident or a house fire, or has one happen to her, let the trauma be*

played out over and over, preferably in your presence or that of a therapist so you can provide the containing, calming environment your child could not maintain when it happened. The feelings do heal, but be sure to get support yourself for your own feelings about it. And do not underestimate the effects on a child of events that adults are used to—for example, medical procedures, a hospital visit or stay, a long separation from home, or the loss of a pet or favorite toy. Some things may be far more traumatic for your child than they would be for you.

A FINAL WORD

Remember, being highly sensitive does not mean being fearful. Yes, the range of conditions in which HSCs can grow up bold and adventuresome are narrower, because they study every situation more carefully and sense danger more readily. Thus what they experience and how they are raised matters more, which makes your role important and rewarding. You are establishing for your child not only courage in the face of uncertainty but an attitude toward life itself— it is usually safe to trust, worth trusting, and good to be alive.

Chapter Nine

School-Age HSCs at Home

Resolving Problems

This chapter helps you cope with the issues that arise with school-age HSCs (ages five to twelve) at home, especially the events that involve the most change and stimulation, such as moves and holidays. We also consider the rarer occurrence of anxiety and depression, and minimizing the overall stress level for everyone in your family, which is also one of the best ways to prevent problems with your HSC at home. Finally, we work with the more difficult HSCs, the minority—those drama queens and pint-size rebels who can be so intense, active, distracted, opinionated, fussy, and irritable that you wonder if this is normal or what further help you need.

SCHOOL AGE—THE TALENTS UNFOLD

Before plunging into potential problems, let's again take stock of some of the joys of raising an HSC, since school age is when these come into full flower. Parents are usually thoroughly enjoying their HSC's curiosity, creativity, and unusual insights about the world. Their child may be unfolding surprising talents in fields such as music, drawing, math, or the study of nature. Many HSCs take up "adult" endeavors such as chess or start their own tiny "business."

For example, Nancy is not an extrovert, but when she has an idea for making money, she can seem like one. When she was seven she made popsicle-stick figures and sold them door-to-door, her mother standing out on the sidewalk. At ten, she writes stories and sells them the same way.

Increasingly, HSCs self-regulate—they pause to check, think about the consequences of their own cautiousness, and decide to go ahead in unexpected ways that solve their difficulties on their own. Catherine, who had never been away from home and does not like meeting new people, had an opportunity to go to France as an exchange student when she was in fifth grade. The few years before had been difficult for her due to ear infections that led to protracted dental work, plus poor teachers in third and fourth grade, so that she was throwing up at the thought of the dentist and was referred to a child psychologist to help her survive tests at school. Yet Catherine was adamant about going to France; she just knew she should. So her parents allowed it, and their daughter was right—the family she stayed with was wonderful. As a high school student she still sees them and has been to France three times since. It seems that even at that early age she was starting to think deeply after she paused to check, and to gain confidence about her own choices.

Parents will also begin to notice their child's awareness of the emotional tone of the family and considerateness of others. For example, when Catherine was three, her brother was born with Down's syndrome and other severe medical problems, so that Catherine's mother was taking him to the doctor almost daily for several years. This affected everyone in the family, of course, but most of all the overwhelmed mother. One day, getting ready for another doctor visit, she was so exhausted that she actually could not find her young son! She sat and cried while Catherine, age five, searched for her brother, who was under the blankets in the bed. Then Catherine sat down with her mother and said, "It's going to be okay, Mother. We're going to be a family." According to Mom, her daughter's words were the turning point for her, the moment when she realized that if her daughter could be that courageous and uplifting, so could she.

But what if your HSC is more trouble than solace? No problem. You are not alone. Later in this chapter you will meet Dinah the drama queen and Chuck the pint-size rebel. Both of whom are HSCs.

YOUR SCHOOL-AGE HSC AT HOME

There are a few problems that may arise at this age that deserve mention. So we'll start by considering the routine issues, moving on to those that are not daily matters but still common, and finally we will consider anxiety and depression, which your HSC may never develop.

Dressing, bedtime, chores, manners, and other daily practices. HSCs generally thrive on order or at least the calm that results from it. With younger school-age children you can have routines, rules, and rewards that help form good habits: "After you have gotten dressed, eaten, and done your chores, you can do whatever you want before we leave for school." Post a list of what has to be done to be ready for school or bed, so that your child can check off each step. After a few weeks it will become habit and you only need to ask, "How are you doing on your checklist?"

Once the habits are established, as a preparation for adulthood, try to shift the responsibility of the smaller matters onto your child as soon as she can handle it (the age to begin varies with the child and the responsibility). Let your child decide what to eat, when to go to bed, what clothes to wear, and even when to wash them or put them in the wash. Then the consequences of not going to bed on time or keeping clothes neat will be taught by life, not by your lectures or discipline, which may seem arbitrary without those life lessons.

In some areas, of course, you may have valid reasons for your strong opinions and therefore strong standards. Sleep is likely to be one of these. HSCs need plenty of sleep; it is part of their down time. If you consistently find your child is not choosing to sleep enough, you may have to return to insisting on an early bedtime and wait a few years for your child to see the connection between sleep and mood.

When it comes to helping around the house, parents usually have to take a different tack. I like the method of family meetings (even for a family of two), especially when there's an HSC in the family who needs to express himself and also find ways to compromise about the preferences of others. In these meetings, everyone agrees on what needs to be done and how the work is to be divided, and if anyone fails to fulfill his or her agreement, there are consequences agreed upon ahead of time by all, related to the failure, and mainly involving making reparations to those affected.

For example, everyone in the family can probably agree that parents are not the only ones who should have to take out the trash, which is produced by everyone, and that not taking out the trash when it's your chore should lead to having to do it two weeks in a row. It should not lead to being grounded or no TV, especially if a parent decides that after the fact and without discussing it with the group—in that case you are teaching how to live under tyranny, not in a democratic group.

Reasonable good manners toward each other can also be agreed upon this way. If everyone in the family agrees that name calling or swearing at another family member is hurtful, a consequence might be a spoken apology and a short written note, to be read at the next family meeting, about why it happened and how the person will avoid that situation in the future. Be sure such consequences are applied to everyone, parents included.

Some issues will require lengthy negotiations and may not seem worth it—unless you consider the real learning to be gained. For example, your HSC wants a quiet house, without yelling; her brother wants to whoop it up when the mood strikes him and feels a good shouting match clears the air. What matters far more than how quiet the house will be is the opportunity for both sides to practice voicing their opinions and listening respectfully to another's, then finding a creative, mutually satisfying solution. With this practice, conflicts can come to seem okay, or even almost good, because family members become closer in the end.

If your HSC does not keep an agreement, it may have been about a matter that was too difficult for him to adhere to. For example, fascination with a new friend or activity may suddenly be making it just too tempting to stay out past the time he was expected home. When an agreement is not kept, always ask why before imposing the consequence. Listen for the story underneath the excuses. You will still impose the consequence, but you may also agree to revise the agreement.

Fighting. This is the age when fighting among siblings and friends can reach a fever pitch. HSCs can be insightfully blunt, and when overstimulated or "pushed to the wall," can strike out with words or blows. Be firm in keeping your standards—for example, no aggression. (I define aggression as words or deeds intended to hurt another, whereas anger is a strong message to stop hurting *me*. Anger establishes my boundary, "go farther and I hurt," but aggression transgresses another's.)

Always begin by giving the two parties, but especially your HSC, twenty minutes of down time. This is *not* a punishment; it is a chance to get calm and think things over. Then bring the two back together to discuss what happened. Try to role model the search for truth and justice and the desire to make amends.

Again, as I said about family disputes generally, the goal is not merely peace but that children learn the principles of negotiating and, if it comes to it, the rules of fair fighting: no name calling, no blaming, stick to the current conflict (not, "You always cheat" or "This serves you right for not doing the dishes last night."). You calm down and then discuss the basic problem, negotiate solutions, listen to each other's position, take turns talking, and try to get to win-win. As I discussed in Chapter 4, until they have these skills, do not abandon two children to fight it out.

Avoid saying that each is equally to blame if you do not know this.

HSCs find it especially difficult to be treated unfairly by parents; they may begin to feel hopeless about being able to get help when they need it, and instead resort to submitting too much or dominating the other child. If fights happen often with a particular friend, try to find out why.

Holidays. Keep these simple and meaningful rather than major productions. Keep visitors under control—not too many, and especially not many "drop ins." *Require* no more than a polite "hello" from your HSC, no matter how aggressive the guest. But *encourage* your child to enjoy visitors, and invite those he likes often.

Holidays are very exciting, especially if they involve gifts, costumes, or special house guests. When there is a spiritual meaning to an event, be careful not to overload your child with its significance or with too much drama or details—give her what she can appreciate this year; the rest can wait for other years. Establish family holiday rituals and routines—HSCs usually enjoy these and traditions make the unusual time of year familiar and soothing rather than just exciting. In short, your HSC will enjoy holidays more if you keep her in her optimal level of arousal by maintaining established or special holiday routines rather than making it new and exciting or increasing her anticipation of surprises and unpredictable gifts to the point that she cannot eat or sleep. It happens to HSCs easily.

Moving. Randall's family moved when he was in first grade. At the new house, Randall kept trying to go to his old room in the old house. He wanted his new room to be *exactly* the same. A little boy across the street would come and ask him to play, but Randall would not go out of the house for months, and when he did he needed a certain videotape to be playing or he could not stay. (The two mothers still laugh about this.) You can imagine how much Randall was trying to keep everything the same, to control his overstimulation, in spite of a huge upheaval in his life.

I wish certain HSCs did not ever have to move. They are a bit like cats, very tied to their territory. They know every mark on the wall in the house, every tree and plant in the yard, personally. They have a feel for the neighborhood for miles around them. Moving them is like transplanting a well-rooted old tree. You do not do it lightly.

If a move is necessary, allow plenty of time for making it work for your HSC. Try to take your child many times to the new neighborhood and home. Before and after the move, take your child to places similar to those at home—similar parks, libraries, even stores. Pack your child's room last and unpack it first. Do not throw out things now. Arrange her furniture and belongings the same as before unless she *wants* a change. Pack a special box of "comfort objects," including her pillow, that can be easily found when you arrive. Let her help you pack it.

Moving day itself is stressful for everyone, so plan what will be best for all of you—to have your HSC present enough of the time to understand the reality of what is happening and maybe to participate and help, or to have him somewhere else for the actual moving day.

Throughout the move, from conception to long after it, talk about what she's feeling, what you're feeling. Explain that grief and regrets are absolutely normal (although you must try not to burden your HSC with too many of yours). "Even when you move from a hut to a palace, you miss the hut a little bit." But you also want to emphasize all the pluses about the palace.

Watch your own stress level, temper, and grief. Stick to routines like family meals, story times, and time for playing catch or whatever you usually do with your child. They will help you as well as your HSC.

Anxiety, depression. It is a fact that when HSCs are under stress—such as not having a single good friend at school, living with a family member who is seriously ill, or there not being enough money because a parent cannot find a job—they are prone to develop anxiety and depression (now seen to be closely linked). Some HSCs will also sink into depression as they realize and try to cope with the terrors and griefs associated with life itself—their growing awareness of the real dangers all around us and the losses that can happen. If your child develops either anxiety or depression, do not assume it is your fault. And even if you have in some way added to your child's stresses, you probably did not have a choice about what you did and certainly did not have a choice about having a sensitive child who would be particularly vulnerable. What matters now is how you play the hand your family has been dealt.

As we discussed in Chapter 7, fears can easily mushroom into permanent anxiety, so you want to reduce fears as much as you can. Fortunately, at this age, your child can understand much more. You can emphasize the small odds of anything dire actually happening. As for that small but real risk (remember, HSCs hate risks), one of the biggest tasks for a sensitive person is to live courageously with a full awareness of the unpleasant possibilities in life. HSCs cannot deny these as well as others can. So you must help with the courage. Do not dismiss the fears, but show how one lives with them reasonably.

At some point, your HSC may show not only unusual anxiety but depression as well, often following a period of anxiety or stress. The signs of depression are sleeplessness or sleeping all the time, lack of energy, lack of pleasure or interest in anything, loss of appetite, or, especially in children, excessive irritability, a sudden increase in misbehavior or "acting out," or a dramatically new level of withdrawal. To qualify as depression (not merely a depressed mood), it must be present most of the day, nearly every day, for two weeks. However, a depressed person can seem fine with others. Only close family members may notice the marked change. Depression is quite common with HSCs; several parents I interviewed mentioned it. They also immediately brought up medications.

I am so glad that I did not have to raise a child when antidepressants were available. My son's moods were intense, but we managed without. Today, parents of HSCs face tough decisions if their child develops persistent anxiety, depression, or irritability. I recommend that you become very knowledgeable about all sides of the issue before you make a decision, so that at least you will not feel misled later. Most of what doctors know about any medication comes from the companies that manufacture them, and those who manufacture medications to handle childhood behavior problems are seeing a large market unfolding. Therefore the drawbacks are often not discussed, and probably not known anyway. But no one can predict the effect of certain medications on developing minds—no children taking antidepressants (or Ritalin) have lived their life span so that they could be compared to those who did not.

Given this lack of research, and the fact that you might hear more of the pros than the cons, I would go slow and try other approaches first, such as temperament counseling for you to see if you can alleviate your child's stress by improving the fit between your parenting and your child's overall temperament traits. You can also visit a child psychologist by yourself or with your spouse to consider what else is happening in the family or yourself that might be affecting your child. If acting alone does not help, bring your child in for therapy, but do so only as a last resort, since at this age children have difficulty understanding why they are being treated and may feel even more anxious and depressed about whatever you seem to have begun to see as an abnormality.

Remember, too, that the short-term effects of medications can be so helpful that, while they are not exactly addicting, they can become difficult to give up because of a fear of the problem returning. So it is important to remember that most HSCs will become a little anxious or depressed at times, for short periods (less than the two-week criterion). Especially if there is an obvious reason, such as a disappointment, loss, or rejection, and if the mood does not last too long or greatly interfere with schoolwork, then it is probably better to let children learn to manage their moods without medication. Learning and doing what it takes to change one's mood develops with practice. Without these skills, they may be taking medications for life, and we do not know the effects of that at all.

Another approach is to use a small amount of medication, bring the child to where the moods are manageable but still there (instead of the usual goal of removing all symptoms) so they can be worked with. Remember that your advice and role modeling can be the best therapy. You might try to find a professional who can coach you in teaching your child "behavior management" or "mood management." For example, you can teach your HSC to handle a depressed or anxious mood. First acknowledge the feeling itself and express empathy. For example, "You seem a little beaten down by things today. It's hard sometimes, isn't it?" Then you might explore the cause if it is not obvious. "Did something upset you this evening?" Try to convey that you are not being nosy, but that understanding the source of a mood can help in finding a way to relieve it.

Once you have empathized and understood a bit, there are several actions you can teach your child to take rather than just accepting the mood passively. One is to check out the reality of the upsetting event: "Why don't you ask your father if he's angry with you?" Another is to think more about what happened, reframing it: "You didn't win this time, but you don't usually play with older kids who have played checkers many, many times." Or you can at least plan to avoid the mood in the future: "I don't know about you, but I make a point of not watching movies like that. Someone made it up, and I guess some people like that sort of stuff. Or they can keep in mind that it's 'just a movie.' But I know a lot of people who avoid movies like that. I sure do."

When working on the cause of the mood does not readily resolve it, as in the movie instance, or the mood persists, you can suggest some of the following:

• *Encourage your child to think about what usually helps her mood, or might, and do that, even if she doesn't feel like it.* "I know you feel like just lying on the couch. But maybe a walk (bath, some time off, some time with a friend, a talk with your dad) would help. Probably it isn't very appealing, but I know I sometimes feel better after doing something I usually like—you know, something nice for myself—even when I didn't want to at first. Times like that, I almost have to force myself."

- *Hint that moods do change on their own and initiating a transition may bring that change sooner.* "Maybe it will seem better in the morning (after you eat, after you get up and take a bath)."
- *Encourage problem solving.* "Let's see if we can think of a way to make this easier for you."
- *Encourage seeking help.* "Perhaps one of us should talk to your teacher (counselor, principal) about this. What do you think?"

Notice what helps your child the most, point this out to her, and see if she implements it on her own next time. Your place is that of a person who can witness her moods and take an active role in their management. Your suggestions will often be ignored or rejected, and that's okay. You may well see them used next time.

Please do not assume now that I am antimedication. Especially if there are unusual stressors impacting your child, or the moods and fears do not stop, these can have their own physiological effects on a developing mind. So medications may be necessary, and how wonderful it is that they are available. Mainly, try to be informed. Get several opinions, or use a team of experts, as described in Chapter 1. Just remember that all the research points to medication being more effective when it is paired with some change in the child's environment or coping skills.

REDUCING THE STRESS IN YOUR HOME

While discussing medical visits in Chapter 8, I mentioned the crucial finding from two different studies that HSCs are healthier and have fewer injuries than other children when their stress level is tolerable. If you decide to keep your HSC healthy and happy by reducing the stress around him, you can look forward to your child's needs changing your entire family for the better. I am sure you do all you can already to protect your family from harmful and somewhat controllable stresses such as accidents, illness, and family dysfunction. There are other stresses we cannot control very much at all—threats from the outside such as the death of a beloved grandparent or news of a terrorist attack. We can only try to protect our children from too much exposure to these threats too early, discuss the risks realistically if they come up, explain what is being done to protect the community, role model how we cope ourselves, and acknowledge that life is not always easy and sometimes requires courage.

What most of us consider less often is the stress that accompanies all of life's opportunities and expectations. Humans today have endless opportunities. We can call anyone anywhere. On the Internet we can learn anything. If we really want to, we can travel anywhere in the world, learn almost any career or skill, and supposedly become any kind of person. Wealthy, famous, wise, spiritual, artistic. You name it. Short on money? Take another part-time job, earn another degree. You can do anything. Or that is the impression we receive, and in our eagerness to help our children, that is the impression we may give them. "You can be anything, do anything. Dare to dream." And so on.

Meanwhile, your HSC will have her own temptations to overdo: Video games, television, and the Internet will offer endless opportunities to learn and be entertained, opportunities often explicitly designed to be as stimulating and alluring to children as possible. Schools will keep offering more and so will after-school organizations (replacing quiet reading or play in the wild places such as a wood, vacant lot, or down by the river, which might have soothed children a bit).

In fact, our minds can conceive anything, but our bodies cannot do everything, and it happens that your HSC will be able to do just a little bit less than others of even the nicest activities and opportunities. Fewer playdates, fewer sports, fewer kids' activities. But almost everyone is trying to do too much these days. HSCs will respond merely a little sooner to stress, warning the others that it will soon be too much for anyone.

Assessing the Stresses in Your HSC's Life

Parenting expert Mary Kurcinka has noted a lengthy list of some of
the stressors in *any* child's life, many of which we do not think
about. We have already discussed birthday parties, travel, holidays,
moves, and medical procedures, plus all the stress of school life,
whether it comes in the form of opportunities or disappointments.
But there is also bad weather, which can keep children housebound
or make going out more nerve-racking, plus weather-related events
such as floods and tornados. There are news stories that are upsetting. And most children play with other children, leading to inevitable upsetting conflicts, tensions around sharing, and the fear of
being teased, rejected, bullied, or wrongly blamed.

Every child also faces the stress of having to let go of childhood
and its comforts, to sooth oneself without them; to learn about pain
and death, not to mention the inevitability of adulthood, however
that looks to them. Finally, there are growth spurts, which happen
about every six months in the early years and last four to six weeks.
As Kurcinka says about these, "The only thing you can really do is
maintain your standards, nurture more, and wait it out. Growth
spurts disappear as suddenly as they appear. One day you realize
your child has achieved a whole new level of skills. The monster is
gone, replaced by a very enjoyable kid."

Now add to these hidden but normal stresses the stress of being
so sensitive to the subtleties and deeper consequences of events, and
of being different from other children. Your HSC may not say "I am
stressed" in exactly those words, but you can read the message in
these behaviors:

- Acting younger again—having trouble with skills that had been
  mastered, like toilet use, getting dressed, or separations (especially true during growth spurts)
- Little things becoming major problems
- Exaggerated emotions—unusual fear, sadness, or irritability

- More physical problems—asthma or allergy attacks, headaches, stomachaches, catching more colds
- Difficulty sleeping, nightmares, oversleeping
- Clinging to you more
- Isolating—hiding in closets, staying indoors

Avoiding or Reducing Stress, Short-Term

There are both short-term and long-term strategies for reducing stress. Most of these I have already mentioned elsewhere, but here I am reminding you to put the short-term ones into practice as soon as you are aware that your HSC is overburdened.

1. *Arrange for your child to have frequent breaks; allow for down time.* Plan quiet times throughout the day for your HSC (and for yourself). Do this to prevent a stress response as well as to handle one after it happens.

2. *Be more nurturing,* during stressful times and all the time, by touching, holding, soothing to sleep, and listening with total acceptance; by providing healthy and satisfying food, sound sleep, time in nature or with animals, and time in or near water. It is no surprise, but research indicates that reactions to the same stress is lower in rats and monkeys receiving good maternal care.

3. *Make the protection of your HSC's sleep a top priority.* The next day is influenced by this more than almost anything else. Chronic sleep loss is extremely hard on HSCs.

4. *Bring in the familiar,* especially during an unusual event. Maintain your routines, bring out familiar toys, play the usual games, go back to places that are old favorites.

5. *Reduce decisions.* I have encouraged giving HSCs decisions in general, but reduce the choices when your child is already overloaded. For example, if she is anxious about what will happen in school, being asked what she wants for breakfast may be too much. So offer what you know would probably be her choice. Then all she has to decide is if she wants that or not. If you sus-

pect even that will be too much, merely check to be sure she is happy with you deciding today. But familiar, easy choices are sometimes stress reducers, too—the sense of control over some aspects of her life can be just what she needs.

6. *Once things are a little better, figure out how this overstressed state might be avoided in the future.*

Reducing Stress, Long-Term

Equally important as managing short-term stress is making long-term adjustments to your family style and your HSC's life experience. Here are some suggestions, although you can probably think of many more that would apply to your family.

1. *Let things become routine,* habitual, or preplanned for both you and your child. This reduces decisions and surprises (there will still be plenty). For example, have meals at the same times, set the table the same way. Plan together, when that makes sense, the menus for the week's meals, the outfits to wear, the errands to be done. Look at the week's calendar to see if anything conflicts or if too much has been planned. Have a daily schedule, at least for weekdays.

2. *Be together.* Humans are social animals, and being together soothes us. Consider whether more of the things you need to do can be done together, like getting dressed in the same room, or your answering e-mail while your child colors beside you. But also find common joys to share. Maybe you and your child like to garden, cook, walk the dog, or bathe together. Of course your HSC will need to be alone sometimes, too. But stick around. And if he prefers solitude all of the time, you may need to lure him out, or to consider whether you have been too rushed, irritable, prying, or insisting on conversation. Quietly doing things side by side can be the best.

3. *Keep nature at the center of your life.* I cannot emphasize this enough. Even if it's a goldfish and a few plants in your apartment,

your child needs nature to stay balanced. We come from nature, our bodies are meant to be in it.

4. *Think and talk about the meaning and purpose of your life.* There are so many legitimate ways to fill a life, by dedicating it to gaining knowledge, doing God's will, helping others, creative expression, new experiences, or family life and friendship. If you know to what your life is dedicated, share that with your child. This clarifies your own priorities so that your child understands where you are headed, and also gives her some idea of how she will make order out of the chaos of opportunity.

On the other hand, if you are uncertain, anxious, or dejected about life, try not to burden a young HSC with that unless she notices and speaks of it. Even then, do not use her as a confidante. Just explain that every grown-up has periods of rethinking and uncertainty, followed by better times. Give her room to develop a perspective on life different from yours. It may help you as well.

5. *Think and talk about how you face the bad things in life.* What is your explanation for calamities and cruelty? Hearing about, fearing, and finally experiencing these are the biggest stressors of life, especially for an HSC. How do you cope with tyrants, loss, pain, death—whatever terrifies you? You have gone ahead of your child, you have learned something; make it easier by sharing this. But be careful of giving pat answers or concrete images of your equivalent of rescuing angels—things that might let him down when tested in a crisis. Some uncertainty or mystery to life is all right; it may, in fact, ring more true to an HSC than a false promise of perfect security.

6. *When you cannot prevent a major stress happening to your child, try to embrace it.* I have never met an adult worth knowing who did not deal with some hardship in childhood. It does build character, depending on how you as a parent help your child understand it. Illness, poverty, family upheavals, bad world news—they can teach life lessons, even provide a spiritual awakening. If you can keep this view, it may help your child. (If you cannot, but your

HSC gains it, then support what you have been privileged to witness.)

Next, we discuss an inescapable stressor for parents: raising the "difficult" or "strong-willed" HSC.

PARENTING THE DIFFICULT HSCs

Much of this book and this chapter may leave the impression that all HSCs will be cautious, considerate, and withdrawn unless their parents take action to loosen them up. But some HSCs show a different side most of the time. For example, Dinah, age nine, is a drama queen in the best as well as worst senses. She is intense, persistent, outspoken, highly creative, and loves to perform. At home she is demanding, difficult, dramatic, and truly fussy. If she does not like the taste of something, or the plans made involving her, everyone hears about it. In fact, everything stops until her feelings are dealt with. She is exquisitely aware of others' feelings, although she seems obstinately uncaring at times—depending on how it affects her, of course.

Given all of this, Dinah seems tough, and she is certainly tough to raise, but fortunately her parents understand that in fact she is very vulnerable underneath the impressive, occasionally overwhelming display. Yes, she has to be handled firmly. Yet punishment is not the key to developing her self-control, as I will discuss later in this chapter.

Sensitive boys can be equally strong-willed and dramatic. Chuck, age nine, the skier and tree climber, can be very nasty with his mother when he is disappointed, and very stubborn when he does not want to do something. At his first consult for braces, he simply refused to open his mouth. Finally they wore him out, telling him, "You will either open or we will hold you down." Later, when a routine was established, Chuck went happily to the orthodontist.

My favorite story about Chuck is his first visit with his priest to discuss his sins. Chuck went dirty, barefoot, in a defiant mood. Not knowing this man, he refused to speak to him, saying, "I'm not telling you anything and you can't make me." The priest agreed. Chuck and Dinah might get along fine.

But Chuck has a soft side, too. He cries easily, tries to mediate every family argument, loves the kindergartner assigned to him to "buddy," befriends kids who are not popular, and speaks up when someone is being teased. Ultimately, I think his priest would be pleased.

Managing the Moods of the Drama Queens and the Tough Rebels

HSCs like Dinah and Chuck, who are dramatic, outspoken, creative, intense, and often tempestuous to live with, are special cases. What is most noticeable is their lack of self-regulation. They often know they are going to be getting themselves into hot water, but they cannot stop their reactions. They are overcome by feelings and opinions that sweep them away, often alienating them from others. They need parents who are rock solid, and no one is that all the time. But the more they feel your solidness, the better. It is also my impression that if they go through a time of seeing a parent emotionally out of control, this affects them in certain ways more than other HSCs. Their own capacity to be out of control seems turned on by the adult's.

This type of child can try the patience of the best-intentioned parents, especially if they are highly sensitive, too. You cannot lose control, however, and become angry or hopeless. Dinah and Chuck can only be held partially responsible for the battles they start. Their feelings are controlling their behavior. But, of course, these feelings are controlling everyone else as well, making others angry. So they should be excused for the trouble they are having but not from gradually learning to do better. For them to be liked and feel good about themselves, for their own happiness, they cannot be allowed to carry on without limits or guidance.

Everything said before about discipline applies here: You set your standards, you stick to them, but you are careful about punishment, which can increase the arousal so much that your message does not penetrate. Assuming your drama queen or fighting rebel is already overexcited, you state the limits and hold firm. Then, or later, try to help them understand why they lost control. "I wonder if you were so upset with us because you were tired?" or "I wonder if all of this might be due to something that happened at school today. Want to talk about it?" But reaching a calmer place may take longer and require more patience than with another type of HSC.

Considering the responsibility and difficulty involved, you should have all the support you can get. You should not manage such a child alone if you are a single parent. You will need to involve a wise close relative or friend and perhaps a professional as well.

The question always arises with these more difficult HSCs as to whether there is a more serious problem to be treated. I would strongly advocate beginning with a temperament approach, since it involves the least labeling and expense, and may be the only real problem. Some temperament trait combinations are just plain difficult, especially those I pointed out in Chapter 2: high activity, high intensity of emotional expression, high distractibility, and low adaptability. The more of these four your HSC has, the more difficult he will probably be, depending on how well these traits fit with you and the school he attends.

Once you or a professional has assessed all of your child's temperament, you need to work with someone skilled at considering what does and does not fit with these trickier-to-handle traits and how to help your child moderate how they are expressed. There may be many behavior problems, but usually it is best to work on only a few at a time. You prioritize, deciding what behaviors need to change first. Imagine three baskets: *A* for "Now or I can't stand it," *B* for "Would sure be nice," and *C* for "Someday." Work on the *A* basket first, which might be rudeness, tantrums, and refusing to go to bed. Establish your standards here and focus on only these. When everyone feels improvement in these, the tension will ease and the others will be easier.

If the problems do not melt away with temperament counseling, you need to seek out other professionals. But beware that if you do that first, or at this point, most professionals do not take a temperament perspective and may blame all of your child's problems on a disorder. In particular, many teachers and counselors are most familiar with attention deficit disorder, either the distractibility type or the hyperactive type. Occasionally an HSC, who naturally notices every little sound or movement, will be highly distractible in distracting environments, and for that reason be diagnosed and treated for ADD/ADHD. But as I said in Chapter 1, such a child will have good concentration when there are no distractions, which is not typical of children with this disorder. Another way to discern what is really the problem is to think about whether this or any other disorder began suddenly, with a new teacher or school. Often a poor fit is the real cause—for example, a teacher who demands that children be highly focused at all times, so that the more your HSC is unable to unfocus, the more aroused and anxious she becomes, decreasing still further her ability to focus. Focusing requires mental energy—energy that is reduced with overarousal. Or an HSC might seem to have ADD or ADHD because a school is too noisy and stimulating.

If improving the fit and management of temperament traits does not seem to reduce the problem substantially within a few months, then you may want your child thoroughly evaluated and tested, as described in Chapter 1. Most ADD and ADHD is diagnosed with a relatively brief questionnaire or observation designed to diagnose that only, but learning disorders, bipolar disorder, childhood depression, and a host of other possibilities need to be eliminated as well.

If your HSC is difficult due to temperament traits, try to bear in mind that these "troublesome" traits can bear great fruits once they have been shaped and pruned a little. There are no great opera divas without high intensity of emotional expression; no great innovators without low adaptability (a refusal to put up with inconvenience that others are used to); no great discoveries without high distractibility (noticing what others do not); no great athletes without high activity.

In sum, home life may be a little difficult now, but think of your family and home as a launching pad for your HSC. With the proper support from you and her own great and growing awareness, your HSC will certainly go far.

Make a list of how your child's sensitivity is blossoming right now—all of the talents, assets, virtues, and plain old nice qualities that you and others are noticing.

Now make a list of the problem areas your child still has at home. Touchy feelings. Rudeness when refusing certain foods or rejecting clothing you have purchased. Difficulty making transitions—stopping an activity, getting up, going to bed. Unwillingness to try new things.

1. Ask your child if she would like to work on one of these.
2. If so, come up with a plan together. Decide a final goal that seems reasonable and agree on the steps along the way.
3. If this is an old issue where you have both failed in the past, try to come up with new, creative answers together—a reason it will work this time. For example, if your child never goes to sleep on time, read up on "day persons" and "night persons." Discuss how she might be a "night person" and think together about how to manage, given that schools require children to be present early in the morning. For example, during the summer and other holidays, she can indulge her true nature, and during the school year you will let her sleep longer and go two hours late to school once a week (if her school will tolerate it). In return, during the school year she will increase her efforts in ways you both agree upon to go to bed earlier every night, not just school nights, to see if her body will find it easier to fall asleep if bedtime is the same each night.
4. Try not to resort to rewards or incentives, except token rewards

like stars or blue ribbons that make success more tangible. Out-line together the benefits of the goal so vividly that accomplish-ing it will be reward enough. If your child's fear begins to interfere, plan smaller steps. If your child loses interest, remind her of what she wanted to accomplish. Discuss how you manage to stick to goals such as dieting or exercising. Perhaps work on your goal the same time your child does. Talk about the value of having willpower or persistence, of expecting a few slips and learning from them what can interfere with sticking to your goal.

Ultimately, leave the task to your child, which is where you be-gan. "It is up to you." You will probably not succeed in forcing the issue anyway, and if you do, when your child is slightly older he will resist even harder your offers of help to change.

For an example of going step by step toward a goal, see the end of "Applying What You Have Learned" in the next chapter.

Chapter Ten

School-Age HSCs
Out in the World

Helping Your Child Enjoy the Classroom and Social Life

This chapter is about HSCs out in the world, especially at school—how outgoing they should be and what to do if they need help forming friendships or getting along in special situations such as sleepovers. We then consider what you can do to assist your HSC in the school environment and classroom, which are usually not designed with the sensitive in mind. We explore the educating of HSCs—for example, their academic perfectionism (or lack of it due to boredom or other intense interests). Finally, we tackle what to do if your HSC is bullied or otherwise tormented at school.

The good news for this chapter is that I have never heard of an HSC who was a major behavior problem at school. These children rarely if ever fight, bully, lie, steal, cut school, try drugs, or insult teachers. At most they might be a class clown or engage in some insightful "back talk." They are usually excellent students, performing beyond their grade level, enjoying learning, and earning their teachers' praise. They are sometimes popular leaders, or at least have one deep friendship and a small circle of like-minded children.

The less-good news is that the school situation is often taxing for HSCs. Even the tough-seeming drama queens like Dinah and the rebels like Chuck, whom you met in the last chapter, do not find it easy. Let's begin with how this type of HSC finds school, since the less difficult HSCs often have similar troubles in the classroom, even though the problems may not be as noticed by their teachers.

Dinah, as is the case for most HSCs, is better one-on-one than in groups. She tries hard to control herself, wanting to please and knowing that her strong reactions can put others off. But her teachers still find her "too sensitive," saying "Dinah's feelings are easily hurt." The fact is, they do not have time to give her the extra help she needs in order to sort through what she feels, what is going on in others' minds, and how to control her first response.

For example, if she is teased or rejected she may rage or cry or both, all of which can delight those out to get her. If she could just "stay cool," it would further her goals of friendship and acceptance. But it will be a few years before she can do this away from home, since at school her parents can only coach from the distant sidelines. Thus she has seemed slow to mature and has had to learn many social lessons the hard way.

Chuck is popular at least. He's the class clown and has already been noticed by the girls, but he's not a great student—he's more interested in studying bugs and wildlife than reading books—so he's frequently distressed by his sense that he is behind his friends academically. Still, he's full of insights and ideas and speaks up in class anyway.

Whether tough and outspoken or quiet and compliant, HSCs find the going rough when they venture into the world, especially the world of school. Let's explore why. Many highly sensitive adults have told me that their home life was happy, their parents were very kind, but school was hell, and they still carry the scars.

WHAT HSCs FACE AT SCHOOL

First, most schools are excruciatingly overstimulating—80 percent of your child's fellow students are non-HSCs, and the classrooms are usually overcrowded, noisy by design as well as because of the loud voices used, and the days are long. At the same time, they are often boring for HSCs, since they grasp their teachers' messages right away, but these have to be repeated over and over to the other students. Then the HSC's mind wanders, returns, and finds she has missed something, which is also troubling.

Second, there are more demands and punishments at school, none of them adjusted for the sensitivity of your child. HSCs are usually very conscientious about meeting every demand of school authorities. When an entire class, or your HSC personally, receives a rebuke or punishment, your child is probably crushed by the intensity of the message, a message designed to get through to the most stubborn nonsensitive child.

Third, it is usually at school that HSCs find social life difficult. Parents say that at home, at a friend's house, or in the neighborhood, their HSC plays with as much eagerness and outspokenness as any other child. But at school, HSCs are a true minority in the ways they behave. For example, they tend to become quiet and observe the highly stimulating environment. They are left out of the interaction—leave themselves out. Furthermore, part of what they observe is cruelty directed toward others or themselves—a further reason to withdraw, or to react strongly in other ways. Any strong reaction sets them apart, and by the time they have figured out the rules and are adjusting better to the quickly changing social scene, the other children have formed friendships and made up their minds about the HSC—this one is afraid, odd, aloof, superior, shy, boring, or whatever. We might say they experience temperament prejudice.

Given the above, your HSC is likely to be anxious at school as well as overaroused due to the overstimulation. Overarousal and high anxiety interfere with the expression of social, academic, and athletic skills. As a result, the association of anxiety with school is eventually justified. Your child is trying to be perfect while the body is in a far from perfect state.

All of this should be taken into consideration if you find that your

school-age child is depressed, sulky, irritable, overexcitable, or withdrawn.

CLASSROOMS—MIRROR OF A CULTURE'S
IDEAL TEMPERAMENT

It is time to place the typical North American classroom in perspective. In Chapter 6, I described the work of Charles Super and Sarah
Harkness of the University of Connecticut, who compared the
arousal and sleep of Dutch and U.S. infants. While in Europe, Sarah
Harkness and her colleagues also compared the classroom environments in various countries with those of the United States. She
found that most European classrooms were orderly and not particularly stimulating. In some countries, especially Sweden, they were
more like a home: The blackboards were hidden, only taken out
when needed, and there were no rows of chairs, but areas arranged
and furnished like living rooms and kitchens where students and
teachers could gather. In all the schools they visited, even in the
poorer eastern European countries, the furnishings were generally in
good repair, neat, clean, well-designed, and aesthetically pleasing.

In short, European classrooms seemed designed to provide a reliable, calming environment in which children could learn at their
own pace and develop good taste. Such places seemed ideal for a
child who was positive in mood and regular in habits—places where
HSCs could learn in peace.

In the United States, in contrast, Harkness found that the typical
classroom was highly stimulating and "print rich"—designed to
pour as much information as possible into students, as fast as possible. Order was less important than there being many activities
available. The furnishings were often not aesthetically pleasing or
well maintained, as if expecting the children not to notice the furnishings or to damage them. The U.S. classroom environment
seemed ideal for a child who was intense, active to the point of be-

ing destructive, hungry for stimulation, highly adaptable, certainly not aware of subtleties, and having a high sensory threshold—in short, not an HSC.

You may not be able to provide your HSC with a European-style learning environment, even if you enroll your child in a private or charter school, but at the very least you will need to have a sense of what your HSC may be coping with.

Homeschooling

There is an option that more and more parents are exploring, and that is homeschooling. For most parents it's not possible because of working during the day, but parents of HSCs probably think of it more, for exactly the reasons I have just enumerated. One could debate endlessly about whether homeschooling is a good idea for children, even HSCs, if public or private schools are also readily available. Yes, there is always the question of having enough children with whom to learn social skills and being toughened up in order to survive in this culture. But I am confident there are times when some HSCs would be better off homeschooled, *if* the home is a good environment. (Unfortunately, sometimes when children are suffering in school, one reason is trouble at home.)

The HSCs to homeschool might be those who must otherwise go to schools that are unusually bad environments physically or socially, those given a teacher who is a very bad fit with an HSC and the parents cannot change the assignment, or those teased or bullied too much because they happen to go to schools where this is not handled well. I am sure there are other examples. So do not dismiss homeschooling as an option if it seems right for you, even if everyone around you disagrees. It is truly a highly individual matter. I wish I had homeschooled my own son from fourth to sixth grade, when public school was most difficult for him. If you are interested, there are excellent homeschooling resources on the Internet (homeschooling without the Internet is difficult to imagine), including the laws that need to be met in each state and how to find a local support group.

SOCIAL LIFE AND SHYNESS

As I explained in the last chapter, shyness for children before ages seven to ten is not a major or lasting problem. But after ten years it tends to lead to low self-esteem, loneliness, and anxiety. The reason is that, beginning in middle childhood, all children—at least in some cultures—see social withdrawal in a very negative light.

However, research points out that having just one good friend is enough to restore self-esteem and social acceptance, especially if the friendship is "validating and caring." And being shy in groups generally does not keep a child from forming individual friendships. So no matter how your child is managing "playground politics," it is worth helping her find a friend outside of school even if you cannot help her while she is there.

Finally, remember that being "shy" at any one time in childhood does not put a child at risk for being shy forever. Sometimes children have a bad year, as when they move or are in a class without friends. When shyness persists year after year, or if your child is being actively teased, rejected, or bullied, you have to become more concerned. Is your child behaving appropriately and effectively?

Meanwhile, what can you do to improve her ability to make at least one friend?

Helping Your Child Find a Friend

First, if your child says he does not have friends, find out if this is true and why. Sometimes an HSC will exaggerate the problem, feeling isolated inside because of feeling different, even if in reality he has several friends or is even quite popular. Remember, just one good friend will do, even if other children have more. But if teachers verify that your child is generally alone during free time, you need to find out the reason. That can probably come from a gentle, open conversation with your child, plus some unobtrusive observing on your part.

Sometimes teachers can help at this point by identifying another child who is friendly or could use a special friend and would be a good match, then pairing them in some activity or seating them together.

When a teacher cannot help, you may be able to. In fact, solving it outside of school first can be a good idea. Friendships often form more easily one-on-one, away from other children and all the playground politics. Select a child who is the same age and, if possible, going to the same school, so they can be in the same class next year if their friendship blossoms. It may help if this child does not yet know yours at school, so your child will not have been labeled in the other child's eyes. This child and yours should have similar interests, something they can talk about or do together, and their families should have some similar values. You might notice such a potential friend at your place of worship or through an activity in which you have involved your child, such as riding lessons, a chess group, art or music workshops, or a sports or performance day camp.

Invite this "good prospect" over. Or better, have your family and the other child's get together for dessert at your home, a picnic, or some family outing. Having the children together at your home or on an outing will make the first stages of getting acquainted less novel and arousing as well as allowing you to observe how your child behaves with a new friend. For example, is she talkative or withdrawn, bossy or allowing herself to be bossed around too much? With this information, you can focus on what your child needs to learn about meeting and getting along with others. Above all, if a friendship does form, try to have the two in the same class the next year. A study of shy kindergartners found that those with a friend in their class whom they knew prior to entering school were accepted more by the other children.

As for making friends at school, discuss the other students in your HSC's class to see if your child has overlooked a good prospect. Your HSC may be rejecting someone because other children do or because of wrongly assuming he will be rejected.

Finally, make your home an attractive place for children of that age, with interesting games and an area that can be messed up and is semiprivate.

Do not accommodate to extremes, however. I have seen parents make their homes so hospitable that their child was upstaged or taken advantage of. All the children knew that kids came over for the easy eats or the cool dad, not to see the child. And do not become too involved in your child's friendship formation or continue after you are no longer needed. Children need privacy, too, and a sense they can handle matters on their own. Children can also be branded as much for their parents' uncool behavior as for their own.

What the Shy Kids Themselves Say About How Parents Help

Psychologists Nathan Fox, Ana Sobel, Susan Calkins, and Pamela Cole studied children from two to seven years of age. At two years, one aspect of the study was to videotape the children in a laboratory while a clown tried to interact with them and while they were presented with a toy robot. At seven, they were observed while playing with three children they had not met before. Later, the seven-year-olds also watched the videos of themselves at two and the psychologists asked them how they felt about shyness generally, how they felt about their behavior as two-year-olds, and, if they had changed, what had changed them.

Those who were cautious at two but outgoing at seven tended to explain their change as due to their parents exposing them to lots of things. In other words, these children themselves were indicating that parents can have an effect on their child's confidence.

By the way, the children who were no longer "shy" (at two they were probably just behaving like HSCs) were more dismayed by the thought of themselves and others being shy than those who had not changed. Those kids who had overcome their caution probably knew their tendency to pause to check was still there and possibly, as a result of their parents' intense effort to change them, felt secretly flawed. But now that you understand the full nature of the trait, you can help your child connect with others without her growing up seeing her caution as a hidden problem that may come back. Yes, her sensitivity may give her a cautiousness that requires some real, safe experiences to reassure her, but sensitivity has too many good aspects to be a flaw.

So let's imagine you sitting down with the children who had become more comfortable in new situations and with strangers. What would they suggest specifically to help you with your child? Perhaps before we hear them tell you how to help your child fit into a non-sensitive world, you will want to decide for yourself if there is anyplace where you want to help change the world instead.

But Before Trying to Change Your HSC, Decide Your Values

Young HSCs are sometimes slow to give up "young" habits such as thumbsucking, carrying a beloved stuffed animal, or crying when you drop them off at school. You may want to do everything you can to see that your child stops these behaviors so he is not teased by those less sensitive children who do not understand. Or you may want your child to be free to express his needs and emotions, developing at his own pace. It's a tough call.

Further, this culture is very appearance-oriented. If you decide that you want your child to fit in, you will need to buy the appropriate clothes. A girl has to manage her weight, developing an athletic look. Boys will also need a competitive style. However, by concentrating your efforts here, you are giving the message that you agree that looking and acting like everyone else should be a top priority in life. Again, it is up to you to make the call.

Now let's raise the stakes. HSCs may shrink back at first from some of what children watch on television (for example, action shows with a great deal of violence); from the gossiping, teasing, and bullying that kids do; from the scapegoating of those who are different; from make-believe play or video games involving killing, torture, or mass destruction. All caring parents are in a bind here, wanting their child to be accepted but not wanting him to become the "average" violent, uncaring, troubled kid. What do you do?

Further, we all have our preferences about what we want our child never to become—addicted to TV and video games, ruthlessly competitive, obsessed with appearances or popularity or sports, limited by outdated gender expectations, overly driven to excel, racially prejudiced, delighted with violence, or indifferent to the feelings of others. Yet if your child is too different from the average child, he will be on the front lines of your chosen battles and will be bound to suffer as a result.

If you want to reduce rigid gender roles, for example, you may find yourself with a sensitive boy who is teased for crying easily or liking to cook and arrange flowers, or a girl who is unable to discuss fashions or tolerate an afternoon of playing with Barbie dolls. Or maybe you want to raise a person who would rather read than watch TV, and so has no idea what the other kids are talking about when they compare notes on last night's shows. Or a child who befriends the class nerd and so receives the same label.

Do you want to change society, starting with your child, or see your child become one of those you wish you could change? It's a question only you can answer, but it has to be considered.

Among other idealistic goals, I wanted my son to eat healthily and in a way that is gentle on the environment, and to me that meant no meat, sugar, or processed wheat. Good luck. He was teased for his brown bread and no-meat sandwiches and ate sugar as often as he could get it. I finally learned to buy fake bologna and use white bread. I gave up on prohibiting sugar.

Once you decide how idealistic to be, how do you implement values not shared by the families around you? You must explain them well to your child, so she can defend them with others. And you can try to choose your child's friends, by getting to know their parents' values (this becomes more difficult as children get older). The friends who share her attitudes and yours will be her allies, and yours, in larger groups. You can also choose a school that fosters your values, if there is one. Even so, your efforts may not seem to be working, or they could backfire. I tried to keep my son from watching TV, and now he writes scripts for the Saturday-morning cartoons. On the other hand, he is still a vegetarian and eats less sugar than I do!

Above all, keep in mind that even though our society favors children who are socially confident, bold, adventuresome, outgoing, and all the rest, you do have a choice about how much to press for your child to develop in these idealized directions. There are other values. You may want to foster a child who turns inward to develop her artistic abilities, the main tool of which is a sensitivity that is not blunted and a self that is highly individuated, original, and creative, one who creates and alters culture rather than consuming and reflecting it. You may hope your child takes a spiritual path, in which case he will need to be at home on "the road less traveled," finding his guidance in ways unseen by others. But such a person may be lonely, finding only a few people who see the unseen as he does. You may believe there are deeper ways of thinking that begin inside or with deep reflection on the outer world. You do not even know exactly what that is, but you know that your sensitive child may know, with enough time and inner space.

However, we do not have to make this a matter of all one or the other. Every artist, theologian, mystic, philosopher, scientist, or depth psychologist needs to get along with people and be ready to go out and speak to strangers about his or her insights. So however much you want to or plan not to shape your HSC to fit in, read the suggestions below. Simply implement those that seem right for your child to the degree that you believe best.

Now Some Tips on Raising a (Relatively) Bold, Socially Accepted HSC

How do you parent an HSC who, like the children in the shyness study, looks back and says, "I used to be a little scared of new people and things, but my parents helped me get over it"?

1. *Expose your child to all kinds of experiences,* just not too many at a time. For example, look together through recreation program catalogs, signing up for anything that appeals to your child. Suggest Scouts. Bring a variety of books into the house that describe everything from fishing and fencing to magic shows and chess. Find out what your child's friends are up to. Look through magazines and the newspapers for kid-oriented events that your child might enjoy (that usually means avoiding crowds). Don't force any of this, or do more than one or at most two at a time, but keep offering opportunities.

2. *Avoid the label "shy" and discourage it in your child.* Shyness is a state of mind, a fear of being judged and found wanting, that happens to everyone. It is not a trait. Reframe your child's self-description this way: "You like to take your time in new situations, or with strangers, but look how much you like to talk to your friends."

3. *Use role-playing,* dolls, puppets, or action figures (that is, make-believe) to help your child learn how to join a group, meet an individual, or be a better friend. But keep it simple and repeat the phrases often. "Hi, I'm Jules. Can I play?" During these rehearsals, if the anxiety goes up, be silly: "Now, Jules, how would you introduce yourself to a school of fish?" Explain that awkward moments happen to all of us and how you just laugh with the others and go on. Tell your most embarrassing moments and laugh at them yourself.

   Be sure you are giving sound advice for interacting with kids of your child's age in these times. *Listen* to how the kids who are your child's age actually do talk with each other.

4. *Realize that entrances into groups are delicate for HSCs.* Suggest that when going up to a group, he can approach the most familiar child first, or draw that child aside, talk, then enter the group with that person. Or approach a child who looks equally hesitant or who is doing something your child likes to do.

5. *Place your child in a teaching or "star" role,* with younger children or in some activity where she always shines. Or one in which she will be admired just for being a girl and being there, maybe a judo class. And at this age a boy in a drama or dance class will probably always have the leading male roles. Find your child's talents and see that she is in settings where she is admired for them.

6. *Help your child develop athletic skills, especially team sports.* These are not always easy for an HSC at first, but if he can persist and develop adequate skills, he will "belong." If he does not, he may struggle with being accepted, at least until high school.

Special Situations—Such as Sleepovers

Special, potentially problematic social situations of all sorts can arise with HSCs—going to camp, belonging to teams or clubs, group lessons. Look at each in a fresh way, seeking novel or gradual solutions that will allow your child to join in without calling undue attention to her temperament, or at least without making it seem like a huge obstacle.

Let's take sleepovers as an example. Then I think you will be able to apply the same kind of thinking to other situations.

If your HSC is likely to be reluctant to sleep in another house, start preparing him before too many invitations have to be rejected. A great deal of "kid politics" and bonding happen at these sleepovers, especially when they involve a group of kids, and it is much better that your child be at some of these than be continually left out.

First, have a child sleep over at your house—one your own child really likes and whose parents are understanding, so that you can explain your need for them to make your child especially comfortable when they reciprocate. There should be some ordinary visits, first at your house, then at the other child's, each one a little longer. For one of these, suggest a sleepover at your place. Do not make the total hours together too long and be sure you enforce their sleeping so your child does not have to.

When the sleepover invitation is reciprocated, be sure it is your child's friend who urges your child to stay. If yours still refuses, when you are alone together, be lightly curious. If he will not tell you the reason, accept that. If he does, do not dismiss it or try to solve it casually. Weigh the reason respectfully, perhaps waiting a day or two to offer your solution.

When your child is ready for the first sleepover away from home, if he is fussy about anything, bring that up with the parents (for example, your child's food preferences) and nonchalantly express your hope that this can be respected without giving your child too much embarrassing attention. And could they point out which bathroom to use and encourage him to use it?

When you drop off your HSC, stay around for a while, visiting with the parents. If your child would like you to, call once to see how he's doing. Agree to a code word that means he wants you to make an excuse to pick him up. And if that is your agreement, speak to your child in person, do not take anyone else's word for it that all is going well.

How would you apply this type of strategy to, say, going to camp? Start with a day camp, then send your child to a sleepaway camp that her friends are going to. See that she will be in a cabin with at least one trusted friend. Talk to the camp counselors about your child's specific sensitivities, including the possibility of acute homesickness. Tell her you are prepared to bring her home after a few days if she is miserable (but do not be surprised if she has you come, then she sends you back home without her).

Other Ways to Promote Social Skills

We have discussed developing your school-age child's friendships and general boldness, as well as an example of dealing with a specific, special situation, sleepovers. Here are a few final pointers before we move on to address other aspects of school life.

1. *Expose your child to more adults.* A child who has been able to gain the respectful attention of adults often has more self-confidence elsewhere, even with peers, and HSCs are frequently quite interested in and interesting to adults. Ask some of your relatives or your own friends to engage in conversations with your child. You can even suggest the topics the two of them might find worth pursuing. (More ways to encourage these conversations are in the activity at the end of this chapter. Also see the discussion of how adults can best encourage a quiet child to speak, in Chapter 8 under "Step-by-Step Help for Your Child in Social Situations.")

   One mother had an agreement with her HSC that she would rescue him from an adult when he was uncomfortable. They had two code phrases that her son could use to signal that he (1) wanted help keeping up an awkward conversation or (2) wanted to escape. What nice sympathy and teamwork.

2. *Play word games that develop quick, spontaneous verbal replies.* Encourage spontaneity as much as you can.

3. *Have your child ask for directions or information when you need it* while out together, or make appropriate phone calls for information. She can order at a restaurant for the family or even make a restaurant reservation with some coaching. If she would like you to drive her somewhere that she could reach on foot, strike a bargain: In exchange for the time you spent driving, she will spend the same amount of time helping you by making those time-consuming little calls to find out a postage rate or the hours a store is open. Or make this all a part of a learning program she has agreed to, as described at the end of this chapter.

4. *Encourage your child to look people in the eye.* Because eye contact is stimulating, HSCs often avoid it. But this can be taken as an unconscious sign of subservience or fear of the other. Have your child practice looking others in the eye with a safe person—you, others in the family, then people less familiar. Give him plenty of praise for doing so—there are not many obvious, inherent rewards in it, but eye contact will help him.

5. *Enlist the help of other adults around your child,* such as teachers, coaches, and other parents, but first find out what they plan to do. Good plans include pairing your child with a friend or a similar child for a task or arranging to have your child stand out in some area that the other kids respect. Being discussed as having a shyness problem or especially good behavior that others should emulate (making her the "teacher's pet") will not help.

6. *Point out progress.* Transformation is a process, not a sudden miracle, so point this out often: "Last year you almost couldn't stand up and speak at all in class, but this year, look how much easier it is for you."

There are two final points: First, do not overdo on social activities. Even extroverted HSCs need far more down time from groups than non-HSCs. Many parents of HSCs said they limited their child's social activities to once a week and avoided soccer teams, Little League, or other high-pressure activities. Second, realize that your HSC may never have more than one friend and never be immune to scapegoating, in control of tears, or able to express to others all that you know he knows. But that goes with having a sensitive, compassionate, creative nature. It is a package deal.

MAKING SCHOOL LIFE FEEL GOOD

Remember Randall, who did not want to go to playgroups or preschool? According to his mother, even at nine he feels "unbelievable anxiety" during most of the summer about the first day of school. Just before going he becomes so anxious "he can't even breathe."

What You Can Do Even Before the First Day

It is a shame Randall has to feel such distress every year. (His mother tries to learn who his teacher will be, to help him know what to expect, but their school district does not disclose that until opening day.) Your child may feel the same terror, so do all you can to help smooth the transition. For example, find out what you can about the various teachers your child at least *could* have the following year.

About teachers: All those I interviewed said that most of their colleagues were of the cookie-cutter type, not very creative and definitely using one teaching style for all children. Indeed, whether consciously or not, many teachers tend to ignore the quieter students, giving the leadership roles to the ones who catch their attention. You need to find the exceptional teachers, those who consider each student's unique needs and assets. One teacher suggested you observe in the classroom those teachers your child might have the next year. You can say to the principal, "My child needs careful placement, and I would like to observe the teachers he might have next year in order to give you my opinion about who would be the best match for him." Principals should be happy to assist you in this. Also, if your child has had a helpful teacher, he or she can suggest who will be best for your child in the coming grades.

Once you have made your choice, during the summer, suggest to the principal the one who seems best for your child. Obviously principals cannot grant all of these veiled requests for specific teachers, but they do want your child to thrive. So it is appropriate to write a letter to the principal saying something like this: "My son Justin is the type of child who works hard in school without needing to be lectured about it. In fact, he does not do well when he hears lots of harsh reprimands during a day, so keep this in mind when placing him in a class. It is my impression that Ms. Kindness would be a good fit for him."

You can also write a letter about your child needing to be in a class with her best friend. You might write this: "Last year Betsy really had to struggle to make friends at school, and I think it distracted her from her schoolwork. But she does have one good friend, Carol Moore, who also attends Lincoln School, so this letter is a request that they be placed in the same class if that is at all possible."

Follow up requests like these with a friendly phone call to be sure they were received and noted.

Before school starts, go there with your child to locate his classroom and the toilets, water fountains, and school offices. Explain the roles of the different adults at school—principal, assistant principal, nurse, and so forth—and who your child can turn to for help with various matters. Introduce your child to the most approachable of these, if that is possible.

What You Can Ask Teachers to Do

Teachers, like principals, want your child to thrive. However, they are busy, and many are not interested in issues of temperament, feeling they cannot or should not give special treatment or become caught up in purely psychological issues. Therefore the more you mention the teacher's goals—that your child learn the material—the more you will be heard.

The teachers I interviewed thought you should feel free to give your child's teachers the "Tips for Teachers" at the end of this book—or give them the entire book—unless you think a particular teacher will not respond positively. Organizations supporting children with learning disorders or ADD/ADHD provide such materials for teachers, and while high sensitivity is not a disorder, it warrants a teacher's attention because of the high achievement potential as well as the vulnerabilities of these students.

You can also become acquainted with the children in your child's class and suggest to the teacher who your child works well with. You can even describe the kinds of assignments your child does best and those that are most difficult. Do not, however, ask that your child be entirely excused from speaking in class or making presentations. All HSCs need to overcome at least some of this fear so that they can share their unusually creative, thoughtful ideas. And studies find that the intelligence of quiet children is consistently underestimated by teachers, who tend to ignore these children during activities and discussions. You do not want that happening to your HSC. But you can suggest that your child's teacher might keep expectations low about class participation until after Halloween or Thanksgiving, when your child is more at home in the classroom.

If you have a good rapport with the teacher, you could also suggest "building up the confidence of all those children like mine who are slower to speak up" by breaking the class up into smaller groups. Perhaps they could start presenting their ideas in groups of two, then three, then four, and so on. Or perhaps your child could give a joint presentation with a friend, and not be among the first or last asked to present, so that she can see how it is done without being anxious for too long.

Other Pointers for Keeping School HSC-Friendly

With HSCs, the small irritations, unexpected changes, or last-minute additions in stimulation are often what turn a nice day at school into a long, stressful one. Do whatever you can to foresee and reduce these extras.

1. *Remember that riding a school bus can be particularly difficult for HSCs.* There is little supervision and high stimulation. Consider driving your child, carpooling, or letting him walk to school so that the day is off to a good start.

2. *Before a class trip, prepare your child for what will happen.* Focus on what she will enjoy, but forewarn her about any potential discomforts, too, and discuss how she will handle them. Be sure she has enough food with her and adequate clothing.

3. *Consider limiting extracurricular activities.* Many parents of HSCs mentioned it. These children need to come home and be alone after school. Whatever activities your child does engage in, the adult coach, leader, or teacher should be a good one for an HSC. Indeed, you might want to choose an activity on the basis of the understanding qualities of a particular adult in charge.

4. *Allow "mental health days,"* another suggestion from several parents. These are days when your HSC can stay home from school and sleep late, nap, and generally relax. The rule here is, do what is best for your child in the long run.

THE ACADEMIC PART OF SCHOOL LIFE

Having considered making and managing friendships and minimizing the discomfort of school life, we can turn to the actual business of learning.

If Your Child Is a Perfectionist

HSCs are usually good students—sometimes too good. For example, they may spend too much time studying for exams and doing homework—that is, more than their teachers expect and more than other students spend who are also earning good grades. Try to find out why before you ask your child to cut back. Is he afraid of the teacher? Competing with another child? Confused about the purpose of homework? (Explain that it is just practice.) Is the work too difficult? Are the assignments confusing? Have you overemphasized exam results or grades? (Ask yourself how you respond to a less than perfect grade. It's easy for a small unpleasant response from you to be a major rebuke to your HSC.) Or, does he just enjoy doing it?

With a perfectionist, you must discuss often the importance of a well-rounded life, of pacing oneself, and not doing more than is needed to get an adequate grade so that there is time left for the other things in life. With a perfectionist, you may need to insist on "mental health" days, giving your child a chance to see that something can be missed, made up imperfectly, and survived. Other tips:

1. *With a younger child, try making deals:* "If you are done with your homework by four, we'll have time to play a game together before dinner."

2. *Offer to look over homework for mistakes,* and do not be a perfectionist yourself, wanting more changed than the teacher would! Your reviewing the homework reduces your child's worry about how terrible it may be and gives you the chance to say something like, "If this were my paper, I would be happy with it as it is." Or "I think your teacher will be quite satisfied with this without copying it over." If you can honestly do so, start with "This is terrific."

3. *Help your child prioritize.* Often there is not time to do every item of homework perfectly or to complete all the parts of an exam. Teach your child to decide what should receive first attention, second, and third, and to accept that the lower priorities may not be done well or even at all. Imperfect schoolwork can be even more difficult to accept when it must be given up because of nonschool priorities, such as having enough sleep, being a good family member and friend, and staying physically fit. Prioritizing is a skill sensitive people will need their entire lives.

4. *Discuss how long something should take* and set a timer to give warnings when half and three quarters of the time is up, so your child can get used to there being limits in what can be done. This will help prepare for timed exams as well.

5. *You can also tell this story:* I graduated Phi Beta Kappa from the University of California, Berkeley, and the night of the initiation dinner the honored speaker was the student with the highest GPA in our entire graduating class of thousands. He described in great detail his four years of sitting in the library every night, Fridays and Saturdays, too, alone, studying, but also watching other students heading off to dates, movies, or basketball games. He ended

his speech by pausing, then saying it is traditional in such speeches to give some advice or to say what one has learned. "I learned that earning this honor was the biggest mistake of my life. I would have gained far more if I had joined the rest of the human race out in the world." We all stood as one to applaud him, knowing exactly what he meant.

Above all, describe your own experiences with accepting limits and errors.

HSCs Who Are Less Than Perfectionists

Or course, some HSCs are anything but perfectionists, at least at first. Their talents may not be academic. They may be bored by school, or have an undiagnosed learning disorder or vision or hearing problem. It is important to evaluate a child who is struggling in school rather than write her off as lacking intelligence or motivation. If we remove the obstacles that have distracted or disturbed them, all children are smart enough and highly motivated to learn—they just do not always want to learn what adults think they need to know.

The obstacle for most HSCs is that they have had a few bad experiences of failing under the pressure of overarousal and henceforth have protected themselves from further criticism and shame, which hit them so hard, by not seeming to care. I faced this problem with my son. Thanks to this self-protecting indifference to praise or criticism, plus sloppy handwriting and hurried work, he was being seen as a below-average student when I knew he was not.

My solution was to become very involved for a few years, seeing that any homework turned in was very well presented, even typed by me when appropriate (but I did *not* do the homework—it had to be brought to me in its final state). Every exam was well prepared for. Every oral presentation had interesting visuals. Every artistic project was done with good materials. This led to my son's work being praised, and from then on he enjoyed doing a good job. His new teachers saw his good grades from previous years and viewed him as a top student before school had even started (it would be nice if this type of bias did not occur, but it does). By middle school, he was being placed in advanced programs, where there were more HSCs and he was more at home socially.

I realize that some parents cannot spend this kind of time with their child. But do remember this is an investment like any other, and since you have already invested a great deal in raising your child, consider putting more resources here for a while if your child is struggling in school. The payoffs can be substantial.

Often HSCs are bored by what is going on in the classroom. While in elementary school, my son estimated that the actual learning in school could be done in about an hour or two per day—the rest was "baby-sitting." He was probably right, and certainly disgusted and not paying attention.

The need to engage their deeper processing of information is vital, yet difficult to solve in elementary school unless there are advanced classes or a teacher who is a bit creative. Copying a picture of Columbus's three ships is not enough for an HSC. He also needs to think (because he is able to, like a muscle aching for use) about how it felt to be on one of those little ships, to see land, to meet Indians, and how that changed the lives of the Spaniards, the Indians, and even us today. You can encourage this deeper, more creative thinking yourself, of course. But it does take time and attention.

Once out of elementary school, there may be more solutions. My son's school allowed him to take textbooks home during the summer, study, and test out of algebra and geometry, which he did with glee. The school administrators had never done it before, but they did not stand in the way. Other parents homeschool or select private schools that can satisfy an HSC's style of thinking.

Generalists and Specialists

Academically, HSCs are often one of two extreme types, the generalist, who is interested in *everything*, and the specialist, who only wants to write poetry or study bugs or such. Both types are associated with giftedness and not a cause for concern, although you can try to restore a little balance. At this age, however, the generalist is often seen as the better student, having good grades in everything. Their problem comes later, when they have to choose a focus.

The specialist is often perceived as a problem by educators, and you may have to intervene more to defend or at least explain your specialist—"I know she isn't keeping up with her writing assignments. She's spending all her time studying bugs!" Then give a picture of your budding entomologist that hints of genius.

Sometimes the specialists can be enticed into other areas by relating the "boring" subjects to their specialty: The entomologist who must write a poem can use insect imagery; the poet who must study bugs will find his poetry enriched by being able to make better metaphors about mayflies, june bugs, and lice. But even if specialists are not good all-around students at this age, they may be on the way to stardom in their specialty, so it's all right to humor them. Indeed, parents may want to find a mentor in their child's field and let this flower blossom.

WHEN YOUR CHILD IS BULLIED OR TORMENTED

So your child has at least one good friend, is able to enjoy and be included in larger groups at times, and has struck the right balance academically between perfectionism and carelessness, specialist and generalist. Then comes one of the most painful moments for parents of HSCs: Your child comes home in tears because of having been bullied, badly teased, or ostracized. And remember, girls have their own special form of torturing each other, by betraying secrets, gossiping, forming threesomes and then excluding one and whispering in her presence, and all the rest.

As I said in Chapter 8, these torments often happen to HSCs because they are a little different so they stand out, they have stronger reactions so it is more rewarding to the bully and his audience, and they are less likely to retaliate so they are safer targets. Handling it is never easy, but here are some ideas.

1. *Be sure it is as bad as it first sounds,* because almost anything you do or even suggest *could* potentially make the problem worse by drawing more attention to your child. Do not minimize the problem either, but just consider whether it is something that might be resolved in a day or two.

2. *Find out what specifically has happened* and what your child fears may happen, having seen what happens to others. That way you know if you are dealing with prevention or intervention.

3. *Discuss cruelty and meanness,* letting your child know it is wrong and she is in the right (if your careful questioning suggests this is so). She needs your full sympathy, support, and perspective as her reality check. At the same time, you can carefully hint at what might be going on inside the mind of the bully, if you have an idea. Is this other child under stress, being bullied by others, embarrassed by poor grades, afraid of being shamed in front of others? Insight into the other may give your child's keen intuition a chance to find a solution.

4. *Discuss how justice can be achieved*—who your child (or you) should complain to, how, and why. A complaint must be firm and effective; merely whining, crying, or taking it can bring on more of the same.

5. *Have your child notice how other kids deal with the bullying, teasing, and so forth.* Do they ignore it, walk away, laugh, defuse comments with sarcasm, get even? Try some role-playing between you of how to handle the troubling situation. But realize that your

HSC may not be capable of the responses other kids make easily. And remember, things an adult might do, like reasoning with a bully or "turning the other cheek," may not work on the playground and only make your child seem more "out of it."

6. *Help your child be less of a target* by dressing appropriately and refusing to tolerate mischief. A thoughtfully taught course in physical self-defense (not aggression), such as judo, can sometimes give a child more verbal confidence. He knows that if a physical fight were necessary, he could win it.

7. *If there is a specific child involved, try to get the two of them together* or "on the same team," in the same social group, for some event or task. An example of that is below.

8. *Do whatever you have to do to see that it stops.* It is very damaging when a child is teased or bullied, not only for the target but for those who do it and witness it. If working with your child does not help swiftly, speak to teachers, principals, or other parents. If the situation is drastic, consider removing your child from school for the duration of the year, or seeking a teacher at your school or a different school that works especially well with these issues which come up in every classroom but are often ignored. The latest thinking is that teachers and administrators should be responsible for creating a non–bully tolerating school culture. Remember, however, that most of the mistreatment could happen when a teacher is not around.

HOW MARILYN HANDLED A BULLY

Marilyn, Randall's mother, handled one bully smoothly by bringing her child and his potential tormentor together. At a school assembly, Randall had been shoved by Jeff, an older boy he did not know. Randall started feeling anxious about this boy and began going out of his way to avoid him. Even when Marilyn dropped her son off at school, if the boy was in the car ahead, Randall would not get out. If the soccer team that Jeff was on was playing Randall's team, Randall would not play.

Marilyn suspected that Randall had seen other kids bullied and imagined he was going to receive the same or worse treatment. So she decided to call Jeff's mother and discuss what was happening. The other mother admitted that she was divorcing Jeff's father and her son was acting out. She was happy to have Marilyn arrange for Jeff to come over, along with two brothers, one who was a friend of Jeff and the other a friend of Randall. She took all four on an outing so she could see that things went smoothly. That day they got to know and understand each other.

Marilyn brought them together several more times, and while Randall and the older Jeff are not about to become close friends, they did later choose to play on the same soccer team. Marilyn's final comment was that it requires a lot of energy and thought to parent an HSC well. Clearly she is working on it.

While this was a mild case of bullying, it might have become more if Jeff or others had had the chance to take advantage of Randall's fears. But by getting to know him, Jeff had to recategorize Randall mentally as an insider, an acquaintance, eventually even a teammate, rather than as an outsider. Alas, all humans seem more comfortable victimizing an outsider if they are going to be mean at all.

SO YOU HAVE MADE IT THIS FAR

Just a reminder of what Randall's mother, Marilyn, has told you: Raising an HSC is hard work but highly rewarding. I might add that it can be a source of growth and character-building in you as well. You will need all the maturity and strength you can muster for the next stage, adolescence. But not for the reasons parents of non-HSCs will tell you.

APPLYING WHAT YOU HAVE LEARNED

As you did at the end of the last chapter, look at the areas where you think your HSC needs to improve—this time out in the world rather than at home. Perhaps this is shyness with strangers (adults, children, or both), lack of friends, or spending too much or too little time on homework. Use the steps described at the end of the last chapter:

Ask your child if she would like to work on one of these issues; if so, come up with a plan together and a final goal that seems reasonable; then agree on the steps needed to get there.

If this is an old issue, try to come up with new, creative answers together—a reason it will work this time. For example, if your child has taken group swimming classes and has not learned to swim, a solution might be private lessons with an instructor that both of you interview, so that he can choose someone he trusts and who is patient. And try not to resort to rewards or incentives, except token rewards that make something more interesting (like getting to keep the coins your child can collect from the bottom of the pool while learning to put his face underwater).

Perhaps your child would really like to become more comfortable speaking to adults she does not know. You might agree on a goal of speaking to one stranger a week, with you present. Later the goal will be two, three, or four a week, and then one person a day, then two.

You might begin with phone calls for information. Then add speaking to a visitor in your home (with you present of course), perhaps her telling the person something about the house, something you two have rehearsed ahead of time: "Our house is fifty years old. How old is yours?" Or "This apartment seems small but we have three bedrooms. How many does yours have?"

Finally, you could take your child to lunch with an adult she has not met (one you have coached to respond with interesting, involved answers to any question your child poses). Again, rehearse what your child will say, such as commenting with polite interest on a person's choice of food: "I like chow mein (or whatever the person ordered), too." And following up with a question: "Do you like Italian food?"

Chapter Eleven
Sensitive Adolescents and Young Adults

The Delicate Task of Launching a Spirited, Seaworthy Vessel

This chapter begins with a reminder of what your sensitive adolescent is facing as he approaches adulthood. Then we consider specifics: getting along together at home; helping your teenager through high school, both socially and academically; plus the handling of that special topic of romance and sexuality. Next comes the actual breaking away, a special moment for HSCs and their parents, and finally we consider your continuing relationship through the young adult years.

THE DEEP WATER AHEAD

The transitional years from childhood to adulthood, about fourteen to eighteen, require far too much of all young people. In about four years we expect them to transform from carefree, innocent kids playing with toys to adults driving a car, earning and managing money, handling their sexuality (and that of those who are attracted to them), and facing the temptations of drugs and alcohol. If they are baby-sitters or camp counselors, they change from being children to being someone who takes care of children.

In addition, they must plan and carry out the first steps of a career or higher education. And if they are in a public high school, they have to spend their days with the broadest cross section of society—those raised well and those whose parents have not done a very good job. They will probably never again have so little choice about those with whom they associate. Meanwhile, in this culture especially, they are expected to be leaving home very soon, to "cut the umbilical cord," "break away." They are not supposed to show grief about the end of childhood, even though it must be present. They face all of this while their body is going through remarkable and unsettling changes as well.

This rapid launching is probably too much for all youths, but it is especially challenging for HSCs. If they do not understand what makes them different from others, they may have to fight off the feeling that there is something terribly wrong with them, because they think they see that they cannot possibly succeed at all of this, when it seems others are. And even if they are full of confidence and self-esteem, they sense the size of the task, the breadth of the ocean they are sliding down into, the fact that all the lines are being removed, yet the hull is untried. The launching is drastic, frightening, and highly exciting. They take every aspect of it with deep seriousness, and this can often prove overwhelming.

Unless highly sensitive adolescents feel thoroughly understood, supported, and free to slow down this transition, they are likely to find a way to avoid a task they feel, consciously or unconsciously, is simply beyond them. They may try to solve the problem by seeking premature closure, such as an early marriage, pregnancy, a dead-end job, or joining a cult, or they will unconsciously find a way to "be excused from this activity" through a physical or mental illness. In extreme situations, some even end their lives.

Of course, most sensitive adolescents, if they are having difficulties, express it in quieter ways. They may have a great reluctance to date, a fierce ambivalence about the parties they feel they must attend yet do not enjoy, or a constant nagging worry about what kind of career or college they will be able to manage. As a result, they may be quietly preoccupied, irritable, or anxious, even while obviously trying to be mature and considerate. Meanwhile, parents, remembering these years as gloriously free and fun (thanks to the amnesia to pain the passage of time provides), may be expecting their teenager to be having "the time of her life" at pool parties, proms, and football games, never guessing how much a sensitive teenager struggles.

The point of all this is not to make you worry, but to make you more aware of what your HSC now faces. You may be a firm believer in being able to answer yes to the question "Do you know where your teenager is right now?" but can you do as well with "Do you know where your teenager is inside right now?" Of course he doesn't always like to be asked or observed. He needs privacy. But if you put yourself in his place and listen and watch for indications of anxious or low moods (irritability being an important one), you can begin to think of what might help.

HSCs—The Ideal Adolescents

The good news about sensitive adolescents, however, is very good— for their parents and their communities. Sensitive adolescents do not present many of the problems other teenagers do. Once they realize what they face, they usually aim to be adult as soon as possible, almost skipping over adolescence. They try to be considerate at home and with others. At school, this may lead them to take strong stands against bullying or any other unfairness they see, including political issues.

With just a little sound information to convince them, they rarely engage in anything illegal, unhealthy, or risky, including drinking or using drugs, unprotected sex, and unsafe driving. Thus, when a sensitive adolescent does use drugs (in more than an experimental way), it often signals that the teenager is trying to overcome anxiety or depression through a type of self-medication. Risky sex may suggest that a girl or boy is under such stress that the unconscious emotional solution is to merge with another person (or with a group practicing unsafe sex) to avoid having an individual life with individual choices. And unsafe driving or other risky behavior is probably a flirting with self-destruction, which for HSCs is generally a cry for help. But again, all of these are exceedingly rare among HSCs with a good support system.

What stands out at this age will often be the HSC's growing talent and depth, so that most are good to outstanding either academically, artistically, or in some other domain for which sensitivity and deep processing are an asset. They may be budding inventors, scientists, chess champions, or computer whizzes. They may be showing an aesthetic sensibility or keenness of insight that would seem to be found only in someone older. They are often involved in unusually caring, interesting friendships. Their inner life is often flourishing, perhaps in the form of a budding spirituality or interest in psychology or philosophy. Frequently they are working on their own now to overcome any behaviors they perceive as a limitation, such as fearfulness, shyness, or a lack of worldly experience and adventures.

What is perhaps most remarkable is the originality of their thinking. But River can make my case better than I.

The Sensitive Taxi Dispatcher

River is nineteen and, in his words, "I'm the observant type." He says he was shy when younger but overcame "all that" when he started working as a dispatcher for a taxi company (a very demanding job, balancing the urgent needs of outspoken drivers and stressed customers). In situations such as starting a new job, "I wait and watch until I know what is allowed, what is not. You get over shyness by learning not to do something stupid." And when something is difficult, "You just get it over with, you get it done." Now *that's* self-regulation.

As for his schooling, River struggled with the stress of public school. He did his first year of high school by correspondence course. He went back to public school for one year, then finished high school by correspondence. Did he miss the social activities? River told me that mainly he had liked playing sports at school and was good at them, but stopped in seventh grade because it stopped being comfortable. Everyone played to win, and if they didn't the coach "chewed them out." Now he has a small circle of close friends he met on his own, so it has worked out fine for him not to be in a public high school.

He found his friends by joining a group doing role-playing in the public park. It is "live action"—you play the characters assigned to you. He says the others who are involved are mostly "geeky" men, but he also found here the people he "clicked with."

Socially, he says he's very diplomatic, but he's also picky about the people he spends time with. "With women," he says, "I'm careful—we're usually not compatible." But he reports that if he's interested, "it goes well."

His greatest problem, he feels, is his sensitivity to those around him. When someone needs help—for example, someone needing a taxi immediately, the big headache on the job—he feels compelled to respond, often acting on his intuition. "It directs me whether I want to be directed or not." One certainly senses that this HSC is not going along with the crowd, as teenagers are usually expected to do. He is thinking for himself.

Is This Kid Sensitive?

River is working as a taxi dispatcher, does role-playing in the park, and in Chapter 1, I mentioned that he asked his mother to take in a homeless man—these are challenging, even risky choices. Yet both his parents and River agree that he is an HSC. The same is true of Janet, nineteen, who has just begun college at Columbia University. She "totally loves" New York City. She also loves football—playing it. She started in eighth grade, feeling "girls can do anything." I also know sensitive teenagers who have biked across the continent alone, taken up hang gliding, swum to shore from Alcatraz Island in San Francisco Bay, and toured India alone. Even if they do not try major feats, many of the adolescent HSCs I interviewed like to attend large concerts or sporting events, mingle in crowds, explore the back streets of a large city, draw attention to themselves through unusual clothing, or do two things at once, such as talking on the phone while cooking—pleasures most older sensitive persons would gladly forgo.

Are these kids really HSCs? Definitely. (Although, of course, some HSCs did not like these things, and many non-HSCs do.) But adolescence is the time in life when HSCs will be most willing to try new things and are least bothered by overstimulation. It is clear from research that small children and older people are the most sensitive in all senses. The low point in the trait seems to be the teens and early twenties. The best evidence of this buffered sensitivity is that somehow even the most sensitive teenager usually likes loud music and will play it even while studying. Trust me, their tastes and listening habits always change by thirty.

This is also the time when they are most bold and downright heroic, going off to join the Peace Corps, trying to make it in the Big City, or starting their own business. You may have seen them questing in foreign lands for the secrets of art, history, or their own ancestry, with only a backpack, a Youth Hostel guide, and a journal, where they will write poems and sketch street scenes. It is an exceedingly important time for HSCs, as they can learn a great deal about the world.

There are probably many causes of this lowering of their sensitivity and caution. There is the physical rush of hormones and maturing of the brain, which must create a new boldness, confidence, and yearning to test all this new capability out in the world. There is their eagerness just to be there, out there, like the moment when you first walked through the gates of Disneyland or a great museum. There is their lack of experience—they do not know just how hard and cold the ground really is when you sleep on it all night. And perhaps nature provides a little hormonal push at this age, too, since all mammals have to separate at least a little from their parents to make room for younger offspring. Finally, HSCs in particular may take on extremely difficult or risky challenges to prove they are not different from others, not the way they secretly know themselves to be, thinking it's a bad thing.

Ideas to Keep in Mind When Dealing with Your Sensitive Teenager

The first rule in conversing with teenagers is to figure out whether you are talking to the adult version or the child version. It's true that they are eager to be adults and to be treated as adults—that *is* the goal. And they frequently think and act like quite outstanding adults. But at other times they regress and act like children and unconsciously want to be treated that way. By now you know how to behave with either a child or an adult. The difficulty is guessing who you are speaking with at the moment.

The problem, too, is that as soon as you respond to the one who has presented herself to you, she may become the other. The adult becomes embarrassed by her slip into childishness, so the child you were speaking with becomes suddenly more adult and insulted by your offering help. Or the child suddenly feels unready to be separate and mature, so that the adult you thought you were speaking to goes back to needing your help and even feeling entitled to it. This unpredictability is not her fault. Transitions like this are not made overnight.

Further, you probably have noticed that you are not dealing with just any adult. A fresh, new adult is both highly inexperienced and overly confident, even grandiose, even arrogant at times. The reason for their arrogance is that, around the age of ten to twelve years, children's brains enter a final growth spurt, making possible the development of their full reasoning ability—what the Swiss psychologist Jean Piaget termed "formal operations." (Although all children have the capacity for formal operations, the ability does not always develop, especially in the uneducated.) Suddenly they are able to reason systematically, apply abstract principles mentally and imagine a range of outcomes, or actually test their hypotheses and consider "objective truth" (which at this age they are confident exists). At school they are, hopefully, receiving constant practice in and praise for these new talents. The newness of this reasoning power makes it seem like an amazing tool, especially to an HSC, who reflects so deeply and so can use this tool so well. They feel as if they can solve all the world's problems, and want to know why the previous generation left them this mess.

Now is the age when you have to be patient as a heron, and insist on a little respect in the meantime. As for respect, honesty, kindness, and all that, your HSC will probably give you all these with only the need for a reminder now and then. At this point, your job is polishing and adding the final touches. However, these final touches, like the spark plugs in a new car, are no small matter if skipped. Even sensitive teenagers can resist doing their assigned and agreed upon tasks—that is, accepting the more onerous responsibilities of adulthood, like taking out the garbage. They resist with such a combination of passive aggressive forgetfulness, emotional blackmail ("I'm just overwhelmed"), and clever reasoning that it can be far, far easier to wash the car or the dishes yourself.

But you cannot quit now. You owe it to civilization and your child's first roommate, not to mention his future spouse. You have to insist on the keeping of agreements, a modicum of good manners, and a display of tolerance (common human decency), especially for hopeless people like yourself, whom he has suddenly discovered are incomprehensibly dumb and uncool. You have to insist, or at least keep working at it, and your teenager has to make it difficult. And the result is "nature's plan": This way, neither of you are as sorry as you expected to be when you finally part company.

What You Can Do

Although sometimes your sensitive teenager may look tough and sound brilliant and confident, stick to the following general principles:

1. *See that your adolescent is talking to you, or at least to some other adult,* such as a school or professional counselor or a sympathetic and interested relative, mentor, coach, or family friend who has taken an interest in your child (try to see that this person understands high sensitivity). You or this other person needs to be giving both the usual empathy, advice, and support, but also a perspective that takes into account this temperament trait. Your child needs to see the long-term potential in being unusually observant, insightful, and original. She also needs to understand the lifestyle adjustments her trait will require of her—for example, taking more down time, opting for less stimulation, watching the arousal level, and right now, accepting that a sensitive person may require more time to make all the adjustments to adulthood.

2. *Keep up your comments about managing overstimulation.* Try not to make them warnings or advice, as this may insult the bold adult inside your HSC. Just make observations. And messages to teenagers often need to be brief—something you can say as they are dashing upstairs or getting out of the car. It also helps to be a bit clever, tongue-in-cheek, or even gently, lovingly sarcastic. For example, "From the look on your face when I mentioned birth control, I'd say you are wrestling with the great Sex Question. Let's see, this year you've learned to drive, taken the PSAT, and gotten your first job. Since you have nothing else you're trying to do, sure, why not expect yourself to solve the mysteries of love?"

3. *Be unstinting in your love as well as your praise of your child's accomplishments.* Now that you may be spending less time together, these are the ways you can signal your support briefly, on the fly. "I love you." "You look terrific." "By the way, I still think your grade on that test in algebra was awesome."

4. *Encourage that reflective nature.* Ask your teenager's opinion often, especially on difficult moral or world-politics issues. You, and your adolescent, will be surprised how much wisdom bubbles up. And rather than insulting your HSC's intelligence with some pat sermon about "just say no" to drugs, alcohol, or cigarettes, ask her to research their effects on the body, in detail. (Here is a gory

point that will appeal: Did you know that if a smoker cuts off a finger, doctors will not try to sew it back on? The capillaries will be too unhealthy. And when alcohol breaks down in the liver, it becomes a toxic substance.) Have your doctor help her find the research. And rather than merely saying you want your HSC to wait another year to learn to drive, have him report to you on the statistics for accidents by new young drivers and the insurance rates for that age before you agree to help him obtain a license.

5. *Express trust rather than worry or doubt.* As often as you can, use my favorite lines for this age: "I trust you to do the right thing" and "Just think it over, then do what seems right." If you want to add a caution, try "I'm sure you have thought of this, but I wonder how you will stay warm on that camping trip."

Maybe you don't quite feel as secure as you're sounding, but how else does one speak to a proud and thoughtful new adult, and how else does anyone who thinks they know everything learn? Expressing doubts when it is not necessary insults their judgment as well as their independence and gets you nowhere fast. Besides, your trust is reasonably well founded, since HSCs by nature look before they leap.

6. *Accept your teenager's need to distance from you.* There is a bitter irony to the fact that as close as you were before, she needs her distance now (this is especially true for mothers and daughters). There will still be long, intimate discussions between you, but only when your child feels she can do it without losing her adult identity. There will probably be more times when you feel utterly rejected, almost revolting to her. "What happened to my loving HSC?"

The truth is, she needs to separate, and it is so much more difficult when the bond is a good one! You know your child so well. If your child says a word, you understand what is going on—the tone of voice is enough. And she is reviewing all her memories of your love, the good times and, above all, your support. Yet she must soon leave all of this behind her, and go with some sense of herself as separate from you, a self of her own that wants something besides being your daughter. To do all of this she needs to have a private inner world where that self can finish developing and discover its purpose, away from your powerful influence.

7. *Never doubt your importance or power.* With an HSC in particular, your opinion still matters and so does your support. My research and that of others finds that fathers are especially important in helping both boys and girls enter the adult world. Even if your HSC seems to ignore your ideas, you will probably see them put into practice soon.

GETTING ALONG AT HOME

Having considered some general issues about what your HSC faces during these years, how you can help, and the basics of communicating with a sensitive teenager, let's consider getting along together at home at this age.

Privacy as Preparation for Leaving Home

Sensitive teenagers definitely need their privacy, a room or at least a walled-off corner of their own where they can unwind and ponder their lives. Ideally, this is also their first experience of having complete control of a space, decorating it (or not) as they wish. But because your child is not quite an adult, you have a right to make some rules about, for example, how often the room will be cleaned and by whom. You should agree on what food is going to be in there, and that nothing is done in there that violates house rules or local laws, such as smoking, drinking, or using drugs. If the rules are broken, one reasonable consequence would be that the door cannot be closed for a while (one parent I know even took the door off completely, which may be going too far).

You might explain that the privacy of your child's room is at this age a privilege earned through trustworthiness. You should not have to worry about what is going on in there. So while everyone should have to ask before entering his room, and no one should go through his drawers without a drastic reason, you might consider having the additional rule that "Who is it?" is the only right response to a knock. And if it is you, the answer should be "Come in" or "Just a minute," not "I'm busy." You are knocking as a courtesy, not to gain permission.

On the other hand, when a child asks to enter your room, you might have the understanding that here access is not automatic—she really is asking permission. That is, parents have privileges their dependents do not have—until those children leave home. Besides being fair to you, this attitude gives your HSC more reason to long for adulthood. (For an HSC, there may not seem to be many reasons to want to grow up.) It also promotes a certain reality about a personal income being the ticket to independence and privilege. Many HSCs would like to put that financial independence off as long as possible, since it seems so difficult. But we all have to learn it: While we accept another's support, we usually end up having to accept their managing our affairs. There is no free lunch for adults; "God bless the child that's got his own."

Give Them All the Responsibility You Can

Hopefully, you have already begun what I described in the last chapter—putting your HSC in charge of as many aspects of his life as possible: food, clothing, sleep schedule, and now activities schedule and homework.

Carin, who runs the calm home I described in Chapter 4, was already using this approach. With her two adolescents, "If they aren't taking care of something, I'm allowed to mention it once. Then I just have to let them mess up." As a result, there is little to hassle them about and they are "easy teenagers."

Not only does this show respect, but you are providing the chance to learn the consequences of inattention, a miserable fact of adult-hood. An unattended wallet can be stolen, an unattended pair of pre-scription sunglasses can be broken. This gives them less of this to learn when they are on their own.

Responsibilities are also abilities learned and used for them-selves, which can bring great pleasure. Teach them to sort their wash, iron a shirt, sew on buttons, mend a seam, and darn a sock (and when not to bother). And teach them to cook! We had fun with this; every Wednesday one of the three of us would cook a gourmet dinner, using recipes never tried before, from print or made up. Whenever my son took his turn, we had some odd, high-calorie combinations (gnocci with chilis, with a side dish of fried matzo balls and caramelized onions). But my son is now an excellent cook.

The First Job, the First Car

If your child can manage it, encourage him to take a part-time job while in high school. Start with him working for you or a family friend, but move him on soon to a job that involves a social security number, punching a time clock, and all the rest. It is a dose of real-ity, and it builds confidence that he can indeed support himself and manage in the world.

Along with a job comes learning to drive and owning a car. All of these are huge steps for an HSC, so timing is everything. My son didn't have his first job until after a year of college, and he learned to drive even later, so I'm not a proponent of rushing things. But see that they happen as soon as they will be comfortable for your HSC.

SURVIVING HIGH SCHOOL

Beginning probably with middle school, your child enters the world of changing classes, dealing with five or six courses and teachers. Just for the experience, go to your HSC's school and be in the halls between classes. Welcome to mayhem. This is what your child is dealing with, not to mention a new physical and social environment each hour, with different academic demands from different types of teachers. The advantage, you can point out to your child, is that if a class is not so good, she will not be there all day. And she *can* escape. You will permit a few days off, and there are always quiet spots—the library, a room not in use, or under a shady tree out front. But sometimes an HSC's survival in high school requires some creative or even extraordinary measures.

Two Stories

Catherine is a high school junior and a typical HSC—articulate, mature, outgoing, yet easily tired by social activities, quick to cry, bothered by loud sounds, and excruciatingly aware of others' needs and feelings. Being very conscientious and aware—"wise beyond her years"—she was placed in a program for gifted children in first grade. But math was more difficult for her (anxiety and overarousal can especially interfere with math performance), and in second grade she was told she would not succeed academically because of her math skills.

Her mother removed her from the program, but once she was in high school, Catherine was drawn back into something similar, again because her sensitivity and intelligence were being noticed. This time it was an international baccalaureate program, designed to give U.S. high school students an education comparable to Europeans' (who tend to gain a better general education in high school but take on a specialty sooner after high school). The program required her to take seven college-level classes, with no holidays, even between semesters.

Catherine was keeping up all right, but finding herself frequently exhausted and in tears. So she decided to withdraw from the program in its last year, after all of her hard work. As she put it, "I want to be the best in my class and the best daughter, so when do I just let my hair down?" Sometimes the only way to get ahead is to stop, turn around, go back, and find a better route.

Janet is a similar HSC—outgoing enough but having only a true friends, liking her time alone, and, again, "mature beyond years." Like Catherine, her sensitivity has helped make her a goc student, so that in her freshman year of high school she was assigned to advanced placement classes (the fast track to the best colleges, allowing you to pass out of some college classes and show your readiness for university-level study). It also happened that while she was in eighth grade, her mother was diagnosed with breast cancer.

Each year of high school was more difficult for Janet. Not academically—that she could manage. But she was also involved in more and more extracurricular activities (colleges like a long list of these, too). She was good at everything, liked it all, but "there was no time to breathe." Unlike Catherine, Janet did not drop out of her advanced program. Instead, in her junior year, Janet started to withdraw. She would stare at pictures of herself in childhood, dreaming of those happier times and wondering if she belonged in this world. She would not talk about any of this, so her mother urged her to write about it.

In her senior year, her mother received a phone call from the guidance counselor that a friend had come in, concerned about Janet. Clearly the pressure combined with worrying about her mother's health had finally worn down her nervous system. Her friend's good sense about speaking up and the guidance counselor's understanding and quick action led to Janet entering psychotherapy and taking an antidepressant, which immediately lifted her depression. She has started college—she's the one at Columbia—and still takes the medication. An HSC in Manhattan? She is determined to handle her sensitivity *her* way.

Helping with the School Part of High School

We'll address the all-important social side of high school later. Here, we'll deal with the academics. See that your child becomes involved with the best, most talented teachers *for her*—those who are teach-

ıe subjects or in charge of the activities she likes (drama, art, ınce fairs, debate, etc.), and the good teachers who truly like her. me of these teachers may even be highly sensitive, themselves. .heir classrooms will be her refuge and their encouragement will be what launches her mind more than anything else. (I think teachers are, as a group, the most important people on the planet.)

About homework: Be highly available to give any kind of assistance, and stay involved for the first few years to see that things are done properly and handed in on time. But give up this responsibility as soon as possible. HSCs need to pay attention to these details, asking if necessary, rather than relying on their often keen but sometimes wrong intuition about what they think is expected. Your goal is for your child to become independent and self-motivated, so that he does homework because it benefits his long-term goals, not because others have insisted on it.

In fact, at this age, most or all of the conflicts should be within the HSC. She wants to do the homework and does not want to do it. She wants to be helpful and does not want to. You can help clarify her reasons for doing and not doing—in the case of homework, the fatigue, boredom, or other interests versus the long-term life consequences of not doing it. You may emphasize the long-term impact— that is usually the adult viewpoint—but do not fail to acknowledge the other side, too.

College or No College Looms Early on the High School Horizon

One reason you want to hand over the reins of responsibility to your child as soon as possible is that soon you will not be around to prod him. You want him to be conscientious and successful in college or on the job, where he will set priorities on his own. While your young adult is learning how to do this, you have to expect that mistakes will be made. It is better that he makes them at home than out in the world all alone.

Unfortunately, colleges' entrance requirements do not al.
many mistakes. Starting with high school, your child's grade
part of a permanent record. So you will have to remember to k
loving your child in spite of her making some costly errors—forge
ting to hand in assignments or not choosing to do projects. The
more you can help her envision her future, the better.

I sat down with my son in ninth grade and said something like the
following:

"I know how much you hate doing most of the schoolwork you're
given. You can't see the relevance and you have so many other interests and talents. But here's the deal: We will help you go to college, but we can't afford to pay for all of your college education at a
good school. You will have to have major financial aid, and that is
only offered to the best students. Every grade you receive from now
on will count. Everything you learn will be on the SATs. We will help
you in every way we can—typing homework, taking you to the library and helping you find resources, sending you to any special
courses you need, defending you when you have difficult teachers.
But whether you go to college is up to you. We are not going to push
you anymore about schoolwork. Remind you, yes, but only once."

Then I talked about the consequences of not going to college
(which are even more relevant for sensitive people, who need all the
degrees they can get in order to have their deeper perceptions respected). "You will probably have to work at a boring job with a boss
who does not allow you much independence, live in a rented apartment your entire life, own an old car, and take very few vacations, or
else work overtime and have little time for yourself." I went on to
describe life with a college degree, and even life with a degree from
a top school. And I added that "If you decide to go to college later on
your own, you will find it difficult to support yourself while in
school."

I went on to say that *"We will love you no matter what you do about
this,* but we want you to know the consequences of your actions during the next four years."

it was heavy-handed talk for an HSC, but if he was inde-
nt enough to fight us over every bit of schoolwork, which he
then he was independent enough to hear the whole truth about
at is fun and what is not when you are forty.

There are now professionals who help high school students find
and apply to appropriate colleges. One of these pros can also give
this lecture to your child. "Here are the facts. You decide." With
most HSCs, it is all they need to hear, but they deserve to hear it. Remember, although HSCs think about consequences, they may not
really *know* the consequences unless you have made them explicit.

But There's More to Life Than Going to the Best College

Do not take my lecture to my son as meaning all HSCs should be
manipulated into going to college. It is intended merely as an example of giving a teenager increasing responsibility over the outcome of
his life. Many HSCs, of course, will not go to college. It simply is not
their life path. And those who do go may stall several years, trying
to find a way around it. Indeed, a year or more off before college or
during it is not a bad idea, except that most kids want to keep up
with their peers.

But since these decisions are often made in high school, I will add
that if your teenager is considering college, I highly recommend that
she apply to private schools, probably small ones, where the faculty
and staff notice if students are struggling academically, socially, or
emotionally before it is too late to help them. If she must go to a
large university, it should be very nearby. It will be enough to handle, without also changing regions of the country, with their subtle
but real cultural and climate differences. Have her try to room with
a friend from her high school, as the range of the mental health and
personalities of roommates at large public schools can make the
usual lottery too much of a gamble for an HSC.

SOCIAL LIFE

Adolescence is a very social time in life. That's why there a
many clubs, gangs, cliques, summer camps, teams, bands and
chestras, school newspapers, and so on. But consider the stimul
tion they bring to an HSC, who before adolescence was probably
used to one classroom, a few neighborhood friends, and staying at
home with you.

How Much Becomes Too Much

Highly sensitive people have to find the right balance between too
many and too little activities out in the world. While your child is
still at home, you can help him find that balance. He will feel
tremendous pressure at this age to do as much as others do, but he
will have that as an adult at work, too, and in every other aspect of
life.

Many parents said they limited their HSC's activities themselves,
and that seems wise at first. But again, you want your child to see
the importance of doing that herself, and that may only come
through trial and error. The same need to set and teach limits applies
to HSCs' desire to help others. Whether it's an upset friend or a wor-
thy charity that involves caring teenagers, HSCs have to learn how
much to take on others' problems before it becomes too much for
them. They have to learn what is their responsibility and what is not.
You can discuss what are the likely outcomes if she helps in one way,
another way, or not at all. Then she decides.

Dealing with the Hurts

Teenagers are notoriously self-conscious and easily hurt by their
peers. In fact, many who study shyness discuss a special kind,
adolescent-onset shyness, which arises in this highly social period

.gers are changing so fast physically and mentally and
comparing themselves to each other and adults. HSCs are
re even more aware of their flaws and of others watching
They may have achieved or at least can feign a maturity that
.es them feel a bit above teenage passions and culture. But they
.e still vulnerable.

What helps? Interests and friends outside of high school are often what save HSCs—for example, hobbies, volunteer work, pets, or
outdoor life, plus like-minded friends who come with these. A close,
loving family is enormously helpful, too. If you have a place of worship, that is often a good place for your HSC as well. In short, you
need other worlds that can dilute and place in perspective the
painful experiences HSCs face in the world of high school.

Fortunately, with every year of high school, social life tends to improve. Often differences and being unique become more of a plus at
this age. At any rate, the "oddballs" and "brains" tend to find each
other and enjoy their special subculture. They often meet up in
drama or art classes, in the computer lab, working on the school paper, or in advanced English, social studies, and science classes,
where their teachers engage them in conversations at their level, or
take them to outside competitions like science fairs where they become stars at last. They are starting to shine in their own way and to
earn new respect. Get to know what opportunities might be lurking
for your HSC at your high school.

My own son and his "different" friends started an alternative
newspaper in high school, *Shadow of a Chained Duck* (after the French
radical paper *La Canard Echaine,* or the Unchained Duck). Of course,
it was soon banned, which made it and my son all the more interesting to his fellow students, who picked it up from the young publishers across the street from school property. In college he briefly
published *The Little Friend,* in which anything would be printed as
long as it met the criteria of offending *someone* (and of course it had
to be witty). The point is, in young adulthood an HSC's truly different way of seeing the world, combined with that burst of heroic

boldness and confidence, can make sensitivity the soci
You and she simply have to be ready for this remarkable
the constraints of younger grades.

Social Life and Sex—You Can't Have One Without the Otl.

Social life at this age can never be adequately discussed if we ignore the way that every time teenagers come together, the facts of their life arise: they have entered puberty, the existence of two genders has become highly relevant, bodies are demanding attention as never before, and sexuality is always a possibility or at least a lively, conscious or half-conscious fantasy. Suddenly boys and girls are trying out being men and women. Rather than playing separately or in groups, they are *dating,* or think they are supposed to. The subject of "going out" or who you are "hanging out with" is a constant concern. Flirting is how you get the ball rolling. Gossiping and locker-room talk is how you know how others are doing.

Highly sensitive adolescents are living in this world whether they like it or not, and are often thrown into extreme ambivalence. They feel the sexual energy in themselves and they want to do what is normal, expected, and makes them accepted. But from the first game of "spin the bottle" or strip poker, they are often fully aware that casual sexuality and touching is not going to work for them. It is too frightening, too arousing, too overwhelming unless the other person is well known, trusted, and mature—not usually the situation on dates or at parties that become sexual.

Personally, I can recall the day and hour when I knew I was not going to be able to handle the sexual playfulness that would be expected of me—it was during a seventh-grade game of "post office." My own solution, and one I have seen other sensitive teenagers take, was to find one boy and stay with him for years (thirteen to twenty-four). That way I could avoid dating completely. No one could say I was not popular because I was not even in the competition. Sexuality could be explored gradually, since we were both fairly sensitive

it. My mother tried frantically to pry us apart so that
ve a "normal" adolescence of dating, partying, meeting
.ferent boys. I would have nothing to do with it.

.itive teenagers must live with a different way of being judged
too. Do you have the right looks, the right figure? Sensitive
.nagers can be especially hard on themselves when they look in
.ne mirror, certain that their differentness is there on their faces, or
that some small blemish is being noticed by others with the same
acuity that they have for such things.

Sensitive adolescents are also distressed by the way dating issues
can turn good friends into competitors or traitors overnight. They
feel shocked and betrayed by gossip, disloyalties, or lies that others
seem to think nothing of. They wonder why they do not have thicker
skins, giving and taking barbs as if it were nothing. But they can't.

One sensitive young adult described how in high school she was
tormented almost daily by a group of older girls because she had
caught the attention of a boy their age whom they had considered
part of "their territory." This girl had felt she could not complain to
anyone and had to endure it for several years. Ten years later she saw
one of the girls in a museum and found herself in a fresh state of the
hopelessness and fear she had felt back then, as if it had all happened only yesterday. These experiences do leave scars.

What can you do as a parent? Again, help your child feel confident about other things besides attractiveness, diluting the whole
issue. It might be writing, art, computers, science, an interesting
part-time job or volunteer placement, or an individual sport (to
avoid more of the same among team members). You can also
encourage him to find like-minded people and be with the other
gender in nondating situations rather than the high-pressured, sexualized atmospheres of dances and parties.

When it comes to sexual activity itself, encourage your child to go
at her own pace. Tell her she can set different limits than others do.
She can resist the pressure, or at least try to a little more than others seem to. This is not about being prudish, although she may fear

she will be seen this way. It does not even have to be ab
It's about what makes her comfortable, what her intuitior
will work for her. It's okay to be intimidated, afraid, an
whelmed by the thought of intercourse or other forms of se.
okay to be chaste.

A few sensitive young adults have told me that they took anoth·
path at this age. Hoping to be accepted and to hide their reluctance,
they had sexual experiences as soon as they could, wanting to get it
over with. Everyone I spoke to regretted it later, seeing it as exactly
wrong for a highly sensitive person. But they did not think they
suffered irreparable damage either. Sometimes one has to learn the
hard way.

Your HSC may be very aware of sexuality, but he may not be well
informed. And especially if you are uneasy, he may be too embarrassed to talk to you about it. So you, or someone, has to bring it up.
All of it. And when it is you, you can also express your values and
what you have learned through your mistakes.

Although HSCs may think a great deal about the consequences of
unprotected sex, they may not really *know* the consequences or how
to prevent them unless you have made all of this explicit. Sexually
transmitted diseases and unwanted pregnancies are too life-altering
for you to make assumptions about what your child knows. For example, make it very clear what life would be like if your child decided
to be a teenage parent (and a conscientious one, of course). Speak of
the positives and the negatives. Provide the information rather than
a lecture. Provide information about sexually transmitted diseases as
well, and be sure it is clear that there is still no cure for AIDS.

When Your HSC Does Not Have Much Social Life

Another difficulty with social life can be getting HSCs out into the
world and more involved with others. If she has at least one good
friend and is going places outside the home, I would relax. Perhaps
she has found a way to make an end run around teenage social angst.

things are more complicated now that the world comes
...s via the Internet. Sensitive boys in particular seem prone
. themselves into a social and intellectual life centered
.. what amounts to a virtual reality. What a perfect solution—
have all knowledge and people at your fingertips (seemingly)
.ile not being overstimulated by that noisy, busy world out there
.eyond your room.

The Internet is wonderful, and no one can be fully prepared for
living in today's world without being at home there. Being a whiz
with computers is a definite asset, too. But you have to be a dummy
(you can quote me, but I doubt it will help) to think it substitutes
for face-to-face learning and relating. All the emotional nuances and
pressures are lost, and the reduced stimulation makes human communication seem deceptively easy. Speaking up in a class, or talking
with a real, live, attractive person of the opposite sex, or taking a
moral stand against an actual crowd, is another matter. Strength of
character is built in that busy, noisy, place out there.

It should suffice to lay out to your child the consequences of entering the adult world without sufficient social and practical experience. Then you devise a plan together to break the habit if your child
admits to an addiction (best not to use that term first yourself). You
may be surprised how much fear is behind the resistance and what
small steps are needed at first. One good friend whom he can try
things with will make a huge difference.

Remember, an authoritarian stand, such as seizing the computer,
will probably not work. There are plenty of computers out there he
can turn to besides the one at home, or he will just leave home and
hole up in some studio apartment. Seduce him out, reason him out,
and patiently wait him out, but I would not try to drive him out. It
must be a shared goal.

In expecting your child to join activities and have friends, but not
too many, do not expect these to be the activities and friends the "average" adolescent "ought" to have. Your HSC may prefer role-playing
games in the park with "geeky" guys, as River did, or studying pho-

tography with a middle-aged professional, or mountain clim
with loner outdoor types. Remember our motto, To have an exce
tional child you must be willing to have an exceptional child.

THE INNER LIFE

Some sensitive adolescents may also be less social because of a very
active inner life. A balance must still be struck between outer and inner—all the inner-specializing traditions say so. But this interest is
also very normal, especially in sensitive people.

Many HSCs have had contemplative or mystical experiences from
an early age. Even without formal religious instructions, they may
have prayed, met angels, heard voices, and experienced the tran-
scendent—and believe me, these HSCs are quite sane and normal.
Others become aware of this aspect of life in young adulthood, and
if your child has no previous exposure to religious ideas, spiritual
practices, and the language of mystical experience, he will be a real
novice.

I have not seen any convincing evidence that anyone can predict
who will be swept away by a sudden conversion or cult. Nor is it *always* a terrible or permanent thing. But it can be devastating for a
parent. The best way to prevent being caught up in nonsense or just
newness is probably exposure and open-minded discussions. Reli-
gions, rituals, teachers, and ideas that are foreign to us are always
more "numinous"—divinely awesome. And we live in a sort of religious "food court," so it pays to discuss the nutritional value of the
menu. A bit of objective—that is, not highly prejudiced—instruction
in comparative religion might help, with your bottom line being,
perhaps, that there are many paths to the same goal, but the one in
which you were raised has the advantage of being deeply cultivated
in your soul. But stay *open-minded* and interested, so your HSC talks
to you about her experiences and ideas.

However your child expresses this aspect of his sensitivity, I be-

it is one of the finest facets of the trait, and when it has prop-
matured, it is one of the most valuable contributions to the
world.

THE LAUNCHING INTO YOUNG ADULTHOOD

Perhaps the most difficult change in life is the one of leaving home
and going out on one's own. But it is even harder for HSCs: We have
discussed throughout this book how difficult any change is for them.
So do not be surprised if your child leaves gradually or several times
instead of the dramatic leave-taking so often envisioned.

The first try at living alone may happen right after high school,
sometimes it is postponed until after college. Going off to college
may seem like the Big Break, and it certainly is psychologically because your child will be on her own there. But no matter how you
prepare them, many HSCs will go off to college and drop out, finding it just too overwhelming. Do everything you can to reframe this
retreat so that it is not a source of shame, but a good idea given
whatever she encountered. Let the drop-out return home or to your
locality and enroll in a local college, even a community college part-
time. Encourage her to work, however, even if part-time. The experience of trying to support oneself on a minimum wage has sent
many a sensitive young adult scurrying back to college and even on
to a graduate or professional school. But having mastered living on
her own first, she will be much more ready for college.

What stands out to me about this age is that both research and
anyone's observation will tell you that HSPs "get it together" later
than non-HSCs. They settle on a career later, and while sensitive
young women may marry younger than non-HSPs (hopefully that
trend is lessening), they often do not find their true life partner until later, after a divorce.

There are many reasons for these delays. They are still building
confidence in themselves as a member of a minority in a world fa-

voring the majority, the non-HSPs. They are making mista
choosing like a non-HSP, then having to give up that choice ar
again. Finally, they are avoiding commitments because they are p
cessing the alternatives more deeply and can better see the cons
quences of an impulsive decision.

What can you do? Listen, listen, listen.

When Your Sensitive Young Adult Asks Your Opinion

When your HSC asks your opinion about his plans for becoming independent, which he very likely may, your job, as always, is to
balance overprotection with encouragement to take on more stimulation, more risks.

When facilitating another's decision making, I like to focus on the
process—helping the person identify all the related issues and feelings—rather than what I think this person should do. Your goal,
therefore, is not only to see that the right decision is made but to see
that your young adult learns how to make future life-changing decisions independently. You teach that a good decision requires gather-
ing all the available information and asking people who might have
more experience with the issues, weighing all this information over
time so that it can incubate, trying out each of the two or more possible decisions as if it was the one you already had chosen in order
to see how it would feel to live with it, then going ahead without too
much looking back.

Now that we have emphasized your objectivity, let's also admit
that sometimes, secretly, you may have a strong feeling that your
child is taking on too much or not enough. Let's discuss these separately.

Scaling Down Plans That Seem Too Audacious

First, what do you do if you feel you need to scale down your child's
plans? He presents you with a plan—he is applying to several jobs,

of his career, over a thousand miles away. He will be working a very competitive, high-pressure atmosphere, and given his tion to being away from his home territory in the past, you suspect he is taking on too much. But you do not want to rain on his parade. What do you do?

1. **Ask questions** to see if he has thought about how he will cope. You might be surprised how thoroughly he has thought it through. If you sense major holes in his thinking, gently ask if he has considered these issues.

2. **Do the pros and cons together,** but from his perspective—you may change your mind.

3. **Suggest smaller steps to the same goal.** For example, taking a similar job closer to home or arranging to start out living with a friend or relation in the area. But again, keep these as vague alternatives that you are musing about or they will become your ideas, not his.

4. **Discuss your concerns as your concerns.** "I worry that you may not be happy in such a very different environment." "I would miss you with you so far from home, and I fear you would miss us, too."

5. **If she is determined to go ahead, discuss how she would understand it if it did not work out.** Often it is not so terrible, and both of you will feel better about the risk if a graceful exit is possible. Agree what that would mean practically and psychologically.

Upscaling Plans That Seem Too Cautious

What if your son seems to be planning to live at home indefinitely and that does not feel right to you? Helping your young adult move out into the world is extremely delicate. You do not want to be rejecting. Anything you say should be from the point of view of what is best for him, not your own need to have him gone or behaving like other kids his age.

What *is* best? Young adulthood is a time of experimenting, having

adventures, and making mistakes before settling down. ⁊
that can leave us with no regrets, or if we don't experim
great regrets. HSCs can understand the long-term conseque
you point them out.

On the other hand, if your child is pursuing an inner life of stt
or self-expression, or exploring the outer world closer to home, wh◖
are you to say that she needs to do otherwise? Try to see it from your
child's perspective and with the general understanding that there are
many ways to live in this world.

1. *Again, be sure you are right that your young adult needs a push.* If
   he is planning to move out at some future point, the number of
   years is the issue, not the leaving itself. Give him time. HSCs
   need more time for this transition. And look at what he is actually doing; if he is becoming a professional cellist, does he have to
   travel around the world and date a dozen women, too? For an
   HSC, inner adventures count as much as outer ones.

2. *Look for a mentor.* If you think your young adult is having an emotional problem, this might be a therapist. Or it might be any adult
   with a similar personality or temperament. Mentors function to
   initiate a child into adulthood, a role that can be difficult for parents simply because they represent home and childhood. Explain
   to this adult what the problem is as you see it and let the two of
   them work on it by themselves.

3. *Consider an initiation.* In traditional cultures these were life-
   altering passages. You go in an *A* and come out a *B*—in this case,
   you come out an adult. Bar and bat mitzvahs still serve this function. High school graduations serve this purpose in a sense, but
   this ritual is purposely secular and rational, lacking "ritual space"
   or lengthy preparation. In some regions of the country you can
   find groups or individuals who will help you with such an initiation, borrowing from Native American rituals such as the vision
   quest for boys to become men or the Navajo Blessing Way for
   girls becoming women.

   Sometimes young adults devise their own initiation—a back-

trip or learning an unusual, challenging new skill. Watch
encourage such an informal initiation. If your daughter does
seem ready to leave home but is interested in an extended trip
some foreign country alone, support this plan. She is working on
her own transition. She is finding something exciting enough to
pull her out of your arms; she is attempting to energize her go-for-
it system. Being an adult is more than living alone and having a job,
or it better be if you want to entice her toward it.

4. *Gently explore the issue* to see whether your son is also concerned:
Is he afraid he will never leave home, or sees no problem with it?
These are very different issues. When fear is the problem you
strive to reduce shame and overarousal, which compounds the
fear, and devise a step-by-step strategy together (see below).

   When he simply does not want to leave but you want him to,
you can discuss how that might affect his life five, ten, and twenty
years from now. As a last resort, discuss your own feelings about
it, if you would not like him to continue to live with you. Do not
make these feelings about him specifically, but explain that at this
stage of your life you need to live without children, or without so
many (or whatever is your honest reason). Remember, if you raise
economic considerations or the extra work his being at home creates, he may simply offer to pay you room and board. But if this
is what you need to be more at ease with him at home, do discuss
money and you may have a deal.

5. *Devise a step-by-step program.* Where will your young adult live?
How will she support herself? How will she feel on her own? Encourage her to work on one of these at a time or a little of each.
They do not have to be accomplished all at once. Your young adult
can begin living alone by moving down the street, moving in with
a friend, or taking an extended trip. Economic independence can
be gained by working part-time at first, with you being available
with loans should they be needed. Emotional independence ar-
rives with the other two, but you can be available for supportive
talks and get-togethers your entire life. "Being on one's own"
does not mean being without family and friends.

NOW, YOUR OWN DEVELOPMENTAL TASK

In closing, I offer the words of a person I deeply respected, advice passed on to me when my son was born. The whole trick now, she said, was just continuing this process of letting him go and helping him let go of me—a process that began when he left my body. "It is this task that most parents cannot master. They treat their children like extensions of themselves. At every age they think their children are younger, weaker, more dependent, and more like them than their children really are. Their children resent it, and instead of the intense closeness the parents sought, they end up with even greater distance than they would have otherwise."

My friend was saying that all parents must learn to cope with a child's changes. But I think parents of HSCs especially need to role model a graceful way with change, so that their children can imitate that and not suffer the subtly debilitating effects of lifelong immaturity. Many HSPs persist with a kind of adult childishness because they abhor the change involved in growing up. Every change means a loss and every loss means grief. If the change is voluntary (as many seem to be, even when they are not), then there is also the problem of risk. Why take the risk? HSPs like none of this. Parents don't either. We do not want the loss and we do not want the risk of something happening to our baby. But we are the ones who must teach our HSPs how to grow up, grow on, and even how to grow old.

Yet letting go does not mean being disconnected, unloving, or not expecting love to be returned. On the contrary, true love and connection happen only when there are two, not one. Children, by nature, should not and ultimately cannot love you if you cannot let them become themselves.

What you will have around age thirty is an adult friend. Maintain the good boundaries and good manners you would have with any friend. Remember, your memories of this adult as a tiny baby, clinging toddler, and adoring five-year-old are fresh, but your young adult does not remember all of that so clearly. Now, if you want the relationship to be strong, you must have shared interests. You need to stay abreast of your child's career and other pursuits. And, of course, know well and love well those sweet grandchildren. If some of them are highly sensitive, you know what to do.

To be informed of new developments regarding highly sensitive adults and children, write to P. O. Box 460564, San Francisco, CA 94145–0564 for *Comfort Zone*, the HSP newsletter, or visit www.hsperson.com.

Twenty Tips for Teachers

1. *Expect that every class will have a wide range of biologically based temperaments and about 15 to 20 percent will be highly sensitive children (HSCs).* As this book explains, HSCs are born with a nervous system that causes them to prefer to observe all the subtleties in a situation and to process all of this information deeply before acting. As a result, HSCs tend to be highly reflective, intuitive, and creative (having a strong sense of how things came to be how they are and what could happen next); conscientious and concerned about fairness and what others are feeling; and aware of subtle changes, details, or "what's missing in this picture." The trait also causes them to be more easily overwhelmed and hurt, both physically and emotionally; slower to warm up or join in; and sometimes quiet and unwilling to speak in class. Do not be misled by their holding back—they offer you an opportunity to develop unusual gifts.

2. *Keep current on the findings about temperament differences and their effects on learning styles.* Regarding HSCs, help parents and other teachers realize that an HSC's genetically based behavioral variation cannot be altered, is perfectly normal (the same percentage with the trait is found in almost every species), and has advantages and disadvantages, depending on the situation.

3. *Work closely with the parents of your HSCs.* They often have useful insights and strategies for working with their children. They

also need reassurance from you: At home they see a bright, competent, outgoing child and fear that at school you will see someone quite different.

4. *If you run into problems with an HSC, consult the child's previous teachers* to learn what strategies worked in the past. Do not assume HSCs are being defiant or are seriously disturbed when they do not respond as you expect. With these children, a good fit between their temperament and their environment is everything. When they are older they will adapt to their world, but at first they need it to adapt to them.

5. *Be creative with HSCs, because they are.* Select curriculum for them from the visual and performing arts; offer creative writing exercises or clever problems to solve. Choose literature that deals with complex moral issues or emotional themes. Because HSCs often have rather adult minds, let them become involved with you at recess or lunchtime, helping you clean or set up class projects. Because HSCs often have close ties with nature, they may thrive with a project involving plants, gardening, or a class pet. And because they are good at grasping others' intentions and nonverbal communications, they may be the best choices to assist students not yet proficient in English.

6. *Watch the arousal level of your HSCs.* Everyone feels and learns best when in their optimal level of arousal—neither over- or underexcited. HSCs are more easily overaroused and overstimulated than other children and need more calm around them and more down time to process their experiences. This is a factor in all of their school efforts. Because recovery from overarousal requires at least twenty minutes, when possible it is better to prevent overarousal in the first place. Further, once school is associated with acute or chronic states of overarousal, a student will dread attending and become overaroused simply by the thought of it.

7. *Balance pushing and protecting.* Studies find that for secure HSCs, small doses of overarousing situations at the start of the school year can leave them *less* prone to overarousal in the same situa-

tions later in the year. But HSCs already highly stressed will be hurt from such pushing. Try to sense when a child is ready to be pushed and when you need to back off. But try to avoid having to completely exempt HSCs from what is difficult for them (for example, oral presentations or taking a turn at bat). This will only discourage them about their future and make them feel flawed. Watch for the right time to ask them to perform; prepare them in stages (a presentation to one other child, then a few more, then reading to the class, etc.); or find an equivalent alternative (at first serving a volleyball may be easier than hitting a baseball). See that each step is successful enough and praised enough by you that they will be eager to try the next one.

8. *Plan ways to prevent unnecessary overarousal in the classroom.* For example, with younger children, switch to calmer activities, take the class for a walk, or offer free choices, encouraging the HSCs to do something quiet. With older HSCs, give them increasing responsibility for finding ways to soothe themselves and manage how they express their reactions. For example, agree ahead of time that in order to prevent overarousal, the HSC may retreat to the "quiet reading corner" (try to have one, set off by low bookshelves) or leave the room for a few minutes to get fresh air, a drink of water, or stand in the hall. If HSCs have trouble asking you questions in front of the class, give them a card to set on their desk to signal that your help is needed. Do not chastise HSCs for needing instructions privately repeated.

9. *Allow HSCs to integrate at their own pace.* In kindergarten and the start of middle school or junior high it may take weeks, months, or even a year for HSCs to adjust to the new environment. Especially when very young, if they don't want to join in, let them take their time. They may simply need to observe for a while. Do not give them too much attention—this will only slow down the process. Do not label this behavior as shyness or fear. Being cautious does not lead to fear unless the caution proves justified. Remember, HSCs are conservative; they do not like to take risks

until they feel safe, and to them their school day already seems full of risks.

10. *When trying to promote class participation, again, keep the arousal low, the child relaxed.* With older HSCs, invite them to speak up in class by reading out loud, if they read well, or first sharing in pairs. Make silences comfortable. Praise them for what they do say without commenting about any difficulty they had. Remain confident that when they feel secure, they will have a great deal to share. Indeed, they often become the most talkative, creative, lively students.

11. *Be aware that sometimes your attention, although it is meant to be helpful, will only increase an HSC's arousal.* For example, it may help to look away rather than watch them when you address them. During times such as show-and-tell, do not put them on the spot with questions. Instead, share your own similar experiences (the name of your own dog, your own trip to the beach this year) and leave room for a response. In classroom discussions, invite HSCs to participate and give them a moment to respond; if they say nothing, then proceed as if nothing unusual has happened or offer a possible response, such as "Maybe you were thinking . . ." or "Would it be right to say that you think . . . ?"

12. *Break tasks into small steps*—with HSCs it will save you time in the long run. If an HSC is becoming anxious, back off and make the task smaller and easier. For example, when preparing a young HSC to go home (a big transition at a time when the child is already tired), the task can be made into many small parts. Do not ask HSCs to "get ready to go home," but to "please find your jacket in the coat room."

13. *Adapt your evaluation procedures to temperaments,* if possible, at least at first. During tests, evaluations, or recitals in class, keep HSCs relaxed if you wish to see their true abilities. By nature they have more information to process in every situation, and that takes time. So does retrieving that information. Deeply processed, complex information is difficult if not impossible to

access in high states of arousal. When there is time pressure or too much attention focused on the student or the outcome, there is always high arousal. Especially at the outset, have a variety of ways for HSCs to demonstrate what they have learned (visual artwork, oral presentations, creative writing, essays, etc.). Start with what is easiest for them, then progress to quizzes for which they are well prepared, untimed tests, and finally timed exams. You want to gradually train them to tolerate more arousing evaluation procedures by making each increment as successful as possible.

14. *Warn HSCs well in advance about changes in classroom routines or the approach of special trips or events.* This way they will adapt easily, rather than creating problems.

15. *Recognize when certain undesirable behaviors may be due to temporary or chronic overarousal.* When overaroused, some HSCs withdraw and seem distracted, dull, forgetful, unmotivated, anxious, depressed, or timid; others will become overly emotional, perhaps teary or irritable; some will be hyperactive or distractable, as if having ADHD, or even quite aggressive. But in each case, when the stimulation is reduced they are fine. When attempting to stop a behavior, first acknowledge to the child the cause of it, perhaps saying "You must be feeling pretty overwhelmed right now." Then suggest ways to handle the overarousal, such as "Perhaps you could use some time in the quiet reading area." And at some point, perhaps later, suggest what to do next time: "When you feel overwhelmed, please tell me before you become so upset."

16. *Never use harsh discipline on HSCs.* They tend to be extremely rule conscious and usually only require gentle, private reminders. For some, just knowing they made a mistake will reduce them to tears. If reprimanded, punished, or embarrassed, they are likely to recall the distress and associate it with you and the subject matter, but have little memory of the information you wanted them to learn.

17. *Look at the classroom environment from an HSC's perspective.* If it is crowded, noisy, hot, cold, stuffy, dusty, glaringly lit, or cluttered, all of this will impact HSCs more. Make whatever improvements you can, because they are warning you of conditions that are affecting all of your students to some degree.

18. *Help HSCs with any social difficulties they may have.* Give them time to solve things on their own, but if an HSC seems to be suffering for several days or is consistently withdrawn, isolated, rejected, teased, or bullied, consider intervening and also warning parents and counselors. HSCs can be slower making friends and need some help (see the next tip). They also may act in ways that other children can misunderstand. Their tears, for example, can be seen as weakness; their need for personal space as fussiness; and their moments of overwhelming frustration as unreasonable anger. Further, they can be favorite targets for teasing or bullying because they are so easy to upset. But the latest thoughts on rejecting, teasing, and bullying are that adults need to create an atmosphere in which the underlying attitudes (differences should be ridiculed, more aggression should be directed toward the least aggressive class members) are replaced by acceptance and respect for everyone. Keep reminding your students that people simply come in different "flavors," and these should not be automatically judged as either weaknesses or tickets to stardom.

19. *Help your HSCs form close friendships.* HSCs thrive in one-on-one relationships and usually need only one good friend for their social and emotional well-being, but that one is essential. Try to have their best friend from last year or from their neighborhood added to your class, seat HSCs together, pair them for tasks so they can get to know each other.

20. *Older HSCs benefit greatly from adult mentoring and recognition of their sometimes exceptional abilities.* Often they are ready quite early to move into adult levels in one or more areas, an important boost to their self-esteem. And they are frequently so in-

spired—by beauty, the need for social justice, their spiritual experiences, or simply their deep emotions—that they will suffer if they cannot find an outlet for self-expression. Encourage them to try different media until they find what suits them (poetry, dance, visual arts, acting, speaking, and writing—and do not forget writing for the school paper, or starting one if none exists).

Resources

BOOKS ON TEMPERAMENT

Carey, William. *Understanding Your Child's Temperament*. New York: Simon & Schuster, 1997.

Greenspan, Stanley. *The Challenging Child*. Cambridge, Mass.: Perseus Books, 1995.

Kurcinka, Mary Sheedy. *Raising Your Spirited Child*. New York: Harper Perennial, 1992.

Neville, Helen, and Diane Johnson. *Temperament Tools: Working with Your Child's Inborn Traits*. Seattle, Wash.: Parenting Press, 1997 (to order: P. O. Box 75267, Seattle, WA 98125; $13.95 paper, $19.95 library).

Shick, Lyndell. *Understanding Temperament Strategies for Creating Family Harmony*. Seattle, Wash.: Parenting Press, 1998 (to order: P. O. Box 75267, Seattle, WA 98125; $13.95 paper, $19.95 library).

Turecki, Stanley. *The Difficult Child*. New York: Bantam, 1989.

———. *Normal Children Have Problems, Too*. New York: Bantam Books, 1994.

A SELECTION OF BOOKS ON PARENTING GENERALLY

Gottman, John M. *Raising an Emotionally Intelligent Child*. New York: Simon & Schuster, 1997.1

Hendrix, Harville, and Helen Hunt. *Giving the Love That Heals: A Guide for Parents*. New York: Pocket Books, 1997.

Kurcinka, Mary Sheedy. *Kids, Parents, and Power Struggles.* New York: HarperCollins, 2000.

Solter, Aletha. *Tears and Tantrums: What to Do When Babies and Children Cry.* Goleta, Calif.: Aware Parenting Institute/Shining Star Press, 1998 (to order: P. O. Box 206, Goleta, CA 93116, or www.awareparenting.com, $12.95).

Stern, Daniel. *Diary of a Baby.* New York: Basic Books, 1990.

TEMPERAMENT WEBSITES

Preventive Ounce: www.preventiveoz.org

Temperament Learning Center: www.kidtemp.com

Behavioral-Developmental Initiatives: www.bdi@primenet.com

Mary Kurcinka: www.parentchildhelp.com

Temperament Project in British Columbia: www.temperament-project.bc.ca

VIDEOS

The Temperament Program: A Video Tape Series
Knowing Your Child: Introduction to Temperament
Understanding Your Sensitive and Withdrawing Child
Child Development Media
5632 Van Nuys Boulevard, Suite 286
Van Nuys, CA 91401
Phone: 818–994–0933
Fax: 818–994–0153

Flexible, Fearful or Feisty: The Different Temperaments of Infants and Toddlers
California State Department of Education Video
To order: 916–445–1260
E-mail: jkristal@kidtemp.com
Website: www.kidtemp.com

Notes

Regarding this book's discussion of the trait of high sensitivity in general in adults, the points addressed herein are well supported by research cited in the five books and articles listed below. The chapter notes, which follow this list, are only of studies about HSCs, children in general, or findings about sensitive adults not cited in these five sources. Thus, when I refer to other research, including my own, it has been published in one of these five works:

- E. N. Aron, *The Highly Sensitive Person* (New York: Broadway Books, 1997).
- E. N. Aron, *The Highly Sensitive Person in Love* (New York: Broadway, 2000).
- E. N. Aron and A. Aron, "Sensory-Processing Sensitivity and Its Relation to Introversion and Emotionality." *Journal of Personality and Social Psychology* 73 (1997): 345–68.
- E. N. Aron, "High Sensitivity as One Source of Fearfulness and Shyness: Preliminary Research and Clinical Implications," in *Extreme Fear, Shyness, and Social Phobia: Origins, Biological Mechanisms, and Clinical Outcomes*, eds. L. A. Schmidt and J. Schulkin (New York: Oxford University Press, 2000), 251–72.
- E. N. Aron, "Counseling the Highly Sensitive Person." *Counseling and Human Development* 28 (1996):1–7.

CHAPTER 1: SENSITIVITY

p. 8   have the trait or you do not: J. Kagan, *Galen's Prophecy* (New York: Basic Books, 1994).

p. 8   others say it is a continuum: e.g., J. Strelau, "The Concepts of Arousal and Arousability as Used in Temperament Studies," in *Tem-*

perament: Individual Differences, eds. J. Bates and T. Wachs (Washington, D.C.: American Psychological Association, 1994), 117–41.

p. 15   fruit flies: J. J. Renger, W.-D. Yao, M. B. Sokolowski, and C.-F. Wu, "Neuronal Polymorphism among Natural Alleles of a cGMP-Dependent Kinase Gene, *foraging,* in *Drosophila," Journal of Neuroscience* 19 (1999):RC28, 1–8; K. A. Osborne, et al., "Natural Behavior Polymorphism Due to a cGMP Dependent Protein Kinase of *Drosophila," Science* 277 (August 8, 1997):834–36.

p. 16   culture encourages only certain ones: M. Mead, *Sex and Temperament in Three Primitive Societies* (New York: Morrow, 1935), 284.

p. 17   small, cumulative effects: R. Plomin, "The Role of Inheritance in Behavior," *Science* 248 (1990):183–88.

p. 21   Jan Kristal's: J. Kristal, *The Temperament Perspective: Working with Children's Styles* (Baltimore: Brookes, in press).

p. 27   psychological or psychiatric disorder: M. van Ameringen, C. Mancini, and J. M. Oakman, "The Relationship of Behavioral Inhibition and Shyness to Anxiety Disorder," *Journal of Nervous and Mental Disease* 186 (1998):425–31.

p. 27   Jerome Kagan: J. Kagan, N. Snidman, M. Zentner, and E. Peterson, "Infant Temperament and Anxious Symptoms in School-Age Children," *Development and Psychopathology* 11 (1999):222.

p. 27   shyness in early childhood: M. Prior, D. Smart, A. Sanson, and F. Oberklaid, "Does Shy-Inhibited Temperament in Childhood Lead to Anxiety Problems in Adolescents?," *Journal of the American Academy of Child and Adolescent Psychiatry* 39 (2000):461.

p. 27   with anxiety disorders: J. Biederman et al., "Psychiatric Correlates of Behavioral Inhibition in Young Children of Parents With and Without Psychiatric Disorders," *Archives of General Psychiatry* 47 (1990):21–26.

p. 27   two studies: W. T. Boyce et al., "Psychobiologic Reactivity to Stress and Childhood Respiratory Illnesses: Results of Two Prospective Studies," *Psychosomatic Medicine* 57 (1995):411–22; L. Gannon, J. Banks, and D. Shelton, "The Mediating Effects of Psychophysiological Reactivity and Recovery on the Relationship Between Environmental Stress and Illness," *Journal of Psychosomatic Research* 33 (1989):165–75.

CHAPTER 2: FASTEN YOUR SEAT BELTS

p. 41   parenting does matter: E.g., J. Belsky, K.-H. Hsieh, K. Crnic, "Mothering, Fathering, and Infant Negativity as Antecedents of Boys' Externalizing Problems and Inhibition at Age 3 Years: Differential Susceptibility to Reading Experience?," *Development and Psychopathology* 10 (1998):301–19.

p. 42   studies done with monkeys: S. J. Suomi, "Genetic and Maternal Contributions to Individual Differences in Rhesus Monkey Biobehavioral Development," in *Perinatal Behavioral Development: A Psychobiological Perspective*, eds. N. Krasnegor, E. Blass, M. Hofer, and W. Smotherman (San Diego, CA: Academic Press, 1987), 397–419.

p. 42   Megan Gunnar: M. R. Gunnar, "Psychoendocrine Studies of Temperament and Stress in Early Childhood: Expanding Current Models," in *Temperament: Individual Differences at the Interface of Biology and Behavior*, eds. J. E. Bates and T. D Wachs (Washington, D.C.: American Psychological Association, 1994), 175–98.

p. 42   In another study: M. Nachmias, M. Gunnar, S. Mangelsdorf, R. Hornik Parritz, and K. Buss, "Behavioral Inhibition and Stress Reactivity: The Moderating Role of Attachment Security," *Child Development* 67 (1996):508–22.

p. 42   Several more studies: Cited in ibid.

p. 42   "A history of responsive . . .": Ibid., 519.

p. 43   it affects each child differently: J. M. Braungart, R. Plomin, J. C. DeFries, and D. W. Fulker, "Genetic Influence on Tester-Rated Infant Temperament as Assessed by Bayley's Infant Behavior Record: Nonadoptive and Adoptive Siblings and Twins," *Developmental Psychology* 28 (1992):40–47.

p. 43   Studies in which parents are trained: L. B. Sherber and S. C. McDevitt, "Temperament-Focused Parent Training," in *Handbook of Parent Training: Parents as Co-Therapists for Children's Behavior Problems*, 2nd ed., eds. J. M. Briesmeister and C. E. Schaefer (New York: John Wiley & Sons, 1998), 301–19; J. R. Cameron, R. Hansen, and D. Rosen, "Preventing Behavioral Problems in Infancy Through Temperament Assessment and Parental Support Programs," in *Clinical and Educational Applications of Temperament Research* (Lisse, Netherlands: W. Swets and Zeitinger, 1989), 155–65.

p. 63 schoolchildren in China and Canada: X. Chen, K. Rubin, and Y. Sun, "Social Reputation and Peer Relationships in Chinese and Canadian Children: A Cross-Cultural Study," *Child Development* 63 (1992): 1336–43.

p. 64 actively override this built-in reaction: S. T. Fiske, "Stereotyping, Prejudice, and Discrimination," in *Handbook of Social Psychology*, 4th ed., eds. D. T. Gilbert, S. T. Fiske, and G. Lindzey (New York: McGraw-Hill, 1998), 357–411.

p. 64 "shy" sons, in particular: R. A. Hinde, "Temperament as an Intervening Variable," in *Temperament in Childhood*, eds. G. A. Kohnstamm, J. E. Bates, and M. K. Rothbart (New York: John Wiley & Sons, 1989), 27–33.

CHAPTER 3: WHEN YOU THE PARENT ARE NOT HIGHLY SENSITIVE

p. 84 Research shows that when it comes to household chores: M. Ross and F. Sicoly, "Ego-Centric Biases in Availability and Attribution," *Journal of Personality and Social Psychology* 37 (1979):322–36.

CHAPTER 5: FOUR KEYS TO RAISING A JOYOUS HSC

p. 116 like depressed people: S. E. Taylor and J. D. Brown, "Illusion and Well-Being: Some Social Psychological Contributions to a Theory of Mental Health," *Psychological Bulletin* 103 (1988):193–210.

p. 120 self-relevant memories: C. J. Showers, "Compartmentalization of Positive and Negative Self-Knowledge: Keeping the Bad Apples Out of the Bunch," *Journal of Personality and Social Psychology* 62 (1992):1036–49.

p. 121 than they do in the United States: S. Kitayama, H. R. Markus, and H. Hisaya, "Culture, Self, and Emotion," in *Self-Conscious Emotions: The Psychology of Shame, Guilt, Embarrassment, and Pride*, eds. J. P. Tangney and K. W. Fischer (New York: Guilford, 1995), 439–64.

p. 123 psychologists Tamara Gerguson: T. J. Gerguson and H. Stegge, "Emotional States and Traits in Children: The Case of Guilt and Shame," Ibid.

p. 122 In most studies: J. P. Tangney, "Shame and Guilt in Interpersonal Relationships," in Tangney and Fischer, *Self-Conscious Emotions*, 114–39.

p. 125 Kochanska and others: E.g., G. Kochanska, "Mutually Responsive Orientation Between Mothers and Their Young Children: Implications for Early Socialization," *Child Development* 68 (1997):94–112.

p. 126 values are internalized best: M. L. Hoffman, "Affective and Cognitive Processes in Moral Internalization," in *Social Cognition and Social Development: A Sociocultural Perspective*, eds. E. T. Higgins, D. Ruble, and W. Hartrup (New York: Cambridge University Press, 1983), 236–74.

p. 127 Kochanska observed: G. Kochanska and R. A. Thompson, "The Emergence and Development of Conscience in Toddlerhood and Early Childhood," in *Handbook of Parenting and the Transmission of Values*, eds. J. E. Grusec and L. Kuczynski (New York: Wiley, 1998), 53–77.

p. 136 Stanley Greenspan's: S. I. Greenspan with J. Salmon, *The Challenging Child* (Cambridge, Mass.: Perseus, 1995).

CHAPTER 6: OFF TO THE RIGHT START

p. 157 A study assigned new mothers: V. A Hunziker and R. G. Barr, "Increased Carrying Reduces Infant Crying: A Randomized Controlled Trial," *Pediatrics* 77 (1986):641–48.

p. 158 Aletha Solter: A. Solter, *Tears and Tantrums: What to Do When Babies Cry* (Goleta, Calif.: Shining Star Press, 1998).

p. 158 advice of Tracy Hogg: Hogg, T: *Secrets of the Baby Whisperer* (New York: Broadway, 2001).

p. 159 The average baby cries: W. B. Carey with M. M. Jablow, *Understanding Your Child's Temperament* (New York: MacMillan, 1997).

p. 159 solves even these cases: W. B. Carey and S. C. McDevitt, *Coping with Children's Temperaments* (New York: Basic Books, 1995).

p. 159 babies who were extremely irritable: M. Papousek and N. von Hofacker, "Persistent Crying in Early Infancy: A Non-Trivial Condition of Risk for the Developing Mother-Infant Dyad," *Child: Care, Health and Development* 24 (1998):395–424.

p. 161 and measures of bodily reactions: T. Lewis, F. Amini, and R. Lannon, *A General Theory of Love* (New York: Random House, 2000).

p. 161 excellent implicit memories: S. Epstein, "Integration of the Cognitive and Psychodynamic Unconscious," *American Psychologist* 49 (1994): 709–24.

p. 161 Since newborns do not: Ibid.

p. 161 Not surprisingly, human infants: Ibid.

p. 162 more active right hemispheres: E.g., N. A. Fox, H. A. Henderson, K. H. Rubin, S. D. Calkins, and L. A. Schmidt, "Continuity and Discontinuity of Behavioral Inhibition and Exuberance: Psychophysiological and Behavioral Influences Across the First Four Years of Life," *Child Development* 72 (2001):1–21.

p. 162 emotional and social knowledge: D. J. Siegel, *The Developing Mind: Toward a Neurobiology of Interpersonal Experience* (New York: Guilford Press, 1999).

p. 162 responding to an imagined you: D. N. Stern, *The Interpersonal World of the Infant* (New York: Basic Books, 1985).

p. 163 Charles Super and Sarah Harkness: C. Super and S. Harkness, "Cortisol and Culture: Preliminary Findings on Environmental Mediation of Reactivity During Infancy." Paper presented at the Occasional Temperament Conference, Westbrook, Connecticut, September 2000.

p. 164 Daniel Stern: Ibid.

p. 165 "sensitivity to rejection . . .": Ibid., 195.

p. 165 some evidence that exposing: M. R. Gunnar, L. Hertsgaard, M. Larson, and J. Rigatuso, "Cortisol and Behavioral Responses to Repeated Stressors in the Human Newborn," *Developmental Psychobiology* 24 (1992):487–505.

p. 166 One pediatrician: W. B. Carey, "Night Waking and Temperament in Infancy," *Behavioral Pediatrics* 84 (1974):756–58.

p. 171 no less likely to be "securely attached": S. Mangelsdorf, M. Gunnar, R. Kestenbaum, S. Lang, and D. Andreas, "Infant Proneness-to-Distress Temperament, Maternal Personality, and Mother-Infant Attachment: Associations in Goodness of Fit," in *Annual Progress in Child Psychiatry and Child Development*, eds. S. Chess and M. E. Hertzig (New York: Brunner/Mazel, 1991), 312–29.

p. 172 Finally, studies of HSCs: Ibid.

p. 172 Moments of attunement: Stern, *Interpersonal World*.

p. 173 ". . . doing or believing": Ibid, 148.

p. 173 ". . . of shareable experience": Ibid, 151–52.

p. 175 reestablishing balance: Siegel, *The Developing Mind*.

p. 176 high "perceptual sensitivity": R. K. Rothbart, S. A. Ahadi, and K. L. Hershey, "Temperament and Social Behavior in Childhood," *Merrill-Palmer Quarterly* 40 (1994):21–39.

CHAPTER 7: TODDLERS AND PRESCHOOLERS AT HOME

p. 190 less trouble when they are older: J. R. Cameron, "Parental Treatment, Children's Temperament, and the Risk of Childhood Behavioral Problems: 1. Relationships Between Parental Characteristics and Changes in Children's Temperament Over Time," *American Journal of Orthopsychiatry* 47 (1977):568–76.

p. 202 experience more headaches: A. Kowal and D. Pritchard, "Psychological Characteristics of Children Who Suffer from Headache: A Research Note," *Journal of Child Psychology and Psychiatry* 31 (1990):637–49.

p. 202 more distressed by injections: L. W. Lee, *The Role of Temperament in Pediatric Pain Response*. Ph.D. dissertation, University of Illinois at Chicago (1993).

p. 202 less well during hospitalizations: D. K. Carson, J. R. Council, and J. E. Gravley: "Temperament and Family Characteristics as Predictors of Children's Reactions to Hospitalization," *Journal of Developmental and Behavioral Pediatrics* 12 (1991):141–47; S. G. McClowry, "The Relationship of Temperament to the Pre- and Post-Behavioral Responses of Hospitalized School-Age Children," *Nursing Research* 39 (1990):30–35.

p. 202 more allergies: I. R. Bell, "Allergens, Physical Irritants, Depression, and Shyness," *Journal of Applied Developmental Psychology* 13 (1992): 125–33.

p. 202 not under stress: W. T. Boyce et al., "Psychobiologic Reactivity to Stress and Childhood Respiratory Illnesses: Results of Two Prospective Studies," *Psychosomatic Medicine* 57 (1995):411–22; L. Gannon, J. Banks, and D. Shelton, "The Mediating Effects of Psychophysiological Reactivity and Recovery on the Relationship Between Environmental Stress and Illness," *Journal of Psychosomatic Research* 33 (1989):165–75.

CHAPTER 8: TODDLERS AND PRESCHOOLERS OUT IN THE WORLD

p. 207 those studying shy children: E.g., J. B. Asendorpf, "Beyond Temperament: A Two-Factorial Coping Model of the Development of Inhibition During Childhood," in *Social Withdrawal, Inhibition, and Shyness in Childhood*, eds. K. H. Rubin and J. B. Asendorpf (Hillsdale, N.J.: Lawrence Erlbaum, 1993), 265–89.

p. 207 Stanley Greenspan's: S. I. Greenspan with J. Salmon, *The Challenging Child* (Cambridge, Mass.: Perseus, 1995).

p. 208 fear begets fear: J. B. Rosen and J. Schulkin, "From Normal Fear to Pathological Anxiety," *Psychological Review* 105 (1998):325–50.

p. 210 less pushy then the average mom: M. Nachmias, M. Gunnar, S. Mangelsdorf, R. Hornik Parritz, and K. Buss, "Behavioral Inhibition and Stress Reactivity: The Moderating Role of Attachment Security," *Child Development* 67 (1996):508–22.

p. 210 fear in children in general: K. Burgess and K. Rubin, "Behavioral and Emotional Consequences of Toddlers' Inhibited Temperament and Parenting." Paper presented at the meeting of the Society for Research in Child Development, Albuquerque, New Mexico, April 1999.

p. 221 A study of reticent children: M. A. Evans, "Control and Paradox in Teacher Conversations with Shy Children," *Canadian Journal of Behavioral Science* 24 (1992):502–16.

p. 222 small and facilities well-kept: A. C. Dettling, S. W. Parker, S. Lane, A. Sebanc, and M. R. Gunnar, "Quality of Care and Temperament Determine Changes in Cortisol Concentrations Over the Day for Young Children in Childcare," *Psychoneuroendocrinology* 25 (2000): 819–36.

CHAPTER 9: SCHOOL-AGE HSCS AT HOME

p. 240 Kurcinka says: M. S. Kurcinka, *Kids, Parents, and Power Struggles* (New York: HarperCollins, 2000), 232.

p. 241 receiving good maternal care: E.g., D. Liu et al., "Maternal Care, Hippocampal Glucocorticoid Receptors, and Hypothalamic-Pituitary-Adrenal Responses to Stress," *Science* 277 (1997):1659–61.

CHAPTER 10: SCHOOL-AGE HSCS OUT IN THE WORLD

p. 253 Sarah Harkness and her colleagues: S. Harkness, C. Super, M. Blom, B. Muller, and B. Moscardino, "The Cultural Meanings of Temperament Dimensions: Findings from the International Study of Parents, Children, and Schools." Paper presented at the Occasional Temperament Conference, Westbrook, Connecticut, September 2000.

p. 255 But after ten years: K. Fordham and J. Stevenson-Hinde, "Shyness, Friendship Quality, and Adjustment During Middle Childhood," *Journal of Child Psychology and Psychiatry* 40 (1999):757–68.

p. 255 research points out: Ibid.

p. 256 A study of shy kindergartners: H. H. Goldsmith, N. Aksan, M. Essex, N. A. Smider, and D. L. Vandell, "Temperament and Socioemotional Adjustment in Kindergarten: A Multi-Informant Perspective," in *Temperament in Context*, eds. T. D. Wachs and G. A. Kohnstamm (Mahwah, N.J.: Lawrence Erlbaum, 2001), 103–38.

p. 257 Psychologists Nathan Fox: N. Fox, A. Sobel, S. Calkins, and P. Cole, "Inhibited Children Talk About Themselves: Self-Reflection on Personality Development and Change in 7-Year Olds," in *Emotional Development in Atypical Children*, eds. M. Lewis and M. S. Sullivan, (Mahwah, N. J.: Lawrence Erlbaum, 1996), 131–45.

p. 268 And studies find: R. P. Martin and J. Holbrook, "Relationship of Temperament Characteristics to the Academic Achievement of First-Grade Children," *Journal of Psychoeducational Assessment* 3 (1985):131–40.

CHAPTER 11: SENSITIVE ADOLESCENTS AND YOUNG ADULTS

p. 281 rarely engage in: E.g., A. Caspi et al., "Personality Differences Predict Health-Risk Behaviors: Evidence from a Longitudinal Study," *Journal of Personality and Social Psychology* 73 (1997):1052–63.

p. 304 settle on a career . . . after a divorce: A. Caspi, D. Bem, and G. Elder, "Continuities and Consequences of Interactional Styles Across the Life Course," *Journal of Personality* 57 (1989):390–92.

Elaine N. Aron Ph.D., is the author of the bestselling *The Highly Sensitive Person* (Broadway Books, 1997), *The Highly Sensitive Person's Workbook* (Broadway Books, 1999), and *The Highly Sensitive Person in Love* (Broadway Book, 2001). A highly sensitive person herself, she holds a master's degree in clinical psychology from York University (Toronto) and a doctorate from Pacifica Graduate Institute. She also studied at the Jung Institute in San Francisco. A widely published research psychologist in the field of family relationships, she has a thriving psychotherapy practice and conducts workshops for HSPs around the country. She divides her time between San Francisco and New York.

The Highly Sensitive Person
How to thrive when the world overwhelms you
Elaine N. Aron

Do you have a keen imagination and vivid dreams?
Is time alone each day as essential to you as food and water?
Are you 'too shy' or 'too sensitive', according to others?
Do you feel overwhelmed by bright lights and noise?

One in every five people is born with a heightened sensitivity: they
are often gifted with great intelligence, intuition and imagination,
but there are also drawbacks. Frequently they come across as aloof,
shy or moody and suffer from low self-esteem because they find it
hard to express themselves in a society dominated by excess and
stress. *The Highly Sensitive Person* offers effective solutions to those
feeling overwhelmed. With numerous case studies, exercises and
advice, Elaine Aron focuses on the strengths of the trait, teaching
HSPs that their sensitivity is not a flaw but an asset.

'This remarkable book speaks clearly to highly sensitive people. It
gives a fresh perspective, a sigh of relief, and a good sense of where
we belong in society.'

JOHN GRAY, author of
Men are from Mars, Women are from Venus

The Secret of Happy Children
Steve Biddulph

Steve Biddulph's highly-acclaimed *The Secret of Happy Children* helps you with parent–child communication from babyhood to teens, revealing what is really happening inside children's minds and what to do about it. You'll find yourself letting go of old negative approaches and freeing up more energy to enjoy your kids and take back your life.

Steve Biddulph tackles issues such as tantrums, shyness, fathering skills, television, food and behaviour, making time for your partner and single parenthood. Humorous, easy to read, sensible and practical, this book helps to make children and parents happier!

'A mix of Billy Connolly and Dr Spock ... Steve Biddulph is a publishing phenomenon.'
The Times

'Steve's advice is easy to follow – and more importantly, it works.'
BBC Family Life Magazine

Steve Biddulph has worked as a family therapist since the 1970s. He is also the author of *More Secrets of Happy Children*, *Raising Boys* and *How Love Works*. He is an internationally respected child psychologist with an ever-increasing following.

Confident Children

Help children feel good about themselves

Gael Lindenfield

Self-esteem, confidence and happiness are essential qualities that children need in order to become self-assured adults. So how do we encourage our children to fulfil their potential and grow up to become happy and confident adults? And how do we avoid the fine line between confidence, arrogance and precociousness?

Gael Lindenfield's classic book provides parents with practical and reassuring advice to help them raise happy and self-assured children, including:

How language and actions can be used to boost self-esteem
Helping your children learn essential social skills
Teaching your children to like themselves the way they are
Developing assertive children who can cope with bullies
Helping your child to overcome shyness

Gael Lindenfield is the bestselling author of *Super Confidence, Assert Yourself, Self Esteem, Self Motivation, The Positive Woman, Managing Anger, Emotional Confidence* and *Success from Setbacks*. She gives workshops throughout the UK and is featured regularly in the media. Her work has been translated into 16 languages.